Making Sense of Large Social Media Corpora

Antonio Moreno-Ortiz

Making Sense of Large Social Media Corpora

Keywords, Topics, Sentiment, and Hashtags
in the Coronavirus Twitter Corpus

Antonio Moreno-Ortiz
University of Malaga
Malaga, Spain

ISBN 978-3-031-52718-0   ISBN 978-3-031-52719-7 (eBook)
https://doi.org/10.1007/978-3-031-52719-7

© The Editor(s) (if applicable) and The Author(s) 2024. This book is an open access publication.

Open Access This book is licensed under the terms of the Creative Commons Attribution 4.0 International License (http://creativecommons.org/licenses/by/4.0/), which permits use, sharing, adaptation, distribution and reproduction in any medium or format, as long as you give appropriate credit to the original author(s) and the source, provide a link to the Creative Commons license and indicate if changes were made.
The images or other third party material in this book are included in the book's Creative Commons license, unless indicated otherwise in a credit line to the material. If material is not included in the book's Creative Commons license and your intended use is not permitted by statutory regulation or exceeds the permitted use, you will need to obtain permission directly from the copyright holder.
The use of general descriptive names, registered names, trademarks, service marks, etc. in this publication does not imply, even in the absence of a specific statement, that such names are exempt from the relevant protective laws and regulations and therefore free for general use.
The publisher, the authors and the editors are safe to assume that the advice and information in this book are believed to be true and accurate at the date of publication. Neither the publisher nor the authors or the editors give a warranty, expressed or implied, with respect to the material contained herein or for any errors or omissions that may have been made. The publisher remains neutral with regard to jurisdictional claims in published maps and institutional affiliations.

Cover illustration: © Melisa Hasan

This Palgrave Macmillan imprint is published by the registered company Springer Nature Switzerland AG
The registered company address is: Gewerbestrasse 11, 6330 Cham, Switzerland

Paper in this product is recyclable.

Contents

1 Introduction 1
   1.1 The Coronavirus Pandemic on Social Media 3
   1.2 Related Research 6
   References 14

2 COVID-19 Corpora 19
   2.1 CORD-19: The COVID-19 Open Research Dataset 19
   2.2 COVID-19 Twitter Chatter Dataset for Open Scientific Research 20
   2.3 The Coronavirus Corpus 22
   2.4 Parallel Corpora 23
   2.5 GeoCoV19 23
   2.6 Chen et al.'s Coronavirus Twitter Corpus (CCTC) 24
   References 27

3 Managing Large Twitter Datasets 31
   3.1 Twitter Content 33
   3.2 Downloading and Managing a Large Twitter Corpus 35
      3.2.1 Anatomy of a Tweet 35
      3.2.2 Downloading and Extracting Data 37
      3.2.3 Data Organization and File Format Selection 40
   3.3 Data Sampling 41
   3.4 Extracting Geotagged Tweets 47

		3.5	Subcorpora. Using Metadata with XML-Aware Corpus Tools	52

3.5 Subcorpora. Using Metadata with XML-Aware Corpus Tools — 52
References — 55

4 Keywords — 59
4.1 The Concept of "Keyword" in Corpus Linguistics — 61
    4.1.1 Experiment: The Keywords of Keywords — 67
4.2 Keyword Extraction Methods in Natural Language Processing — 73
    4.2.1 Machine Learning Approaches — 73
    4.2.2 Unsupervised Approaches — 74
    4.2.3 Graph-Based Approaches — 83
4.3 Comparing Keyword Sets — 86
4.4 Keyword Extraction Using Word Embeddings — 95
    4.4.1 Experiment: Comparing Keywords from Two Countries Using KeyBERT — 96
References — 99

5 Topics — 103
5.1 "Traditional" Topic Modelling Methods — 106
    5.1.1 Experiment: LDA vs NMF for Topic Modelling — 108
5.2 Embeddings-Based Topic Modelling — 115
    5.2.1 Experiment: Extracting COVID-19 Topics Using BERTopic — 118
5.3 Dynamic Topic Modelling — 132
References — 136

6 Sentiment — 141
6.1 Sentiment Analysis Methods — 142
    6.1.1 Deterministic Methods — 144
    6.1.2 Probabilistic Methods — 145
6.2 Experiment: Sentiment Analysis of the CCTC by Country — 146
    6.2.1 Tweet Classification and Sentiment Over Time — 147
    6.2.2 The Sentiment Lexicon of the Pandemic on Twitter — 152
6.3 The Role of Emojis in the Expression of Sentiment — 160
References — 164

7	**Hashtags**	169
	7.1 Hashtags in the CCTC	171
	References	179
8	**Lessons Learned and Key Takeaways**	181
Index		187

List of Figures

Fig. 3.1	Data structure of a tweet	36
Fig. 3.2	Total English tweets over time (aggregated by week)	39
Fig. 3.3	English country-geotagged tweets aggregated by week	47
Fig. 3.4	Number of geotagged tweets by country	48
Fig. 3.5	Word usage trends of the India 2020 subcorpus	54
Fig. 3.6	Word usage trends of the India 2021 subcorpus	55
Fig. 4.1	Sketch Engine's attribute selection for keyword extraction	89
Fig. 4.2	Top 50 single-word keywords for February 2020 (TR left, SE right)	90
Fig. 4.3	Top 50 single-word keywords for August 2020 (TR left, SE right)	93
Fig. 4.4	Top 50 single-word keywords for September 2021 (TR left, SE right)	94
Fig. 5.1	LDA topic visualization of the U.S. subcorpus	111
Fig. 5.2	Number of documents assigned to topics in the US subcorpus	120
Fig. 5.3	Interactive topics-documents map	131
Fig. 5.4	Selecting specific topics in the topics map	132
Fig. 5.5	Topics over time visualization (U.S. global)	134
Fig. 5.6	Football-related topic evolution over time (U.K.)	134
Fig. 5.7	COVID-19 "vaccination" topic evolution over time (U.S.)	135
Fig. 5.8	COVID-19 "vaccination" topic evolution over time (India)	135
Fig. 5.9	Timeline of topic "Brexit vs COVID-19" (U.K.)	136
Fig. 6.1	Sentiment timeline (U.S.)	149
Fig. 6.2	Sentiment evolution in the U.S., U.K., and India	150

Fig. 6.3	Sentiment evolution in Canada, Australia, and South Africa	150
Fig. 6.4	Topics over time for India showing the vaccination topic	154
Fig. 6.5	Sentiment over time—'help'	159
Fig. 6.6	Sentiment over time—'protest'	159
Fig. 6.7	Frequency of emojis (per 1,000 words) across countries	161
Fig. 6.8	Sentiment over time—'😭' (*loudly crying emoji*)	162
Fig. 7.1	Frequency of #BlackLivesMatter and #BLM (per 1,000 words)	177
Fig. 7.2	Frequency of #DictatorDan vs. #IStandWithDan (per 1,000 words)	178
Fig. 7.3	Heatmap of #mentalhealth by country	179

List of Tables

Table 3.1	Corpus extraction statistics	39
Table 3.2	Central tendency measures of daily number of retweets	44
Table 3.3	Daily retweets in the corpus by range	45
Table 3.4	Corpus samples used in the study	45
Table 3.5	Processing times of some operations	46
Table 3.6	Distribution of geotagged tweets by country	48
Table 3.7	Tweet and word counts of the geotagged corpus samples by country	50
Table 3.8	Top 50 countries by volume in the geotagged corpus	51
Table 4.1	Top 20 single-word keywords extracted from the book *Keyness in Texts*	70
Table 4.2	Top 20 multi-word keywords extracted from the book *Keyness in Texts*	72
Table 4.3	Unsupervised keyword extraction methods (U.K. Week 2)	78
Table 4.4	Unsupervised keyword extraction (U.K. Week 31)	79
Table 4.5	Unsupervised keyword extraction methods (U.K. Week 85)	80
Table 4.6	Reference corpus keywords extraction (U.K. Week 2)	81
Table 4.7	Reference corpus keywords extraction. (U.K. Week 31)	82
Table 4.8	Reference corpus keywords extraction. (U.K. Week 85)	82
Table 4.9	Monthly keywords intersections (TextRank ∩ Sketch Engine)	88
Table 4.10	Top 50 multi-word keywords for February 2020	91
Table 4.11	Top 50 multi-word keywords for August 2020	93

Table 4.12	Top 50 multi-word keywords for September 2021	95
Table 4.13	KeyBERT results for July 2021 Australia	97
Table 5.1	Corpus used in the experiments in this chapter	106
Table 5.2	Result of tweet pre-processing	109
Table 5.3	Top 15 LDA and NMF topics (United States)	112
Table 5.4	Top 15 LDA and NMF topics (United Kingdom)	113
Table 5.5	Top 15 LDA and NMF topics (India)	114
Table 5.6	Quantitative results of BERTopic's analysis	119
Table 5.7	Topics in the U.S., U.K., and India subcorpora using Llama 2	121
Table 6.1	Corpus used in the experiments in this chapter	147
Table 6.2	Sentiment classification with transformer-based classifier	148
Table 6.3	Sentiment timeline correlations between country pairs	151
Table 6.4	Top 50 negative words for the week 26-04-2021 in India	153
Table 6.5	Top 25 negative lexical items in the 6 top countries by volume	156
Table 6.6	Top 25 positive lexical items in the 6 top countries by volume	158
Table 6.7	Top 25 emojis per country ranked by frequency (per 1,000 words)	163
Table 6.8	Idiosyncratic uses of emojis by country	164
Table 7.1	Top 50 hashtags by country	172
Table 7.2	Country-specific hashtags	176

CHAPTER 1

Introduction

Abstract This chapter contextualizes the book in terms of aims, methods, contents, and audience. It first discusses the impact of the COVID-19 pandemic on all aspects of society, and the crucial role that social networks played as a means to disseminate information and share feelings and ideas between users. Finally, a comprehensive summary of the most outstanding research related to this book is offered, focusing on those works that employ similar techniques to the ones used here.

Keywords Social media corpora · Social media analysis · COVID-19 pandemic · Corpus-based research methods

The general aim of this book is to offer a comprehensive overview of available techniques and approaches to explore large social media corpora in general, illustrating them with Chen's (2020) Coronavirus Twitter corpus. Thus, the book pursues a double objective. First, a fundamentally methodological one, in which I describe in detail a number of methods, strategies, and tools that can be used to access, manage, and explore large Twitter/X[1] corpora; these include both user-friendly applications, such

---

[1] In April 2023 Twitter's legal name was changed to X Corp. In this book, I will refer to the company as Twitter/X to avoid confusion, and because all corpora discussed or used in the book were compiled prior to this name change. For the same reason, I will refer to them as Twitter corpora or datasets.

© The Author(s) 2024
A. Moreno-Ortiz, *Making Sense of Large Social Media Corpora*,
https://doi.org/10.1007/978-3-031-52719-7_1

as Sketch Engine (Kilgarriff et al. 2014) or Lingmotif (Moreno-Ortiz 2017), and more advanced methods and libraries that involve the use of data management skills and custom scripts. These tools and methods, on the other hand, are applied to explore one of the largest Twitter datasets on the COVID-19 pandemic publicly released, covering the two years when the pandemic had the strongest impact on society. Consequently, the second important objective is to seek out, identify, and describe this impact, and how it is reflected in the language on social media.

Therefore, this book is intended to be both a methodological guide for language researchers—understood as all those who use language and textual resources in general as a data source in their research, whichever their field of application—as well as a reference for researchers in other fields who are interested in the impact of the pandemic on society and its reflection on social networks across the English-speaking world.

The tools and methods discussed in this book are described with enough technical detail for readers to apply them to their own datasets, but not so much that the description obscures the practical applications. In order to facilitate the understanding and actual application of these techniques to other datasets, the text provides user-friendly descriptions of technicalities regarding data manipulation and algorithms. In addition, all datasets and data analysis results are made freely available as a companion online data repository.[2]

Given the significance and magnitude of the COVID-19 pandemic, a large amount of related research has been produced since it started, including work similar to the one in this book. Section 1.2 contains a review of a representative selection of such studies. This study differs from these in several key aspects. Firstly, the scope is significantly larger, as I tackle the analysis of two years of pandemic (2020–2021); also, given the extended time span covered by the data, this study attempts to provide both synchronic and diachronic analyses, as I will be using timestamped data over a period of two years. Consequently, the corpus is significantly larger than those used in most of the, often rushed (Hyland and Jiang 2021), studies that have been published on the topic, thus posing a number of methodological and technical issues. Secondly, although references to the medical, social, psychological, economic, and educational aspects of the pandemic are inevitable in such a significant event, the

---

[2] Moreno-Ortiz, A. (2024). LSMC Datasets. https://doi.org/10.17605/OSF.IO/H5Q4J.

main focus of this book is the communicative perspective of language as a vehicular instrument of all those aspects. Thirdly, this study is highly methodological in nature, as it attempts to compare tools, techniques, and methods that are available to the language researcher in order to extract linguistic and conceptual information from very large social media corpora. Because of the emphasis on language use, I will also offer a diatopic perspective, which is made possible by the geotagged subset of tweets available in the focus corpus.

To sum up, the goal of this work is to provide methodological and practical cues on how to manage and explore the contents of a large-scale social media corpus, such as Chen et al.'s (2020) Coronavirus Twitter corpus. The primary goal is to compare and evaluate, in terms of efficiency and efficacy, available methods to extract language-focused information from large-scale social media corpora, fundamentally keyword extraction, topic modelling, and sentiment analysis. Detailed descriptions of various approaches to completing these tasks are provided, and results are compared to provide the necessary criteria for determining the benefits and drawbacks of each, as well as their suitability to various research scenarios.

1.1 The Coronavirus Pandemic on Social Media

The COVID-19 pandemic has been a determining factor in the lives of all humans in the second decade of the twenty-first century, in all aspects of our existence, especially in regard to health, social relationships, politics, the economy, and, of course, language. Until the arrival of the pandemic, concepts and terms that were foreign or altogether unknown to most of us ('pandemic', 'variants', 'antigen test', 'community spread', 'contact tracing') became progressively commonplace in our mental lexicon and everyday language. Unlike previous pandemics, the coronavirus used the sky highways to spread across the globe at an unheard-of pace, becoming a global health issue in a very short time.[3] Likewise, the information highways quickly became flooded with news and data regarding the virus, the disease, and the social and economic impact that the event brought about. Also, given the widespread use of social networks by citizens all over

---

[3] As of September 2023, the pandemic has claimed over 6.8 million lives (https://www.arcgis.com/apps/dashboards/bda7594740fd40299423467b48e9ecf6) [Accessed 21 September 2023].

the world, these information exchange hubs quickly became the obvious choice of many to learn about the pandemic, share their reactions, opinions, and emotions, or just reach out to the world. The "community spread" of the virus was as fast as that of the perceptions about the virus, and the vast range of social implications it triggered.

Social networks have indeed revolutionized the way we communicate and disseminate information. They have enabled people to connect across geographical boundaries, share ideas, and exchange information in real time (Boyd and Ellison 2007). This has not only increased the efficiency of communication but also democratized access to information, allowing anyone with internet access to create and share content (Castells 2009). In the business world, social networks have generated new marketing and customer engagement opportunities. Businesses are able to promote their products, interact with consumers, and collect valuable data for market research (Kaplan and Haenlein 2010), thus contributing to the expansion of e-commerce, with platforms such as Facebook and Instagram incorporating capabilities that allow users to buy and sell products directly (Zhan et al. 2016).

These powerful and enabling features are not without drawbacks. Social networks have been used to mobilize political protests, influence public opinion, and even interfere with elections (Tufekci 2017). The term 'fake news' has crystallized the now common practice of spreading misinformation among the general public, in such a way that it is sometimes not easy to tell facts from fiction, truthful from false information. In turn, this situation has, among other things, contributed to the current climate of political polarization in many societies (Allcott and Gentzkow 2017).

The coronavirus pandemic significantly amplified the importance of social networks in contemporary society. As people around the world were forced into lockdowns and social distancing measures, social networks became a lifeline for many, serving multiple purposes, including communication, information dissemination, and emotional support. Again, the dark side of social networks reared its ugly face from the very beginning. Even at the onset of the pandemic researchers were able to identify certain trends; as Depoux et al. (2020) state,

> Within weeks of the emergence of the novel coronavirus disease 2019 (COVID-19) in China, misleading rumours and conspiracy theories about the origin circulated the globe paired with fearmongering, racism and mass

purchase of face masks, all closely linked to the new 'infomedia' ecosystems of the 21st century marked by social media. A striking particularity of this crisis is the coincidence of virology and virality: not only did the virus itself spread very rapidly, but so did the information —and misinformation— about the outbreak and thus the panic that it created among the public. (p. 1)

Similarly, Rosenberg et al. (2020) note that social networks, specifically Twitter/X, have played a significant role in the medical world, a trend that was magnified during the pandemic. This includes both positive and negative aspects. On the positive side, it has become a forum where medical professionals exchange ideas, information, and commentary, facilitating fast spread of valuable information. However, unlike traditional medical educational resources, Twitter/X's free-flow of messages and ideas is not vetted or peer-reviewed, and therefore can pose a risk of harm. In particular, misinformation, information overload, and even hysteria are mentioned as the most immediate consequences.

It is debatable whether the negative effects of social networks during the pandemic outweighed the positive ones, but it is a fact that global use of social media sites soared. For example, according to a survey of social media users in the United States, 29.7% of respondents spent an additional 1–2 hours per day on social media. A further 20.5% utilized social media 30 to 60 minutes longer than usual per day.[4] Similarly, the share of TikTok users rose from 10% before the COVID-19 pandemic to 28% after it in users aged 15–25, and from 4 to 12% in the general population.[5]

The increase in the number of posts on Twitter was also significant. Haman (2020) reports a weekly growth rate of 1.5% in the number of followers experienced by the accounts of state leaders after March 9, 2020. Ahmed et al. (2021) also note that during the first year of the pandemic, social media participation and interaction increased dramatically, as it provided a forum for individuals to share their perceptions and perspectives on the medical, economic, and social crisis.

---

[4] https://www.statista.com/statistics/1116148/more-time-spent-social-media-platforms-users-usa-coronavirus/#statisticContainer [Accessed 4 March 2023].

[5] https://www.statista.com/statistics/1207831/tiktok-usage-among-young-adults-during-covid-19-usa/ [Accessed 4 March 2023].

As of 2021, there were 4.26 billion social network users around the world, a number projected to increase to almost six billion by 2027.[6] Additionally, social networking sites generate the most user engagement (Chong and Park 2021). In terms of social network market share, Twitter/X is in third position (6.82%) in 2023, after Facebook (36.64%) and YouTube (27.01%).[7] However, Twitter/X has considerably more media coverage, as politicians worldwide use this network to communicate their messages, both as an amplifier of their party's ideology and a substitute that allows them to express a more individualised message (Silva and Proksch 2022). This interaction, in turn, causes the public to react and generate political content themselves.

In addition, the defining characteristic of Twitter/X versus other social media networks is the availability of its data by means of an API (Application Programming Interface), a set protocols provided by Twitter that developers can use to access and download its data. This is the reason why most of the research on social networks has utilized this Twitter as a data source.

1.2 Related Research

The COVID-19 pandemic and its effect on society has been studied using social media content, and user-generated content in particular, from a wide range of perspectives and fields of study, including keyword extraction, topic modelling, and sentiment analysis, the main methods that are described in this book. However, most of these studies are limited in the time span they considered, the geographical scope, and/or the type of methods and techniques employed, the likely reason being that many researchers rushed to publish results of studies during the first months of the pandemic given the significance of the event.

In this section, I aim to describe this body of research in order to shed light on what type of studies utilize the methods discussed in this book, while at the same time describe some results obtained by studies that use similar methods to the ones discussed here. In the literature review that

---

[6] https://www.statista.com/statistics/278414/number-of-worldwide-social-network-users/ [Accessed 4 March 2023].

[7] https://www.dreamgrow.com/top-10-social-networking-sites-market-share-of-visits/.

follows, a distinction is apparent according to the field of study that motivated the research and, consequently, the techniques that were employed. Whereas researchers in (corpus) linguistics fundamentally employ "off-the-shelf" tools and methods common in the field, including distant and close reading techniques (word frequency, keyword extraction, concordancing, multi-dimensional analysis, qualitative analysis), researchers in the social sciences skewed towards strictly distant reading, i.e. quantitative methods and tools developed within Natural Language Processing (NLP), such as topic modelling and sentiment analysis. Accordingly, the results obtained are of a different nature.

This section is intended to illustrate the kind of research that can be conducted employing the techniques and tools described in this book, as well as to contextualize its actual content. It begins with some relevant research works in the social sciences, followed by those in corpus linguistics.

As a typical piece of research in the social sciences, Boon-Itt and Skunkan's (2020) study aimed to determine the public's awareness of COVID-19 pandemic trends and to identify significant themes of concern expressed by Twitter/X users in English. They gathered a total of 107,990 tweets relating to COVID-19 between December 13, 2019, and March 9, 2020. Over the limited time of their study, they used keyword frequency, sentiment analysis, and topic modelling to identify and investigate discussion topics. The study concluded that sentiment analysis and topic modelling can produce useful information about the trends in the discussion of the COVID-19 pandemic on social media, which is in fact, applicable to any corpus.

In a similar study, but including geographical stratification, Dubey (2020) collected 50,000 tweets from 11 countries every 4 days, from March 11 to March 31, 2020, using several search keywords and performed sentiment and emotion analysis using the NRC Emotion Lexicon (Mohammad and Turney 2010, 2013). The study presents word clouds of tweets from each country, which visually represent the most used terms and primary topics of conversation in each country.

The study by Ahmed et al. (2021) provides evidence on how the pandemic has not only triggered a significant global public health crisis, but also other problems, such as economic crisis, job loss, and mental anxiety. They analysed the sentiment of Twitter users at various time intervals to identify trending topics, and generated sentiment-related word clusters from several conceptual categories.

Kruspe et al. (2020) provide a cross-linguistic analysis of tweets posted in several European countries during 2020. The corpus consisted of approximately 4.6 million geotagged tweets in 60 different languages. The tweets were not filtered by subject, so many of them were unrelated to COVID-19. This was intentional, as the researchers were interested in the effect of the pandemic on people's mood in general, not just in relation to the outbreak. The study used an automatic method for sentiment analysis, training a neural network on the Sentiment140 dataset (Go et al. 2009), which contains around 1.5 million tweets collected through keyword search, and then annotated automatically by detecting emoticons. They found that there was a general downward trend in sentiment in the last few months corresponding to the pandemic, with clear dips at times of lockdown announcements and a slow recovery in the following weeks in most countries. Prior to February 2020, the use of pandemic-related keywords was uncommon, and the increase in Covid cases in each country correlates with an increased usage of those terms. The sentiment of tweets began as extremely negative at the onset of the pandemic, and then gradually became more positive. Nevertheless, it remained significantly below the average sentiment in most nations. They also found that there was a slight improvement in sentiment in the majority of countries towards the end of the period examined. As we will see in Chapter 6 these findings are in line with the sentiment analysis results presented in this book.

Mujahid et al.'s (2021) study combined sentiment analysis and topic modelling to investigate the efficacy of online education by analysing the sentiment of its stakeholders using Twitter data. It utilized machine learning techniques for annotation and topic modelling to identify e-learning issues, as expressed on Twitter by students, teachers, and other administrators. The dataset consists of 17,155 tweets, collected by searching for tags such as 'coronaeducation', 'covidneducation', 'distancelearning', and 'onlinelearning'. Tweets were classified using the sentiment lexicons provided by TextBlob (Keen et al. 2023), VADER (Hutto and Gilbert 2014), and SentiWordNet (Baccianella et al. 2010) and using several machine learning classification algorithms (LSTM, CNN, CNN-LSTM, and biLSTM), with and without data balancing with Synthetic Minority Over-sampling Technique (SMOTE). Topic modelling was used to identify the issues associated with e-learning, revealing that the top three issues are the uncertainty of campus opening date, children's inability to comprehend online education, and the lack of efficient networks for online education.

Lyu et al (2021) carried out a study aimed at examining Twitter conversations about COVID-19 vaccines between March 11, 2020, and January 31, 2021, in order to identify the most prevalent topics and sentiment regarding vaccine-related issues and analyse the evolution of these topics and sentiment over time. The corpus consisted of approximately 1.5 million unique tweets collected from March 11, 2020 through January 31, 2021. The authors used the topic modelling implementation of the Latent Dirichlet Allocation (LDA) algorithm in the R *textmineR* package (Jones et al. 2023) to generate an initial labelling for the topics. After carefully reading through a sample of tweets from each topic, they refined the machine-generated labels to provide a more accurate, concise, and consistent description of each topic.[8] As in Dubey's study, sentiment and emotion analysis were performed using the NRC Emotion Lexicon (Mohammad and Turney 2013), thus assigning scores to various emotions, including anger, fear, anticipation, trust, surprise, sadness, happiness, and disgust. The study revealed that among the sixteen distinct topics, vaccination-related opinions were the most prevalent and remained so over time. As global vaccine development progressed, the dominant subjects also shifted. Instructions on how to obtain the vaccine became the most-discussed topic at the beginning of January 2021. Also, the discussion of COVID-19 vaccination on social media was largely influenced by significant news events. The increasing positivity and predominance of trust over time suggests that social media discussions may indicate greater acceptance of COVID-19 vaccines in comparison with previous vaccines.

Using data from Reddit, Melton et al. (2021) also carried out a study combining sentiment analysis and topic modelling to examine public opinions regarding the COVID-19 vaccine. The corpus consisted of approximately 9,000 Reddit posts, which collectively obtained over 600,000 upvotes. The researchers combined these two techniques in a novel way: first they classified posts from a sentiment perspective using the TextBlob toolkit (Keen et al. 2023), which offers both a subjectivity score

---

[8] In Chapter 5 of this book a more advanced method for labelling extracted topics is presented which provides high-quality titles employing state-of-the-art Large Language Models.

and sentiment classification. Then they used LDA-based topic modelling in two different ways: first, they used the global time-series dataset to extract topics over time, and then they extracted the topics from the sentiment-classified posts. The results indicate that the public sentiment in Reddit communities is generally positive regarding discussions about the experiences with receiving the vaccine, although keywords and topics were identified that indicate some reluctance among users. They did not find significant changes in sentiment over time, which they attributed to a potential bias in the Reddit communities and/or strict community guidelines that result in the removal of certain posts, thereby creating an echo chamber. Unsurprisingly, they found topic modelling hard to evaluate, as the quantification through the coherence and perplexity scores is not a good indicator of performance in topic extraction. This is something that we will revisit in Chapter 5, as it is an important issue in topic modelling in general. The results of the LDA analysis revealed a total of five optimal latent topics. The first four topics appear to be closely related to a more comprehensive discussion of the vaccine, safety concerns, efficacy, and potential side effects. Topic 5 appeared to be centred on much broader terms, information (e.g. news, source, question), and a direct mention of vaccination-related concerns. Autism was also identified as a topic, presumably in reference to the antivaccine movement's fixation on the myth that vaccines cause this disorder.

News articles is undoubtedly the other major source of data to analyse text using "distant reading" techniques, such as keyword analysis, sentiment analysis, and topic modelling. Ghasiya and Okamura (2021) used a corpus of over 100,000 COVID-19 news headlines and articles from January 1, 2020, to December 1, 2020, in order to examine the key topics, trends, and themes of English-language COVID-19 news articles across four countries (UK, India, Japan, South Korea). For topic modelling they used *top2vec* (Angelov 2020), which is able to jointly generate embedded topic, document, and word vectors. As we will see in Sect. 5.2, *top2vec* has a number of advantages over traditional topic modelling techniques, such as LDA, as it makes the task simpler by doing all pre-processing (stop-word removal, stemming, lemmatization) automatically, and, importantly, it does not require prior knowledge of existing topics to produce a good topic model (Le and Mikolov 2014). For sentiment analysis, they used a RoBERTa-based (Vaswani et al. 2017) sentiment classifier. Similarly to Melton et al.'s (2021) approach, they also used the output of the classified headlines to extract positive and negative topics. They found that the economy, education, and sports were the sectors most affected by the COVID-19 pandemic. The United States topped every dataset for two reasons: first, it was the country most severely affected and, second, due to the global significance of the presidential elections. The study also revealed that the United Kingdom's media had strong negative attitudes regarding the pandemic and other related issues. In the Indian dataset, the negative headlines were only slightly more frequent than positive ones, whereas in Japan the difference was significantly bigger, with 57.38% negative and 42.61% positive headlines. South Korea had the most positive data of the four countries, with 54.47% positive and 45.52% negative headlines.

On the other hand, the body of corpus linguistics research exhibits some important differences as compared to the social sciences. Corpus linguistics researchers focus primarily on newspaper text rather than social media, the corpora tend to be smaller, and the methods more qualitative in nature. For example, in a special issue of the *International Journal of Corpus Linguistics*, Hyland and Jiang (2021) investigate the language used in COVID-19 scientific publications, given the deluge of papers that were hastily published immediately after the onset of the pandemic, which had certain negative consequences. The authors argue that the urgency and competition surrounding COVID-19 research led to an increase in the use of promotional language, or *hyping*, in scientific papers. They used a corpus of 1,000 COVID-19 research papers published in the first seven months of 2020, and compared it to a reference corpus of 1,000 papers from the same journals in 2015. They used the *AntConc* (Anthony 2023) concordancing software to analyse the frequency of certain features in the texts, such as boosting markers, affective markers, and self-mentions, that is, markers of what is usually referred to as *hyping language*. The results indicated that these markers were significantly more recurrent in the COVID-19 papers than in the reference corpus. The authors discovered that the former were more assertive and definitive in their presentation of results, with a steady increase in hyping features over time. They also discovered that scientists were more "present" in their texts, frequently highlighting the potential future value of their research and its potential contribution to the resolution of the pandemic.

In the same volume, Dong et al. (2021) explore the changes in the use of attitudinal markers in academic and media discourse on COVID-19, with a view to understanding how the use of these markers correlates with the reported cases of the disease. They used two different methodologies; on the one hand, a discourse dynamics approach in order to analyse language according to the evolution of discourse over time and, on the other, they applied Appraisal Theory (Martin and White 2005) to describe and explain the way language is used to evaluate, adopt stances, construct textual personas, and manage interpersonal positioning and relationships. The authors also used LOESS regression, a non-parametric method that uses local weighted regression to fit a smooth curve through points in a scatter plot. The corpus for this study consisted of academic articles and media reports related to COVID-19; the former were sourced from the COVID-19 Open Research Dataset (CORD-19), while the latter were obtained from the BYU Coronavirus Corpus (Davies 2021); both these corpora are described in Chapter 2. The authors ensured the comparability of the two corpora at different observation points by segmenting the media corpus in accordance with the size of the CORD-19 academic corpus in the same period. They found a complex and intricate interaction between the use of affect markers in both corpora with regard to the four types of reported cases of COVID-19: total cases per million, new cases per million, total deaths per million, and new deaths per million. The use of the variable 'new cases per million' was found to strongly correlate with the occurrence of affect markers in the academic corpus at some observation points, whereas the variable 'new deaths per million' was also found to correlate strongly with appreciation markers in the academic and media corpus in some periods. They also identified a fluctuating correlation between judgement markers and the reported cases of COVID-19, in both the academic and media corpora.

As an example of research that focuses on government communication, Gallardo-Pauls (2021) carried out an analysis of risk communication in the context of emergencies. She proposes a discursive model for risk communication, focusing on the Spanish context during the COVID-19 pandemic. The paper examines the communication strategies used by the Spanish government during the pandemic, focusing on the discursive elements that contribute to the perception and understanding of risk. The corpus used in the study consists of the communication materials and strategies used by the Spanish government during the pandemic, including press conferences, official statements, and other forms of public communication. The research identified several dangers associated with risk communication, including complexity of the risk's description, ambiguity in data interpretation, and the domino effects of risk. A distinction is made between 'old' and 'new' risks, with the former being natural risks and the latter being technological or human-made. The paper proposes a discursive model for risk communication that takes into account these risks and aims to improve the effectiveness of communication during emergencies.

Within Critical Discourse Analysis, Florea and Woelfel (2022) analysed a corpus of news reports from four major global TV news providers—CNN, BBC, DW, and RT—covering the COVID-19 pandemic from its outbreak to mid-crisis in 2020; they analysed a total of 12 dataset reports consisting of approximately two million words, to which they applied multi-level content analysis and Proximization Theory (Cap 2013). They used the *Catpac Pony* software package to identify the occurrence of concepts and the semantic relationship among the highly frequent clusters. The results suggest that the news texts surrounding the COVID-19 pandemic formulate a particular type of discourse on suffering that individualizes the sufferer, sets out the course of action, and turns the pandemic into a global cause for action. The negative values of the pandemic, among which they highlight the devastating economic impact, were found to legitimize the proximal discourses of suffering and safety.

As an example of a corpus-based study that focuses on gender and political communication, Power and Crosthwaite (2022) aimed to investigate the crisis communication during the pandemic of two political leaders, Jacinda Ardern, Prime Minister of New Zealand, and Scott Morrison, Prime Minister of Australia. The authors aim to understand how these two leaders' communication styles differed and how these differences might be related to their gender identities. The corpus consists of statements published by these two PMs during 2020, focusing on those that made reference to the pandemic by using the search terms "covid*", "coronavirus", and "pandemic" at least once. They focused on monological genres, as the proportion of dialogical genres was much higher in one of the leaders (Morrison). The corpus was divided into subcorpora reflecting the leader's identity and the relative status of the epidemic curve in each country. The reduced size of the corpus (24,083 tokens in total) allowed the authors to use the *Scattertext* (Kessler 2017) visualizer to compare the keywords associated with each PM. Thus, the results of the quantitative analysis are presented in the form of Scattertext's keyword comparisons charts for the entire corpus and for specific periods of the pandemic (initial case period, steep curve-rising periods, curve flattening periods, and flat curve periods). Guided by the quantitative results, they then produced a qualitative analysis based on Stokoe's (1998) gender conceptualization framework and transitivity analysis (Halliday and Matthiessen 2014) in order to ascertain whether the observed differences were gender-motivated.

This study is a good example of how extraction and visualization of quantitative data can be an entry point to detailed qualitative analysis, as it provides critical cues on what to focus on. Keyword extraction is probably the most useful quantitative method to quickly obtain insights from a corpus since keywords somehow condense the corpus' contents. Chapter 4 of this book focuses on this topic, exploring the different concepts, approaches, methods, and tools.

References

Ahmed, Md Shoaib, Tanjim Taharat Aurpa, and Md Musfique Anwar. 2021. Detecting Sentiment Dynamics and Clusters of Twitter Users for Trending Topics in COVID-19 Pandemic. *PLOS ONE* 16: e0253300. Public Library of Science. https://doi.org/10.1371/journal.pone.0253300.

Allcott, Hunt, and Matthew Gentzkow. 2017. Social Media and Fake News in the 2016 Election. *Journal of Economic Perspectives* 31: 211–236. https://doi.org/10.1257/jep.31.2.211.

Angelov, Dimo. 2020. Top2Vec: Distributed Representations of Topics.

Anthony, Laurence. 2023. AntConc (Version 4.2.0). Tokyo, Japan: Waseda University.

Baccianella, Stefano, Andrea Esuli, and Fabrizio Sebastiani. 2010. SentiWordNet 3.0: An Enhanced Lexical Resource for Sentiment Analysis and Opinion Mining. In *Proceedings of the International Conference on Language Resources and Evaluation*, 2200–2204. Valletta, Malta.

Boon-Itt, Sakun, and Yukolpat Skunkan. 2020. Public Perception of the COVID-19 Pandemic on Twitter: Sentiment Analysis and Topic Modeling Study. *JMIR Public Health and Surveillance* 6: e21978. https://doi.org/10.2196/21978.

Boyd, Danah m., and Nicole B. Ellison. 2007. Social Network Sites: Definition, History, and Scholarship. *Journal of Computer-Mediated Communication* 13: 210–230.https://doi.org/10.1111/j.1083-6101.2007.00393.x

Cap, Piotr. 2013. *Proximization. pbns.232*. John Benjamins Publishing Company.

Castells, Manuel. 2009. *Communication Power*. Oxford University Press.

Chen, Emily, Kristina Lerman, and Emilio Ferrara. 2020. Tracking Social Media Discourse About the COVID-19 Pandemic: Development of a Public Coronavirus Twitter Data Set. *JMIR Public Health and Surveillance* 6: e19273. https://doi.org/10.2196/19273.

Chong, Miyoung, and Han Woo Park. 2021. COVID-19 in the Twitterverse, from Epidemic to Pandemic: Information-Sharing Behavior and Twitter as an Information Carrier. *Scientometrics* 126: 6479–6503. https://doi.org/10.1007/s11192-021-04054-2.

Davies, Mark. 2021. The Coronavirus Corpus: Design, Construction, and Use. *International Journal of Corpus Linguistics* 26: 583–598. John Benjamins Publishing Company. https://doi.org/10.1075/ijcl.21044.dav

Depoux, Anneliese, Sam Martin, Emilie Karafillakis, Raman Preet, Annelies Wilder-Smith, and Heidi Larson. 2020. The Pandemic of Social Media Panic Travels Faster than the COVID-19 Outbreak. *Journal of Travel Medicine* 27: taaa031. https://doi.org/10.1093/jtm/taaa031.

Dong, Jihua, Louisa Buckingham, and Hao Wu. 2021. A Discourse Dynamics Exploration of Attitudinal Responses Towards COVID-19 in Academia and Media. *International Journal of Corpus Linguistics* 26: 532–556. John Benjamins. https://doi.org/10.1075/ijcl.21103.don.

Dubey, Akash Dutt. 2020. Twitter Sentiment Analysis during COVID-19 Outbreak. SSRN Scholarly Paper. Rochester, NY. https://doi.org/10.2139/ssrn.3572023.

Florea, Silvia, and Joseph Woelfel. 2022. Proximal versus Distant Suffering in TV News Discourses on COVID-19 Pandemic. *Text & Talk* 42: 327–345. De Gruyter Mouton. https://doi.org/10.1515/text-2020-0083.

Gallardo-Pauls, Beatriz. 2021. Riesgos de la comunicación de riesgo: un modelo discursivo para la comunicación de riesgo en emergencias. *Círculo de Lingüística Aplicada a la Comunicación* 88: 135–154. https://doi.org/10.5209/clac.77761.

Go, Alec, Richa Bhayani, and Lei Huang. 2009. Twitter Sentiment Classification Using Distant Supervision. *CS224N Project Report, Stanford*.

Ghasiya, Piyush, and Koji Okamura. 2021. Investigating COVID-19 News Across Four Nations: A Topic Modeling and Sentiment Analysis Approach. *IEEE Access: Practical Innovations, Open Solutions* 9: 36645–36656. https://doi.org/10.1109/ACCESS.2021.3062875.

Halliday, M. a. K., and Christian M. I. M. Matthiessen. 2014. *An Introduction to Functional Grammar*. Routledge.https://doi.org/10.4324/9780203783771.

Haman, Micahel. 2020. The Use of Twitter by State Leaders and Its Impact on the Public During the COVID-19 Pandemic. *Heliyon* 6: e05540. Elsevier. https://doi.org/10.1016/j.heliyon.2020.e05540.

Hutto, C., and E. Gilbert. 2014. VADER: A Parsimonious Rule-Based Model for Sentiment Analysis of Social Media Text. In *Proceedings of the International AAAI Conference on Web and Social Media*, 216–225.

Hyland, Ken, and Feng (Kevin) Jiang. 2021. The Covid Infodemic: Competition and the Hyping of Virus Research. *International Journal of Corpus Linguistics* 26: 444–468.https://doi.org/10.1075/ijcl.20160.hyl.

Jiang, Julie, Xiang Ren, and Emilio Ferrara. 2021. Social Media Polarization and Echo Chambers in the Context of COVID-19: Case Study. *Jmirx Med* 2: e29570. https://doi.org/10.2196/29570.

Jones, Tommy, William Doane, and Mattias Attbom. 2023. textmineR: Functions for Text Mining and Topic Modeling (version 3.0.5).

Kaplan, Andreas M., and Michael Haenlein. 2010. Users of the World, Unite! The Challenges and Opportunities of Social Media. *Business Horizons* 53: 59–68.

Keen, Peter, Matthew Honnibal, Roman Yankovsky, David Karesh, and Evan Dempsey. 2023. TextBlob: Simplified Text Processing.

Kessler, Jason. 2017. Scattertext: A Browser-Based Tool for Visualizing How Corpora Differ. In *Proceedings of ACL 2017, System Demonstrations*, 85–90. Vancouver, Canada: Association for Computational Linguistics.

Kilgarriff, Adam, Vít Baisa, Jan Bušta, Miloš Jakubíček, Vojtěch Kovář, Jan Michelfeit, Pavel Rychlý, and Vít Suchomel. 2014. The Sketch Engine: Ten Years On. *Lexicography*: 7–36.

Kruspe, Anna, Matthias Häberle, Iona Kuhn, and Xiao Xiang Zhu. 2020. Cross-Language Sentiment Analysis of European Twitter Messages During the COVID-19 Pandemic. In *Proceedings of the 1st Workshop on NLP for COVID-19 at ACL 2020*. Online: Association for Computational Linguistics.

Le, Quoc, and Tomas Mikolov. 2014. Distributed Representations of Sentences and Documents. In *Proceedings of the 31st International Conference on International Conference on Machine Learning—Volume 32*, II-1188-II-1196. ICML'14. Beijing, China: JMLR.org.

Lyu, Joanne Chen, Eileen Le Han, and Garving K. Luli. 2021. COVID-19 Vaccine-Related Discussion on Twitter: Topic Modeling and Sentiment Analysis. *Journal of Medical Internet Research* 23: e24435. https://doi.org/10.2196/24435.

Martin, James R., and Peter R. R. White. 2005. *The Language of Evaluation: Appraisal in English*. Basingstoke: Palgrave Macmillan.

Melton, Chad A., Olufunto A. Olusanya, Nariman Ammar, and Arash Shaban-Nejad. 2021. Public Sentiment Analysis and Topic Modeling Regarding COVID-19 Vaccines on the Reddit Social Media Platform: A Call to Action for Strengthening Vaccine Confidence. *Journal of Infection and Public Health* 14. Special Issue on COVID-19—Vaccine, Variants and New Waves: 1505–1512. https://doi.org/10.1016/j.jiph.2021.08.010.

Mohammad, Saif M., and Peter D. Turney. 2010. Emotions Evoked by Common Words and Phrases: Using Mechanical Turk to Create an Emotion Lexicon. In *Proceedings of the NAACL HLT 2010 Workshop on Computational Approaches*

to *Analysis and Generation of Emotion in Text*, 26–34. Association for Computational Linguistics.
Mohammad, Saif M., and Peter D. Turney. 2013. Crowdsourcing a Word-Emotion Association Lexicon. *Computational Intelligence* 29: 436–465.
Moreno-Ortiz, Antonio. 2017. Lingmotif: Sentiment Analysis for the Digital Humanities. In *Proceedings of the 15th Conference of the European Chapter of the Association for Computational Linguistics*, 73–76. Valencia, Spain: Association for Computational Linguistics.
Mujahid, Muhammad, Ernesto Lee, Furqan Rustam, Patrick Bernard Washington, Saleem Ullah, Aijaz Ahmad Reshi, and Imran Ashraf. 2021. Sentiment Analysis and Topic Modeling on Tweets about Online Education during COVID-19. *Applied Sciences* 11. Multidisciplinary Digital Publishing Institute: 8438. https://doi.org/10.3390/app11188438.
Power, Kate, and Peter Crosthwaite. 2022. Constructing COVID-19: A Corpus-Informed Analysis of Prime Ministerial Crisis Response Communication by Gender. *Discourse & Society* 33: 411–437. Sage Publications Ltd.
Rosenberg, Hans, Shahbaz Syed, and Salim Rezaie. 2020. The Twitter Pandemic: The Critical Role of Twitter in the Dissemination of Medical Information and Misinformation During the COVID-19 Pandemic. *Canadian Journal of Emergency Medicine* 22: 418–421. Cambridge University Press. https://doi.org/10.1017/cem.2020.361.
Silva, Bruno Castanho, and Sven-Oliver Proksch. 2022. Politicians Unleashed? Political Communication on Twitter and in Parliament in Western Europe. *Political Science Research and Methods* 10: 776–792. Cambridge University Press. https://doi.org/10.1017/psrm.2021.36.
Stokoe, Elizabeth H. 1998. Talking about Gender: The Conversational Construction of Gender Categories in Academic Discourse. *Discourse & Society* 9: 217–240. Sage Publications Ltd. https://doi.org/10.1177/0957926598009002005.
Tufekci, Zeynep. 2017. *Twitter and Tear Gas: The Power and Fragility of Networked Protest*. Yale University Press.
Vaswani, Ashish, Noam Shazeer, Niki Parmar, Jakob Uszkoreit, Llion Jones, Aidan N. Gomez, Łukasz Kaiser, and Illia Polosukhin. 2017. Attention Is All You Need. In *Proceedings of the 31st International Conference on Neural Information Processing Systems*, 6000–6010. NIPS'17. Long Beach, CA, USA: Curran Associates Inc.
Zhan, Liuhan, Yongqiang Sun, Nan Wang, and Xi Zhang. 2016. Understanding the Influence of Social Media on People's Life Satisfaction Through Two Competing Explanatory Mechanisms. *Aslib Journal of Information Management* 68: 347–361. Emerald Group Publishing Limited. https://doi.org/10.1108/AJIM-12-2015-0195.

Open Access This chapter is licensed under the terms of the Creative Commons Attribution 4.0 International License (http://creativecommons.org/licenses/by/4.0/), which permits use, sharing, adaptation, distribution and reproduction in any medium or format, as long as you give appropriate credit to the original author(s) and the source, provide a link to the Creative Commons license and indicate if changes were made.

The images or other third party material in this chapter are included in the chapter's Creative Commons license, unless indicated otherwise in a credit line to the material. If material is not included in the chapter's Creative Commons license and your intended use is not permitted by statutory regulation or exceeds the permitted use, you will need to obtain permission directly from the copyright holder.

CHAPTER 2

COVID-19 Corpora

Abstract The COVID-19 pandemic has had a profound effect on all aspects of society. As a component of this society, the academic and scientific community is not an exception. Numerous datasets have been compiled and made available over the past three years as a result of the extensive data collection efforts conducted by academics. Text corpora, as a rich source of information that is liable to be used for scientific inquiry, were compiled and made available from the onset of the pandemic. They differ in many aspects and compilation criteria, including origin, size, intended applications, text typology, and availability. This chapter is intended to provide a list of the most important text resources, together with some relevant research works that have used them.

Keywords COVID-19 corpora · CORD-19 · Coronavirus Corpus · Twitter Chatter Dataset · Parallel corpora. GeoCoV19

2.1 CORD-19: THE COVID-19 OPEN RESEARCH DATASET

The CORD-19 corpus (Wang et al. 2020) is the result of the collaboration of scientists from several institutions and companies, including The White House Office of Science and Technology Policy (OSTP), the National Library of Medicine (NLM), the Chan Zuckerburg Initiative (CZI), Microsoft Research, and Kaggle, coordinated by Georgetown University's Center for Security and Emerging Technology (CSET). The final version of CORD-19 was released on June 2, 2022, and contains over 1 million scholarly articles, of which over a third are full texts, totalling about 1.5 billion words.

The dataset was started in 2020 as an urgent initiative meant to facilitate the application of Natural Language Processing and other AI techniques to generate new insights in support of the ongoing effort to combat the disease. The dataset consists predominantly of papers in medicine (55%), biology (31%), and chemistry (3%), which together constitute almost 90% of the corpus.

It was created by applying a pipeline of machine learning and NLP tools to convert scientific articles into a structured format that can be readily consumed by downstream applications. The pipeline includes document parsing, named entity recognition, coreference resolution, and relation extraction. The original PDF documents were parsed using the Grobid tool to generate the JSON-based S2ORC (Lo et al. 2020) final distribution format. Coreference resolution and relation extraction are performed using a combination of rule-based and machine learning methods.

The great relevance of this knowledge resource cannot be overstated, as it has been used by clinical researchers, clinicians, and the text mining and NLP research community, who have generated a considerable body of research, including information extraction, text classification, pretrained language models, and knowledge graphs. It has also been used in diverse NLP shared tasks and analysis tools.

2.2 COVID-19 TWITTER CHATTER DATASET FOR OPEN SCIENTIFIC RESEARCH

This dataset, created by Banda et al. (2021), consists of over 1.12 billion tweets (at the time of publishing the paper)[1] related to COVID-19 chatter generated from January1, 2020, to June 27, 2021. The term *chatter* in the context of social media data refers to the ongoing

---

[1] The dataset itself (Banda et al. 2023) can be accessed on https://zenodo.org/record/7834392 [June 2, 2023].

conversation or discourse happening on the platform. As with most Twitter corpora, the authors used Twitter's streaming API with the Tweepy Python library to identify and download COVID-19-related tweets suing a set of keywords ('coronavirus', 'wuhan', 'pneumonia', 'pneumonie', 'neumonia', 'lungenentzündung', 'covid19'). They also relied on a number of collaborators to expand the tweet collection. For pre-processing they used the Social Media Mining Toolkit (SMMT) (Tekumalla and Banda 2020a), and decided to keep the retweets, as the intention of this corpus is to be able to trace the interactions between Twitter users, although a clean version with no retweets, intended for NLP researchers, is also available. The authors decided to include, together with the corpus, a number of Python scripts to read files and generate n-grams from the text. This dataset is intended to be instrumental in advancing research in various fields, including epidemiology, social sciences, and NLP.

The corpus has been well received by the research community, with 211,773 downloads as of June 2023, and has been used in a good number of publications. For example, Tekumalla and Banda (2020b) attempted to identify discourse related to potential drug treatments available for COVID-19 patients from Twitter data. They highlight the difficulties derived from the high number of misspellings of drugs (e.g. "hydroxychloroquine"). To deal with this issue they combined four different methodologies to acquire additional data. Firstly, a machine learning approach called QMisSpell, which relies on a dense vector model learned from large, unlabelled text. Secondly, they used a keyboard layout distance approach for generating the misspellings. Thirdly, a spelling correction module called Symspell, which corrects the spelling errors at the text level before text tagging. The authors demonstrate the importance of dealing with constant misspellings found in Twitter data and show that with a combination of methods, around 15% additional terms can be identified, which would have been lost otherwise.

2.3 The Coronavirus Corpus

The Coronavirus Corpus (Davies 2021) contains approximately 1.5 billion words of data in about 1.9 million texts from January 2020 to December 2022.[2] The corpus is in fact derived from the NOW (News on the Web) Corpus, which currently contains 17.4 billion words.[3] Initially, the NOW Corpus was based on links from Google News; every hour of every day, Google News was queried to find online newspaper and magazine articles published within the preceding 60 minutes. This search would be repeated for each of the twenty English-speaking countries considered by the author, and the URLs from Google News were stored in a relational database, along with all of the pertinent metadata (country, source, URL, etc.). Every night, scripts would download 15,000–20,000 articles, clean, tag, and remove duplicates before merging them with the existing NOW Corpus. Due to changes in Google News, the procedure was modified in the middle of 2019 to collect URLs using Microsoft Azure Cognitive Services. New magazine and newspaper articles from the previous 24 hours are retrieved daily for each of the twenty English-speaking countries. In addition, Bing is queried daily to find new articles published within the previous 24 hours for 1,000 distinct websites.

The Coronavirus Corpus provides the same query tools available for all corpora on English-Corpora.org, such as advanced searching, concordancing, and views of the frequency of words and phrases over time. Users can also browse the collocates of words and phrases and compare the collocates to see how particular topics have been discussed over time.

This corpus has been used in several studies, especially those interested in the linguistic perspective. One such example is the study by Dong et al. (2021) described in Sect. 1.2 above; another example is the one by Montkhongtham (2021), which aimed to examine the use of if-conditionals expressing options and possibilities during the pandemic. The extracted if-conditionals were classified according to Puente-Castelo and Monaco's (2013) framework of if-typology, and the grammatical aspects of all the verb strings were examined in terms of tense, aspect, sentential modality, and voice. They concluded that speech act conditionals were most frequently used to offer specific recommendations for combating the pandemic.

---

[2] https://www.english-corpora.org/corona/ [Accessed 15 May 2023].
[3] https://www.english-corpora.org/now/ [Accessed 15 May 2023].

2.4 Parallel Corpora

Roussis et al.'s (2022) is the best example of the few existing parallel corpora on COVID-19. It is a collection of parallel corpora with English as the main language, as all of them are EN-X language pairs. The primary data source they used was the COVID-19 dataset of metadata created with the Europe Media Monitor (EMM)/Medical Information System (MedISys) processing chain of news articles. The MedISys metadata were parsed to select datasets spanning 10 months (December 2019 to September 2020) and located the articles in several languages for a total of about 57 million URLs. The source HTML content was retrieved and processed to get the raw text. All documents were merged into one for each language and period, and subsequently tokenized into sentences using NLTK (Bird et al. 2009). In total they obtained 150 million sentences in 29 languages. Then they applied the LASER toolkit on each document pair to mine sentence alignments for each EN-X pair and, finally, the parallel data for each period were concatenated to form a single bilingual corpus per language pair.

Overall, the final dataset comprises over 11.2 million sentence pairs in 26 EN-X language pairs. It is offered both in TMX (Translation Memory Exchange) and CSV formats. It covers 22 of the 24 official EU languages, as well as Albanian, Arabic, Icelandic, Macedonian, and Norwegian. Obviously, there are great differences between low-resources languages and those with a high speaker base, with Icelandic having just a few sentence alignments, in contrast to 1.5 million for Spanish.

2.5 GeoCoV19

A well-known problem with Twitter/X datasets is that only a tiny proportion of them are geotagged. Lack of geolocation information may or may not be an issue to researchers, depending on their objectives. Location information, however, may be inferred from other data. Qazi et al. (2020) used a variety of strategies to geotag a large number of tweets downloaded for 90 days starting February 1, 2020. The dataset, dubbed GeoCov19 by the authors, contains over 424 million geolocated tweets. The authors' objective was to create a resource that allows researchers to study the impact of COVID-19 in different countries and societies. They used four types of data from a tweet: geo-coordinates (if present), place, user location, and tweet content. They adopted a gazetteer-based approach and used Nominatim, a search engine for OpenStreetMap data, to perform geocoding and reverse geocoding. They set up six local Nominatim servers on their infrastructure and tuned each server to handle 4,000 calls/second. In the absence of coordinates, toponym extraction from the mentioned data fields and the tweet's text was employed. They followed a 5-step process for toponym extraction: pre-processing, candidate generation, non-toponyms pruning, Nominatim search, and majority voting.

The evaluation of their toponym extraction approach showed that the lower the granularity (i.e. higher administrative level), the better the accuracy scores. At the country level, for both user location and tweet content fields, the accuracy scores at 0.86 for user location data and 0.75 for tweet text. By far, the tweet's text was the data that produced the most results, followed by user location, place, and geo-coordinates.

The final tweets dataset covers 218 countries and 47,328 unique cities worldwide, and several types of locations, such as hospitals, parks, and schools. In terms of languages, the corpus contains tweets in 62 languages, English being clearly the top one, with 348 million tweets, followed by Spanish and French.

2.6 Chen et al.'s Coronavirus Twitter Corpus (CCTC)

This is the corpus used in this study. The authors did not name their corpus in any particular way, so, in order to avoid confusion, I will refer to it as *CCTC* (Chen's Coronavirus Twitter Corpus). Chen et al. (2020) compiled this corpus as an ongoing collection of COVID-19-related tweets. Twitter's API and the *Tweepy* Python library were used to compile tweets since January 21, 2020. The searches were conducted using trending accounts and keywords such as 'coronavirus', 'corona', and 'COVID-19'. While the dataset contains tweets in over 67 languages, Chen et al. (2020) concede that there is a significant bias in favour of English tweets. The dataset is available on GitHub as a collection of text files with just the Tweet IDs.[4] The repository also includes a Python script ('hydrate.py') that facilitates downloading the actual tweets via the Twitter API. This is because Twitter specifically forbids the distribution

---

[4] https://github.com/echen102/COVID-19-TweetIDs [Accessed 18 May 2023].

of Twitter/X data by third parties. In Sect. 3.2, we provide more details regarding the "tweet hydration" process.

This corpus has also been extensively used in previous research, with 320 citations as of June 2023,[5] in a wide variety of research fields, including medicine, sociology, linguistics, and engineering.

For example, Bahja and Safdar's (2020) study aimed to analyse the spread of misinformation through social media platforms concerning the effects of 5G radiation and its alleged link to the pandemic, which at some point led to attacks on 5G towers. The authors applied Social Network Analysis (SNA), topic modelling (specifically LDA), and sentiment analysis to identify topics and understand the nature of the information being spread, as well as the inter-relationships between topics and the geographical occurrence of the tweets. They found that the majority of the topics speak about the conspiracy behind the pandemic, and that the source of the misinformative tweets can be tracked using SNA.

An interesting study with important social implications is the one by Bracci et al. (2021). The authors sought to understand how the pandemic has reshaped the demand for goods and services worldwide in the shadow economy, particularly the Dark Web Marketplaces (DWMs). They analysed 851,199 listings from 30 DWMs directly related to COVID-19 medical products and monitored the temporal evolution of product categories including Personal Protective Equipment, medicines (e.g. hydroxychloroquine), medical frauds, tests, fake medical records, and even ventilators. They also compared the trends in the listings in their temporal evolution with variations in public attention, as measured by tweets and Wikipedia page visits of products advertised in the listings. They found that listing prices correlated with both variations in public attention and individual choices of a few vendors, with prices experiencing sharp increases at key points in the timeline, which also correlated with user attention as reflected on tweets and Wikipedia searches.

In psychology, the study by Aiello et al. (2021) aimed to identify and understand the psychological responses of the population, thus contributing to the research line of measuring the effects of epidemics on societal dynamics and the mental health of the population; the paper also aimed to provide a starting point for developing more sophisticated tools

---

[5] https://publichealth.jmir.org/2020/2/e19273/citations [Accessed 18 May 2023].

for monitoring psycho-social epidemics. In order to identify medical entities and symptoms, the authors used the GloVe (Pennington et al. 2014) and RoBERTa (Vaswani et al. 2017) word embeddings in a Bi-LSTM neural network architecture to train a model trained on the Micromed database from manually labelled entities. The thematic analysis of tweets identified recurring themes in the three phases of epidemic psychology: denial, *they*-focus, and business-as-usual in the refusal phase; anger vs. political opponents, anger vs. each other, science, and religion in anger phase; *we*-focus, authority and resuming work in the acceptance phase. They also tested Strong's (1990) model of epidemic psychology.

In politics, Jiang et al. (2021) used an early version of the CCTC (until July 2020) to study the polarization of discourse regarding the pandemic, and identify and describe the structure of partisan echo chambers on Twitter in the United States, in an effort to understand the relationship between information dissemination and political preference, a crucial aspect for effective public health communication. To achieve these objectives they created an innovative language model, which they dubbed Retweet-BERT, a sentence embedding model that incorporates the retweet network, inspired by Sentence Transformers (S-BERT) (Reimers and Gurevych 2019). The model is based on the assumption that users who retweet each other are more likely to share similar ideologies; it was evaluated thoroughly, achieving strong performance (96% cross-validated AUC). They identified three different Twitter user roles: information creators, information broadcasters, and information distributors. Right-leaning users were found to more likely be broadcasters and distributors than left-leaning users, and therefore were noticeably more vocal and active in the production and consumption of COVID-19 information. As for echo chambers, they found them to be present on both ends of the political spectrum, but they are especially intense in the right-leaning community, as their members almost exclusively retweeted like-minded users. In contrast, far left and nonpartisan users were significantly more receptive to each other's information.

Li et al. (2021) used Chen et al.'s corpus to extract tweets produced by non-governmental organizations, which use Twitter to form communities and address social issues. They analysed a total of 2,558 US-based NGOs, which published 8,281,600 tweets. They focused on the NGOs' distinctive networked communities via features such as retweets and mentions, and how the discourse evolves as new social issues appear.

The authors found that, over time, as NGOs discussed the COVID-19 crisis and its social repercussions, distinct organizational communities arose around various topics. In addition, the use of social media helped eliminate geographical and specialization barriers, allowing NGOs with diverse identities and backgrounds to collaborate. They also observed that the patterns of tie formation in NGO communities largely mirrored the predictions of Issue Niche Theory.

The current version of the corpus at the time of writing (version 2.106, July 2023) contains over 2,77 billion tweets. English is the top language (64.3%), followed by Spanish (11.09%), Portuguese (3.78%), and French (3.7%).

The CCTC corpus is not without flaws: the authors acknowledge that there are some known gaps in the dataset due to Twitter API restrictions on data access and the collection of data using Twitter's streaming API, which returns only 1% of the total volume, so the number of collected tweets is dependent on network connection and filter endpoint. Additionally, the list of keywords used by the streaming API was modified and expanded as related terms (such as "lockdown" and "quarantine") emerged, which explains the sudden increases in the number of tweets at specific times (see Fig. 3.2).

Despite these shortcomings, it is quite possibly the most valuable available resource to study the impact of the pandemic in the world through the voices of social media users. Its sheer size, over 32 billion tweets for the years 2020 and 2021 alone, compensates some of the limitations. For example, even though only a tiny proportion of tweets are geotagged (less than 0.01%), the absolute number of geotagged tweets is enough to undertake contrastive studies that require this information.

The corpus is described in more detail in the following chapter, where specific figures are provided, along with the strategies and techniques followed to manage such a large dataset.

References

Aiello, Luca Maria, Daniele Quercia, Ke Zhou, Marios Constantinides, Sanja Šćepanović, and Sagar Joglekar. 2021. How Epidemic Psychology Works on Twitter: Evolution of Responses to the COVID-19 Pandemic in the U.S. *Humanities and Social Sciences Communications* 8: 179. https://doi.org/10.1057/s41599-021-00861-3.

Banda, Juan M., Ramya Tekumalla, Guanyu Wang, Jingyuan Yu, Tuo Liu, Yuning Ding, Ekaterina Artemova, Elena Tutubalina, and Gerardo Chowell. 2021. A Large-Scale COVID-19 Twitter Chatter Dataset for Open Scientific

Research—An International Collaboration. *Epidemiologia* 2: 315–324. Multidisciplinary Digital Publishing Institute. https://doi.org/10.3390/epidemiologia2030024.

Bahja, Mohammed, and Ghazanfar Ali Safdar. 2020. Unlink the Link Between COVID-19 and 5G Networks: An NLP and SNA Based Approach. *IEEE Access* 8: 209127–209137. https://doi.org/10.1109/ACCESS.2020.3039168.

Banda, Juan M., Ramya Tekumalla, Guanyu Wang, Jingyuan Yu, Tuo Liu, Yuning Ding, Katya Artemova, Elena Tutubalina, and Gerardo Chowell. 2023. A Large-Scale COVID-19 Twitter Chatter Dataset for Open Scientific Research—An International Collaboration. *Zenodo*. https://doi.org/10.5281/zenodo.7834392.

Bird, Steven, Ewan Klein, and Edward Loper. 2009. *Natural Language Processing with Python*, 1 ed. Beijing; Cambridge, MA: O'Reilly Media.

Bracci, Alberto, Matthieu Nadini, Maxwell Aliapoulios, Damon McCoy, Ian Gray, Alexander Teytelboym, Angela Gallo, and Andrea Baronchelli. 2021. Dark Web Marketplaces and COVID-19: Before the Vaccine. *EPJ Data Science* 10: 1–26. SpringerOpen. https://doi.org/10.1140/epjds/s13688-021-00259-w.

Chen, Emily, Kristina Lerman, and Emilio Ferrara. 2020. Tracking Social Media Discourse About the COVID-19 Pandemic: Development of a Public Coronavirus Twitter Data Set. *JMIR Public Health and Surveillance* 6: e19273. https://doi.org/10.2196/19273.

Davies, Mark. 2021. The Coronavirus Corpus: Design, Construction, and Use. *International Journal of Corpus Linguistics* 26: 583–598. John Benjamins Publishing Company.https://doi.org/10.1075/ijcl.21044.dav

Dong, Jihua, Louisa Buckingham, and Hao Wu. 2021. A Discourse Dynamics Exploration of Attitudinal Responses Towards COVID-19 in Academia and Media. *International Journal of Corpus Linguistics* 26: 532–556. John Benjamins. https://doi.org/10.1075/ijcl.21103.don.

Jiang, Julie, Xiang Ren, and Emilio Ferrara. 2021. Social Media Polarization and Echo Chambers in the Context of COVID-19: Case Study. *Jmirx Med* 2: e29570. https://doi.org/10.2196/29570.

Li, Yiqi, Jieun Shin, Jingyi Sun, Hye Min Kim, Yan Qu, and Aimei Yang. 2021. Organizational Sensemaking in Tough Times: The Ecology of NGOs' COVID-19 Issue Discourse Communities on Social Media. *Computers in Human Behavior* 122: 106838. https://doi.org/10.1016/j.chb.2021.106838.

Lo, Kyle, Lucy Lu Wang, Mark Neumann, Rodney Kinney, and Daniel Weld. 2020. S2ORC: The Semantic Scholar Open Research Corpus. In *Proceedings of the 58th Annual Meeting of the Association for Computational Linguistics*,

4969–4983. Online: Association for Computational Linguistics. https://doi.org/10.18653/v1/2020.acl-main.447.

Montkhongtham, Napanant. 2021. A Coronavirus Corpus-Driven Study on the Uses of If-Conditionals in the Pandemic Period. *rEFLections* 28: 33–58. King Mongkut's University of Technology Thonburi School of Liberal Arts.

Pennington, Jeffrey, Richard Socher, and Christopher Manning. 2014. GloVe: Global Vectors for Word Representation. In *Proceedings of the 2014 Conference on Empirical Methods in Natural Language Processing (EMNLP)*, 1532–1543. Doha, Qatar: Association for Computational Linguistics. https://doi.org/10.3115/v1/D14-1162.

Puente-Castelo, Luis Miguel, and Leida Maria Monaco. 2013. Conditionals and their Functions in Women' Scientific Writing. *Procedia—Social and Behavioral Sciences* 95: 160–169.

Qazi, Umair, Muhammad Imran, and Ferda Ofli. 2020. GeoCoV19: A Dataset of Hundreds of Millions of Multilingual COVID-19 Tweets with Location Information. *SIGSPATIAL Special* 12: 6–15. https://doi.org/10.1145/3404820.3404823.

Reimers, Nils, and Iryna Gurevych. 2019. Sentence-BERT: Sentence Embeddings Using Siamese BERT-Networks. In *Proceedings of the 2019 Conference on Empirical Methods in Natural Language Processing*. Association for Computational Linguistics.

Roussis, Dimitrios, Vassilis Papavassiliou, Sokratis Sofianopoulos, Prokopis Prokopidis, and Stelios Piperidis. 2022. Constructing Parallel Corpora from COVID-19 News using MediSys Metadata. In *Proceedings of the Thirteenth Language Resources and Evaluation Conference*, 1068–1072. Marseille, France: European Language Resources Association.

Strong, Philip. 1990. Epidemic Psychology. A Model. *Sociology of Health & Illness* 12: 249–259. Wiley Online Library.

Tekumalla, Ramya, and Juan M Banda. 2020a. Social Media Mining Toolkit (SMMT). *Genomics & Informatics* 18: e16–. https://doi.org/10.5808/GI.2020.18.2.e16.

Tekumalla, Ramya, and Juan M Banda. 2020b. Characterizing Drug Mentions in COVID-19 Twitter Chatter. In *Proceedings of the 1st Workshop on NLP for COVID-19 (Part 2) at EMNLP 2020*. Online: Association for Computational Linguistics. https://doi.org/10.18653/v1/2020.nlpcovid19-2.25.

Vaswani, Ashish, Noam Shazeer, Niki Parmar, Jakob Uszkoreit, Llion Jones, Aidan N. Gomez, Łukasz Kaiser, and Illia Polosukhin. 2017. Attention Is All You Need. In *Proceedings of the 31st International Conference on Neural Information Processing Systems*, 6000–6010. NIPS'17. Long Beach, CA, USA: Curran Associates Inc.

Wang, Lucy Lu, Kyle Lo, Yoganand Chandrasekhar, Russell Reas, Jiangjiang Yang, Doug Burdick, Darrin Eide, et al. 2020. CORD-19: The COVID-19 Open Research Dataset. In *Proceedings of the 1st Workshop on NLP for COVID-19 at ACL 2020*. Online: Association for Computational Linguistics.

Open Access This chapter is licensed under the terms of the Creative Commons Attribution 4.0 International License (http://creativecommons.org/licenses/by/4.0/), which permits use, sharing, adaptation, distribution and reproduction in any medium or format, as long as you give appropriate credit to the original author(s) and the source, provide a link to the Creative Commons license and indicate if changes were made.

The images or other third party material in this chapter are included in the chapter's Creative Commons license, unless indicated otherwise in a credit line to the material. If material is not included in the chapter's Creative Commons license and your intended use is not permitted by statutory regulation or exceeds the permitted use, you will need to obtain permission directly from the copyright holder.

CHAPTER 3

Managing Large Twitter Datasets

Abstract This chapter provides a thorough discussion of Twitter/X corpora in terms of compilation and management. Twitter corpora differ from other types of corpora in many aspects, as they are composed of a very large number of very small documents (tweets), each with a slew of metadata, that can be downloaded through scripts that make use of available APIs, which calls for certain tools and techniques. The type of language used in social media is also very different from other, more standard genres, both in form and content. When this is coupled with large-size corpora, effective sampling techniques are necessary, which are discussed at length in this chapter. Finally, a description is given of using geotagged data and subcorpora creation and management.

Keywords Twitter/X data management · Sampling methods · Corpus sampling · Geotagged tweets · Subcorpora management

A Twitter corpus differs considerably in format from other text corpora. A regular corpus is usually distributed as either a collection of plain text files or, if metadata is included, a set of XML files. Corpus creators decide what (if any) metadata is to be added to the actual data. In a corpus of literary texts, for example, these may include information like author, publishing date, genre, edition, etc. These data categories are additions that describe the text, which is the actual data to be explored, and their primary function is to organize, catalogue, and serve as search criteria. They usually need to be added manually, although sometimes data categories may be inferred or extracted from the original texts (chapters, page numbers, etc.); regular expressions—i.e. advanced text pattern matching—are very helpful to automatically remove such unstructured data from the actual text and encode it as usable metadata. In terms of size, the proportion of data (the actual text) vs. metadata (data about the text) falls heavily on the former: for each of the documents in a corpus the bulk of the data is the document itself, the metadata usually being a very small proportion of each text.

With Twitter data, the situation is reversed in both aspects. Although not apparent to users, each tweet consists of a short text (280 characters maximum) and a slew of metadata that provide additional information about that tweet (user, date, number of retweets, etc.); in fact, there is a lot more content in a tweet's metadata than in the tweet's text. This is why the term *dataset* is often used to refer to Twitter corpora, as this term refers to any structured collection of data of any kind (numerical, textual, multimodal), whereas a text corpus is any collection of texts which minimally contains plain text and may or may not contain further metadata. Thus, in the context of this book, both terms (corpus and dataset) are generally treated as synonyms, as we are dealing a Twitter dataset/corpus, which, by definition, contains structured text and metadata.

The conciseness feature of tweets is probably its most differentiating one, as it determines a very particular type of communication form that differs from other traditional "compressed" language genres, such as telegrams or newspaper headlines. Optional multimedia elements, such as hypertext links, user mentions, and hashtags, provide the means to expand the message in ways previously not available.

Some of these features (multimedia objects, hypertext links) are common to most—if not all—modern social networking sites. However, Twitter/X has several differentiating features. The first one is related to the aforementioned size restriction. Facebook allows up to 63,206 characters in regular posts, while Instagram has a limited text length of 2,200 characters.[1] But it is the social aspect of the social networking site (SNS) that truly distinguishes Twitter/X from others. By default, a user's tweets

[1] https://sproutsocial.com/insights/social-media-character-counter/# [Accessed 25 May 2023].

are public, and any other user may optionally be notified of new posts after "following" them, and automatically receive every tweet in their feed. Twitter users can block specific users, who will stop receiving their tweets in their feed; however, that does not mean that the blocked user will not be able to access the tweets, as they can use third-party apps and websites, therefore blocking someone really works in the opposite direction: the user who blocks will stop receiving tweets from the blocked user, who will, in turn, not be able to reply to their tweets. In contrast, both Facebook and Instagram users need to approve a follower's request before they can view their content (in the case of Instagram this is only true of private accounts, as public ones require no approval to follow).

Thus, Twitter's "openness" of content has largely determined its success as a data source for researchers. Twitter has, since the beginning, offered an API (Application Programmer's Interface) to allow developers to access their data. This favourable scenario, however, changed in March 2023, with Twitter's new API policy. Although free access is still present, it considerably limits the number of tweets to be downloaded (1,500 per month); they also offer two paid licences, a "basic" one, with a 10,000-tweet download limit, and an "enterprise" licence that can be tailored to specific needs. They also offer an academic research licence that needs to be applied for and meet several eligibility criteria, subject to approval by Twitter/X on an individual basis.[2]

Whichever the current—or future—limitations, existing Twitter datasets will remain to be available, and, despite the new limitations, there is little doubt that new ones will be created and made available.

3.1 Twitter Content

Although some of the characteristics of this SNS have been mentioned in passing in previous sections, it is important to understand how Twitter data is obtained, structured, and processed, to be aware of the possibilities and limitations that existing Twitter corpora present.

Since its inception, Twitter has significantly evolved, adding new features and implementing modifications to enhance the user experience and the quality of public discourse on the platform. The first *tweet* was published in July 2006 by Jack Dorsey, one of the platform's creators; it

---

[2] https://developer.twitter.com/en/products/twitter-api/academic-research [Accessed 2 June 2023].

read "just setting up my twttr." Initially, tweets were limited to 140 text characters and multimedia elements were not allowed, a feature that was added in 2012. This is the reason why Twitter was dubbed a *microblogging* site, as the idea was to be used to share users' concrete ideas or status updates by publishing a number of short daily posts. The next year, the company went public on the New York Stock Exchange under the ticker symbol "TWTR". In 2015 Twitter doubled the number of characters allowed in a tweet, which remains limited to 280 as June 2023, except for Chinese, Japanese, and Korean, for which the original limit of 140 characters was kept, as these languages can convey more content in fewer characters than Western languages.

Along with the ability for developers to access content via an API, this strict length limit is probably the most defining characteristic of Twitter, as it encourages users to be concise and to the point. This characteristic has in fact shaped a unique style of communication on the platform. For example, the expression of sarcasm is sometimes not easy to identify, and users recurrently need to resort to paratextual methods, such as the use of the hashtag #sarcasm to make their intentions explicit (Bamman and Smith 2015).

Irony, sarcasm, and other figurative language types are known to be pervasive on Twitter (Sulis et al. 2016), which poses a serious challenge to sentiment analysis and related natural language processing tasks, such as emotion detection. In fact, sarcasm detection is an active NLP area of research itself, and researchers dedicate entire datasets—e.g. Khodak et al. (2018)—and shared tasks—e.g. Ghosh et al. (2020)—to this particular topic.

The character limit is by no means the only problem that makes this task difficult, the lack of acoustic markers is probably the most limiting factor to achieve good results in these tasks (Woodland and Voyer 2011). Although researchers have employed a number of strategies to overcome this problem, the state of the art in sarcasm detection is far from optimal. Plepi and Flek (2021), for example, achieved state-of-the-art performance by using graph attention networks (GAT) to leverage both a user's historical tweets and social information from their conversational neighbourhood in order to contextualize the interpretation of a post. Therefore, detecting sarcasm on Twitter requires sophisticated strategies that take into account not just the tweet's content but also the user's profile. Since this approach is not easily implemented on an isolated Twitter dataset, irony and sarcasm detection remains an issue that affects a proportion of tweets that have been measured at 10% (Moreno-Ortiz and García-Gámez 2022).

Another issue that has been well documented is the presence of potentially misleading information, which became a noticeable problem during the COVID-19 pandemic and the US elections, leading Twitter to add warning labels to suspicious tweets in 2020. Several specific corpora have been compiled to deal with this issue in dedicated shared tasks. For example, FEVER: Fact Extraction and VERification (Thorne et al. 2018) is a manually annotated dataset that consists of 185,445 claims generated by altering sentences extracted from Wikipedia and subsequently verified without knowledge of the sentence they were derived from. More relevant to this book is COVIDLies (Hossain et al. 2020), a dataset of 6,761 expert-annotated tweets to evaluate the performance of misinformation detection systems on 86 different pieces of COVID-19-related misinformation.

Evidently, issues such as the use of figurative language and, especially, misinformation, are aspects that need to be taken into account when carrying out any analysis of Twitter data, but which do not invalidate results, as they should be considered the exception rather than the norm. Irony and sarcasm are often used as devices to create humour, as the entertainment aspect of social networks is clearly an important motivation for users. In fact, Tkáčová et al. (2021) mention that social networks were a useful source of entertainment for teens during COVID-19 lockdowns. Also, although the presence of sarcasm affects the performance of sentiment classifiers, it is rather irrelevant for keyword and topic extraction, as is the presence of misinformation tweets, since the object is not to identify the user's stance on the topic, but the topic itself.

3.2 Downloading and Managing a Large Twitter Corpus

3.2.1 Anatomy of a Tweet

Processing a "raw" Twitter corpus involves dealing with each tweet individually, using a loop to read them sequentially, and extracting the actual data that we need. Each tweet contains a large amount of data fields, most of which may be irrelevant. Figure 3.1 shows a screenshot displaying part of the hierarchical data structure of a tweet.

```
v  ≡ tweet = {dict: 25} {'created_at': 'Tue Jan 21 22:45:27 +0000 2020', 'id': 1219752899636613121, 'id_str': '1219752899636613121', 'full_text': 'R
   01 'created_at' = {str} 'Tue Jan 21 22:45:27 +0000 2020'
   01 'id' = {int} 1219752899636613121
   01 'id_str' = {str} '1219752899636613121'
   01 'full_text' = {str} 'RT @AnneKPIX: @CDC has activated its emergency operations center. \nThey expect more US cases.\n#coronavirus'
   01 'truncated' = {bool} False
  > ≡ 'display_text_range' = {list: 2} [0, 106]
  v  ≡ 'entities' = {dict: 4} {'hashtags': [{'text': 'coronavirus', 'indices': [94, 106]}], 'symbols': [], 'user_mentions': [{'screen_name': 'AnneKPIX', 'name': 'A
     v ≡ 'hashtags' = {list: 1} [{'text': 'coronavirus', 'indices': [94, 106]}]
        v ≡ 0 = {dict: 2} {'text': 'coronavirus', 'indices': [94, 106]}
             01 'text' = {str} 'coronavirus'
          > ≡ 'indices' = {list: 2} [94, 106]
             01 __len__ = {int} 2
          01 __len__ = {int} 1
     > ≡ 'symbols' = {list: 0} []
     > ≡ 'user_mentions' = {list: 2} [{'screen_name': 'AnneKPIX', 'name': 'Anne Makovec', 'id': 18650514, 'id_str': '18650514', 'indices': [3, 12]}, {'scree
     > ≡ 'urls' = {list: 0} []
        01 __len__ = {int} 4
     01 'source' = {str} '<a href="http://twitter.com/download/android" rel="nofollow">Twitter for Android</a>'
     01 'in_reply_to_status_id' = {NoneType} None
     01 'in_reply_to_status_id_str' = {NoneType} None
     01 'in_reply_to_user_id' = {NoneType} None
     01 'in_reply_to_user_id_str' = {NoneType} None
     01 'in_reply_to_screen_name' = {NoneType} None
  > ≡ 'user' = {dict: 44} {'id': 1110906564158869505, 'id_str': '1110906564158869505', 'name': 'нυєяco-\хаΟнестυzомα_тℓатοαιι##', 'screen_nan
     01 'geo' = {NoneType} None
     01 'coordinates' = {NoneType} None
     01 'place' = {NoneType} None
     01 'contributors' = {NoneType} None
  > ≡ 'retweeted_status' = {dict: 24} {'created_at': 'Tue Jan 21 19:09:49 +0000 2020', 'id': 1219698632217116673, 'id_str': '1219698632217116673', 'id_str': '1219698632217116
```

Fig. 3.1 Data structure of a tweet

In all, a tweet contains 141 data fields (attribute-value pairs), many of which are nested data structures themselves, such as arrays. For example, in the figure's tweet, the `entities.hashtags` field consists of a list-type value of cardinality 1, which contains an array of two attributes, `text` and `indices`, and the latter contains a list of two numerical values.

This complex, hierarchical data structure is obviously not easy to manage, and most data are irrelevant or missing. Missing information is a major problem, as some potentially useful data regarding the geographical location of the user or place of publication recurrently fall into this category. In fact, researchers have developed strategies to overcome this problem (Qazi et al. 2020).

Therefore, the first step to process a Twitter corpus consists of selecting the data fields that are relevant to our research, and then save the simplified data structure in a suitable format. Tweets are downloaded as a JSON object, a data exchange format that has gained popularity due to its expressive power (as opposed to CSV) and simplicity (as opposed to XML). However, CSV (comma/tab-separated values) may be preferable for our simplified version, as it is more readily usable with certain data processing libraries, such as Pandas. Alternatively, XML is necessary if we plan to use the resulting corpus with XML-aware corpus processing tools, such as Sketch Engine (see Sect. 1.5). Finally, JSON is probably the best option if we need to store hierarchical data structures; also, converting JSON to XML is rather straightforward.

3.2.2 Downloading and Extracting Data

Due to copyright issues, Twitter corpora cannot be distributed directly, that is, including the original tweets information. Instead, a Twitter corpus is usually made publicly available as lists of "tweet IDs", a string of 18 numerical characters that uniquely identify each Twitter object.[3] This means that accessing a publicly available Twitter corpus involves downloading the original content from Twitter, using its API, by way of each individual tweet ID contained in the distribution, a process known as *tweet hydration*. In the case of the CCTC, the corpus is distributed as a set of *gzipped* text files containing the IDs of each tweet. A Python script ("hydrate.py") is included that downloads the tweets using Twitter's streaming API.

An additional hurdle is Twitter's bandwidth limitations: download will stop if these limits are exceeded. In order to circumvent this, the download process must be paused at regular intervals. Therefore, it takes an average of 12 days to download each month of the original CCTC corpus (the initial months are faster, but it takes longer as the download moves forward in time). The corpus is then downloaded as a collection of *gzipped* JSON Lines files, where each JSON Line contains a complete tweet.

These compressed JSON Lines files contain all tweets in all languages. Therefore, the first step is to extract the tweets from the original files.

For this study, a custom Python script was used to extract only the English tweets, keeping specific information for each tweet (tweet ID, user, date, and text). This script uses several parameters that can be customized to change its behaviour (language to extract, time period, minimum number of words, etc.).

Another important aspect of Twitter/X corpora is the high proportion of duplicates, either because they are retweets or copy—pasted. One data

---

[3] Twitter's tweet detail route has the form https://twitter.com/{userName}/status/{tweetId}. The original tweet can be visualized by using the hyperlink https://twitter.com/anyuser/status/{tweetId}, which automatically converts {username} to the correct user.

field present in the tweet's structure that can be used to deal with this situation is "retweet_status". However, this is not so straightforward in practice because there is no certainty that the original tweet is included in the dataset. The method used by the extraction script resorts to adding each tweet to a daily Python dictionary using the tweet's text as the key, which makes it impossible to have two identical tweets. Thus, we avoid saving retweets or repeated tweets; instead, only one instance of each tweet per day is saved, along with a counter indicating the number of times that tweet occurs during that day.

Additionally, the script applies a number of pre-processing operations on the original text in order to remove hyperlinks and problematic characters such as newlines, tabs, and certain Unicode characters (e.g. typographic quotes). It also ignores tweets with fewer than the minimum number of words specified (3 by default).

Finally, the script generates a log file that includes details about the extraction process along with important statistics:

- Processed tweets by day.
- Saved tweets by day.
- Processed words by day.
- Saved words by day.
- Repeated tweets by day.
- Totals.

These data are printed to the console for each day at runtime and saved as a text file at the end of the extraction process. Since the data are saved in tab-separated format, it can be copy—pasted in a spreadsheet to generate data visualizations, such as the one in Fig. 3.2, where the daily data have been aggregated by week using a pivot table.

Table 3.1 summarizes the data in absolute figures.

In summary, the English portion of the CCTC for the years 2020 and 2021 consists of nearly 1.12 billion tweets and over 32 billion tokens. The "compressed" form used to store it, however, offers considerable savings. If the number of tweets was to be used as an estimator of the size of the corpus, the employed method (saving one instance of each unique tweet per day) offers a space saving of 68.45%. The advantage is not simply a considerably reduced storage size, but, more importantly,

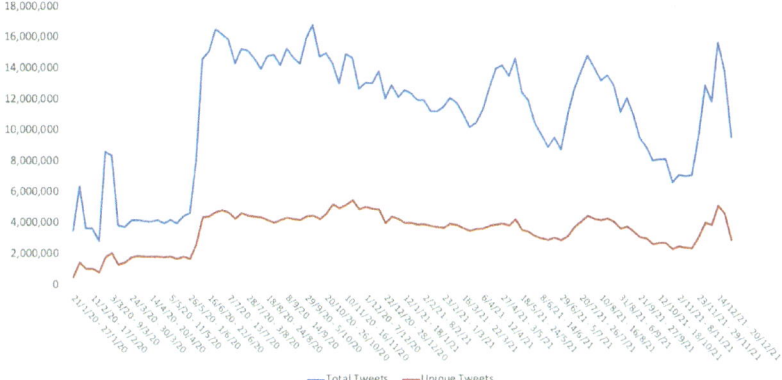

Fig. 3.2 Total English tweets over time (aggregated by week)

Table 3.1 Corpus extraction statistics

	Total	Daily average
Tweets (all langs.)	1,771,847,788	2,495,080
Tweets (English)	1,117,379,746	1,573,774
Stored Tweets (English)	352,556,633	496,559
English Words[4]	31,292,640,403	44,074,141
Stored Words	9,134,879,457	12,866,027
Retweets (English)	752,751,659	1,060,214
Short Tweets (<3 words)	12,071,454	17,002

reduced processing time for any operation subsequently performed on the data, an aspect that becomes critical when dealing with large corpora.[5]

---

[4] Word counting can be achieved in multiple ways, and results may vary considerably. The figures presented here were arrived at by using the Python split() method, which converts a string into a list of items using a specified separator (space by default). Although using a language-specific tokenizer undeniably achieves better results, this method is the fastest and allows on-the-fly word counting during the extraction process with acceptable accuracy.

[5] The optimal method to store and query a large corpus is indexing, but this involves a server-side database management system backend and associated frontend software, a complex hardware and software infrastructure which only makes sense to develop and

3.2.3 Data Organization and File Format Selection

The original distribution of the CCTC stores each hour worth of data in one file, thus having 24 files for each day, for a total of 17,040 files for the years 2020 and 2021 (a total of 710 days, starting February 21). During the process of extraction by language, unique tweets were stored for a given day into a single file (710 files in total). The result is as many files as there are days in the corpus, with each line representing a single tweet containing a reduced set of data fields. JSON Lines was chosen as the storage format, although CSV or TSV is also a good choice. All files were compressed with *gzip*, as this format allows fast, on-the-fly decompression during opening. A few examples of a data line are given in (1) to (6) below. All the data are extracted from the original tweet except the retweet counter ("n").

1. {"text": "A man who lives in Snohomish County, Washington, is confirmed to have the first US case of Wuhan coronavirus", "user": "cnnbrk", "date": "Tue Jan 21 19:42:55+0000 2020", "id": "1219706962851569665", "n": 75}
2. {"text": "BREAKING: First confirmed case of the new coronavirus has been reported in Washington state, CDC says.", "user": "ABC", "date": "Tue Jan 21 19:14:03+0000 2020", "id": "1219699699520876544", "n": 6}
3. {"text": "Dear friends, please spare a few minutes, and read about the #NovelCoronaVirus, and the ongoing epidemic in #Wuhan China…and now being recorded in other cities and countries. Do not spread fear. Spread the right information. And protect yourself and others.", "user": "Fredros_Inc", "date": "Tue Jan 21 21:41:31+0000 2020", "id": "1219736807832682498", "n": 12}
4. {"text": "😀 😀 😀. Remember when Ford cut a billion dollars from Toronto's public health 😒? . A good portion of that was infectious and communicable disease surveillance and treatment programs. Wuhan virus ain't nuthin' ta f' wit. 😀. #cdnpoli #onpoli.", "user": "StephenPunwasi", "date": "Tue Jan 21 23:01:00+0000 2020", "id": "1219756813140275200", "n": 66}

---

deploy for large-scale projects. The method I describe here is meant to be an optimal non-indexed alternative.

5. {"text": "PLEASE SHARE. First Case of Mystery Coronavirus Found In Washington State CDC via @YouTube", "user": "PeaMyrtle", "date": "Wed Jan 22 00:30:58+0000 2020", "id": "1219779453901058049", "n": 1}
6. {"text": "🚨🚨🚨 This Isn't True 🚨🚨🚨 Killer Chinese virus comes to the US, CDC says via @MailOnline", "user": "amandadonnell14", "date": "Tue Jan 21 19:01:15+0000 2020", "id": "1219696475858440197", "n": 3}

The online repository for this book[6] contains the extracted corpus in distributable form, that is as a collection of TweetIDs (*dehydrated*). The files, one for each day, have the extension ".tsv" (tab-separated values), and contain two data fields: "tweet_id" and "n", where "n" is the number of times that the tweet occurs in the original corpus on that particular day.

For some of the exploration tasks that I present in the following chapters, the geotagged subset of the corpus will be used, whose extraction process and statistics are described in Sect. 1.4.

3.3 Data Sampling

Given the size and organization of the corpus (large daily collections of tweets) sampling becomes extremely important. Although sequential, unindexed processing of each and every tweet in the corpus is possible (whether for keyword extraction, topic modelling, or sentiment analysis), it would be extremely impractical, as the processing time may extend for days or even weeks. Not only that, it may be unnecessary altogether, as a properly extracted sample may return the same or very similar results. This is true of all large corpora, but especially of social media corpora, as Twitter data consists primarily of short texts, many of which are merely repetitions of one another (retweets). Preparing the data and employing a consistent sampling method, as well as a representative sample size, is crucial for optimizing the storage and processing of data.

The importance of choosing the appropriate data sampling technique cannot be overstated. According to Boyd and Crawford (2012), "just because Big Data presents us with large quantities of data does not mean

---

[6] Moreno-Ortiz, A. (2024). LSMC Datasets. https://doi.org/10.17605/OSF.IO/H5Q4J.

that methodological issues are no longer relevant. Understanding sample, for example, is more important now than ever" (p. 668).

Data sampling refers to the set of methods used to select a subset of units from the target population. Although many definitions of sampling exist, the one by Brown (2012) is particularly suited to our context:

> Sampling is the act of choosing a smaller, more manageable subset of the objects or members of a population to include in an investigation in order to study with greater ease something about that population. In other words, sampling allows researchers to select a subset of the objects or members of a population to represent the total population. Sampling is used in language research when the objects or members (hereafter simply objects or members, but not both) of a population are so numerous that investigating all of them would be unwieldy. Such objects of study might include the total populations of all ESL learners, TOEFL examinees, essay raters, words, cohesive devices, and so on. (p. 1)

Our "objects of study" are tweets and the words that they contain, and the population is the full corpus. This creates an interesting paradox, as a corpus is usually defined as a sample of a language (Sinclair 2004) and the concept of representativeness enters into play. The notion of a *subcorpus* is also relevant in this context. A subcorpus is a part or section of larger corpus, but it is usually selected according to one or more directed criteria that define the content of that section, such as date, genre or media.[7] Sampling, however, attempts to extract a representative, usually random subset that can be used with the statistical certainty that the results do not differ significantly from those that would have been obtained from the population (i.e., the entire corpus).

There are numerous sampling methods, which are typically divided into two categories: probability and non-probability sampling. The primary distinction between these is that the latter selects units using a non-random and therefore subjective or intentional method, such as applying one of the abovementioned criteria for subcorpus creation. In the following sections of this chapter, I discuss the creation of time and location-based subcorpora, a good example of non-probability sampling.

---

[7] https://www.sketchengine.eu/my_keywords/subcorpus/ [Accessed 15 May 2023].

Probability sampling, on the other hand, is based on the randomization principle, which is the best way to obtain statistical representativeness. There are, however, several methods to implement probability sampling (Beliga et al. 2015; Siddiqi and Sharan 2015): (i) simple random sampling, (ii) systematic sampling, (iii) stratified sampling, (iv) cluster sampling, (v) multistage sampling, (vi) multiphase sampling, and (vii) proportional-to-size sampling. Two of these methods are especially relevant to our objective: simple random sampling, which is the most commonly used due to its simplicity, and proportional-to-size (PPS) sampling.

Simple random sampling basically requires a list of all the units in the target population, and all population members have the same probability of being selected for the sample. A drawback of this method is that the random drawing may lead to the over- or underrepresentation of small segments of the population: since all of the members of the sampling frame can be randomly drawn, it leaves to fate to which extent a particular group will be represented—or if it is at all—in the sample (Kamakura 2010).

Consequently, ensuring representation may require more sophisticated sampling techniques, such as *proportional-to-size sampling*. This method requires a finite population of units, in which a size measure "is available for each population unit before sampling and where the probability of selecting a unit is proportional to its size" (Skinner 2016, 1). Therefore, the likelihood of being included in the sample increases as the unit size grows.

Systematic sampling utilizes intervals to determine the number of sample units, which is determined by dividing the number of units in the population by the desired sample size. Although this scheme is frequently preferred due to its simplicity and convenience, it runs the risk of not being representative of the population, for instance if there is a periodic feature in the population's arrangement that coincides with the chosen sampling interval. Moreover, this method does not permit an impartial estimator of the sampling design variance (Bellhouse 2014).

Stratified sampling is based on the division of a population into strata. This ensures that each stratum is appropriately represented in the same proportion in the sample as in the sampling frame. This process improves the efficiency of sample designs in terms of estimator precision, as it allows the division of a heterogeneous population into internally homogeneous subpopulations (strata) whose sampling variability is smaller than that for the whole population (Parsons 2017).

Cluster sampling divides the population in groups, which are subsequently selected randomly in order to represent the total population. Then, all the units found in the selected clusters are included in the sample (Levy 2014). This method is especially useful in what Kamakura (2010) defines as "mini-populations", each having its own features and characteristics.

Multistage sampling involves the selection of a sample within each of the selected clusters (Shimizu 2014) and requires, at least, two stages: (i) selection and identification of large clusters (primary sampling units), and (ii) selection of units from within the selected clusters (secondary sampling units). A third optional stage is formed by tertiary sampling units, which are selected within the secondary sampling units.

Multiphase sampling is based on the (i) collection of basic information from a large sample of units, and the (ii) collection of more detailed information. It must be distinguished from multistage sampling: in multiphase sampling, "the different phases of observation relate to sample units of the same type, while in multistage sampling, the sample units are of different types at different stages" (Lesser 2014, 1).

Since our corpus consists of a daily set of unique tweets, each of which has a frequency indicator with the number of times it was retweeted, we can use this counter to apply proportional-to-size sampling. Thus, the probability of a tweet to be included in the sample grows proportionally with the number of times it was retweeted.

To describe the statistical distribution of the number of daily retweets (in fact, duplicate tweets, whether retweeted or not), Table 3.2 shows the descriptive statistics of the number of duplicates of a random day (June 20, 2021).

Table 3.2 Central tendency measures of daily number of retweets

N	318,926
Mean	3.2782
Median	1
Mode	1
Std. Deviation	46.7324
Variance	2,183.91
Range	17,029

On this particular day there are 318,926 unique tweets, with 3.28 average number of duplicates, but with a very large range, standard deviation, and variance, which indicates that the distribution is greatly spread and skewed. The median and mode of 1 suggest that the vast majority of daily tweets are unique. To provide a more accurate image of these numbers, Table 3.3 provides counts of daily retweets by ranges.

Using proportional-to-size sampling, several samples were extracted from the full corpus to use in the experiments described in the following chapters, the assumption being that working with smaller, fixed-interval samples is more practical and efficient than working with the rather unwieldly numbers of the full corpus. Table 3.4 summarizes the number of tweets and tokens contained in the full corpus and in each of the extracted samples.

To extract these samples, the corpus is taken as a time series of day intervals. The sample extraction script takes several parameters, including

Table 3.3 Daily retweets in the corpus by range

Number of retweets	Count
1	248,787
2–10	60,481
11–50	7,536
51–100	1,081
101–500	899
501–1,000	84
>10,000	58

Table 3.4 Corpus samples used in the study[8]

	0.1% sample	0.5% sample	1% sample	Full corpus
N tweets (stored)	923,550	3.94 mill	7.25 mill	352,56 mill
N tweets (repres.)	1,11 mill	5.53 mill	11.01 mill	1.12 bill
N tokens (stored)	28.75 mill	109.3 mill	199.37 mill	9.13 bill
N tokens (repress.)	31.24 mill	156.35 mill	312.75 mill	31.29 bill
Space saving	16.42%	28.69%	34.45%	68.45%

[8] Along with the full corpus, the three samples are included in the book's repository as collections of tweet ID's.

sample percentage and time period in number of days. All the samples in this study used daily time periods and the proportional-to-size ("pps") sampling method, but the script can use any number of days as a time period and two alternative sampling methods: "random", which retrieves a simple random sample of the desired percentage of tweets, and "top", which extracts the top retweeted tweets. The PPS and top methods use the frequency information obtained during the tweet extraction process.

As with the full corpus, samples are stored as gzipped JSONL files (one file per day, one JSONL document per tweet), with the text, date, and frequency of each tweet included in each JSONL document. With this system, considerable processing time is saved. Thus, instead of processing the actual number of tweets (many of which are the same text because they are retweeted or copied and pasted), we can simply multiply results by the tweet's frequency. To give an idea of how this system optimizes processing, Table 3.5 provides a summary of the processing times of some operations, such as sample and keyword extraction.

These processing times indicate that even though the sample extraction time is comparable for the 0.1%, 0.5%, and 1% samples, sample size becomes an important factor in the keyword extraction task: in the case of the 1% sample, this task alone took over 48 hours, compared to the almost 6 hours needed for the 0.1% sample.

Table 3.5 Processing times of some operations[9]

Task description	Sample	Time taken
0.1% sample extraction	Full corpus	00:58
0.5% sample extraction	Full corpus	01:03
1% sample extraction	Full corpus	01:05
Keyword extraction	0.1%	05:57
Keyword extraction	1%	48:32

---

[9] All times are given in hh:mm format. All tasks were run on an Intel Core i7-7400 3.0 GHz CPU (4 cores) on Ubuntu Linux 20.04 Server 64-bit. During the keyword extraction process other text items, such as entities, mentions, hashtags, and emojis, were also extracted, thus adding considerable overhead processing time.

3.4 Extracting Geotagged Tweets

The creators of GeoCov19 (Qazi et al. 2020), one of the few geotagged COVID-19 Twitter corpora available (described in Sect. 2.5), mention that only 1% of the tweets contain actual latitude/longitude coordinates. However, this figure is much smaller in reality, as they mention that only 378,772 tweets in their dataset of 452 million were actually geotagged (i.e. 0.084%). This is in fact very similar to what we find in the CCTC corpus.

In order to extract the geotagged portion of the English corpus, a script was created which only extracted tweets where the language was English and the `place.country_code` data field was not empty. This returned a total of 8.2 million tweets distributed in 242 different countries. As with the full English dataset, they were saved with the date information per day. The timeline, shown in Fig. 3.3, has a very similar profile to the overall English corpus (see Fig. 3.2), which indicates that the time distribution of geotagged tweets is almost identical.

An additional script was used to obtain statistics by country. Table 3.6 summarizes the data, and Fig. 3.4 visually displays the top ten countries by number of tweets.

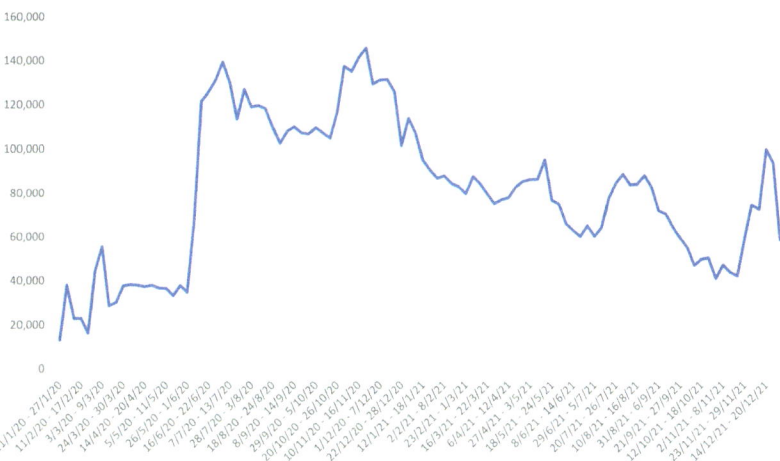

Fig. 3.3 English country-geotagged tweets aggregated by week

Table 3.6 Distribution of geotagged tweets by country

Country	Number of Tweets
U.S.A	3,984,700
U.K.	1,418,550
India	684,902
Canada	451,562
Australia	279,842
South Africa	180,177
Ireland	131,432
Nigeria	100,451
Philippines	73,230
Malaysia	55,224
Rest of the World	845,299
Total	8,205,369

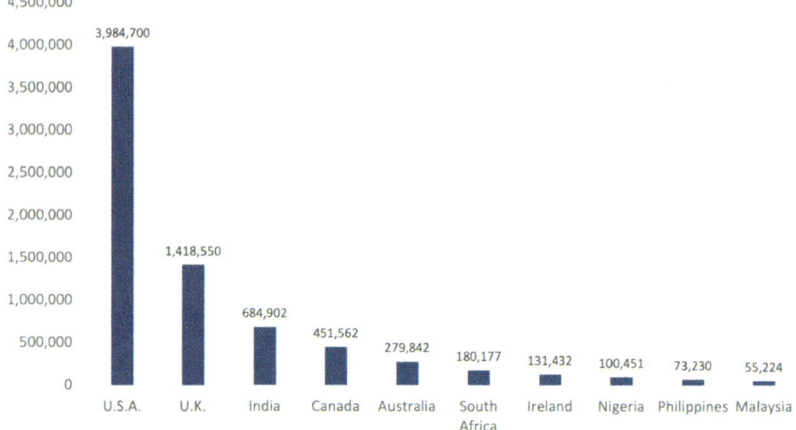

Fig. 3.4 Number of geotagged tweets by country

The United States alone generated almost 4 million tweets, that is, almost half of all the geotagged tweets (8.2 million). It must be remembered that this distribution may or may not be representative of all the English tweets; this is probably because these countries generated most of the tweets about the pandemic, but it can also be due to device configurations that allow the client application to read and post the country of origin. It does mean, however, that any study of English tweets will be skewed towards the most prolific countries, particularly the United States, the United Kingdom, and India, which account for 74.2% of the total volume.

The geotagged corpus obviously requires a different data structure to include the country code. (7) to (12) below are sequential JSON Lines randomly taken from the file corresponding to January 17, 2021.

7. {"country_code": "CA", "timestamp": "Sun Jan 17 00:02:51+0000 2021", "user": "RunnertheFirst", "id": "1350594395431706627", "text": "Has the reporter been arrested?"}
8. {"country_code": "US", "timestamp": "Sun Jan 17 00:03:01+0000 2021", "user": "cbwebster", "id": "1350594435931889669", "text": "If this doesn't make you think. 😒🤬 #CNN #COVID19 #coronavirus #CovidDeaths #CoronaVirusUpdates #planecrash"}
9. {"country_code": "US", "timestamp": "Sun Jan 17 00:03:19+0000 2021", "user": "trenttarbutton", "id": "1350594515518824448", "text": "COVID finally got me 😒"}
10. {"country_code": "US", "timestamp": "Sun Jan 17 00:03:25+0000 2021", "user": "Chrissy287", "id": "1350594538319065093", "text": "Poor guy these people are just trying to make a living there is nothing worse than someone who refuses to wear a mask in a pandemic"}
11. {"country_code": "GB", "timestamp": "Sun Jan 17 00:03:25+0000 2021", "user": "Gerfome", "id": "1350594540630138882", "text": "Not hearing any world news now on BBC, or other media outlets. Don't hear about what's happening in the EU. Proper mushroomed we are now, but I bet we all know the latest UK covid statistics 💻😒!"}
12. {"country_code": "US", "timestamp": "Sun Jan 17 00:03:32+0000 2021", "user": "dago_deportes", "id": "1350594569516187648", "text": "@LeviHayes21 Haha I know there's a game but didn't know if covid restrictions applied"}

As for the number of words, the entire geotagged corpus consists of nearly 198 million words (counted using the abovementioned split() method). Although this is a much more manageable figure, it may still be too large to apply some methods that require intensive computing, such as embeddings-based topic modelling, which is explored in Sect. 5.2. Thus, a script was created that extracts a daily random sample by country proportional to the number of tweets of that country in that day. The script takes several parameters, including the list of country codes whose tweets are to be sampled and the percentage of the desired daily sample. The list of country codes can be left empty to sample all countries in the corpus, and if 100 is selected as the percentage of the sample, all tweets for the specified country or countries will be extracted. The script also generates a log file that includes statistics on the read and written data, including number of tweets and number of words for each of the sampled countries.

Table 3.7 shows the statistics of the samples used in this book: 10%, 25%, and 50% of the top ten English-speaking countries.

Table 3.7 Tweet and word counts of the geotagged corpus samples by country[10]

Country	10% Sample		25% Sample		50% Sample	
	Tweet count	Word count	Tweet count	Word count	Tweet count	Word count
US	398,155	9,284,908	995,902	23,203,999	1,992,177	46,440,738
UK	141,523	3,643,566	354,371	9,109,664	709,099	18,250,060
IN	68,176	1,843,429	170,974	4,625,236	342,276	9,260,158
CA	44,836	1,151,059	112,612	2,890,685	225,587	5,774,809
AU	27,651	689,914	69,685	1,741,967	139,745	3,490,755
ZA	17,702	363,857	44,782	925,200	89,914	1,857,860
IE	12,826	325,490	32,593	830,523	65,757	1,673,491
NG	9,724	213,876	24,843	544,349	50,054	1,102,390
PH	7,000	151,902	18,050	392,518	36,442	790,565
MY	5,212	101,639	13,549	264,614	27,437	534,765
TOTAL	732,805	17,769,640	1,837,361	44,528,755	3,678,278	89,175,591

[10] Along with the full geotagged corpus, the three samples are included in the book's repository as collections of tweet ID's in TSV format with two data columns: "tweet_id" and "country_code".

Although all these countries have English as a first language, not all countries included in the corpus do. In fact, Germany is in 14th position by number of tweets published in English in the Geotagged section of the CCTC, after Kenya. Table 3.8 offers the ranked list of the top 50 countries present in the corpus, including the exact number of tweets and the percentage of the whole corpus. The top 10 countries selected for the samples make up 92.31% of the entire geotagged corpus.

Table 3.8 Top 50 countries by volume in the geotagged corpus

Country	Tweets	Percent (%)	Country	Tweets	Percent (%)
U.S.A	3,984,700	49.98	Mexico	15,838	0.20
U.K.	1,418,550	17.79	Brazil	15,721	0.20
India	684,902	8.59	Singapore	14,504	0.18
Canada	451,562	5.66	Belgium	14,066	0.18
Australia	279,842	3.51	China	14,056	0.18
South Africa	180,177	2.26	Botswana	12,329	0.15
Ireland	131,432	1.65	Switzerland	11,798	0.15
Nigeria	100,451	1.26	Sri Lanka	11,506	0.14
Philippines	73,230	0.92	Trinidad and Tob	9,768	0.12
Malaysia	55,224	0.69	Zimbabwe	9,276	0.12
New Zealand	48,116	0.60	Sweden	9,126	0.11
Pakistan	47,735	0.60	Saudi Arabia	8,721	0.11
Kenya	46,846	0.59	Namibia	8,074	0.10
Germany	35,094	0.44	Israel	7,862	0.10
Uganda	30,841	0.39	Hong Kong	7,659	0.10
Ghana	29,151	0.37	Nepal	7,430	0.09
Spain	28,213	0.35	Turkey	6,771	0.08
France	24,364	0.31	Bahamas	6,318	0.08
Netherlands	23,940	0.30	Portugal	6,083	0.08
Indonesia	21,021	0.26	Bangladesh	6,040	0.08
Italy	20,424	0.26	Korea	6,001	0.08
Jamaica	20,273	0.25	Colombia	5,877	0.07
UAE	19,278	0.24	Taiwan	5,779	0.07
Thailand	17,476	0.22	Zambia	5,776	0.07
Japan	16,299	0.20	Myanmar	5,660	0.07

3.5 Subcorpora. Using Metadata with XML-Aware Corpus Tools

The described JSONL format chosen to store the corpus is suitable for processing the data with the custom tools that we will be using in this book, but other formats are required to use the data effectively with different tools. XML (Extensible Markup Language), in particular, is a standard text exchange format that is used by many text processing tools.

Like JSON, XML is capable of encoding metadata together with the text. (13) to (17) are examples of XML-encoded tweets from the geotagged corpus.

13. <doc date="2021-05-01" country="US" id="1388488549922598915">Planned Parenthood? We're a pro-life institution. Vaccinations? We're pro-choice.</doc>
14. <doc date="2021-05-01" country="US" id="1388283084072787971"> I literally have covid for the 3rd time….how in the fuck???</doc>
15. <doc date="2021-05-01" country="US" id="1388521299698495491">May gone be the month I stay my ass home 😭😩 I been away from home like weeks out out of April smh</doc>
16. <doc date="2021-05-01" country="GB" id="1388381954714832899">Koreans are immune to Covid—fact. (The Japanese call them the "Garlic Eaters").</doc>
17. <doc date="2021-05-01" country="IN" id="1388539225767772161">Sir i need an oxygen bed for a corona positive relative in dehradun. Plz help sir. Regards</doc>

XML-aware corpus tools, such as the web-based corpus suite Sketch Engine (Kilgarriff et al. 2014), are able to read the metadata and offer certain extra functionalities, such as the creation of subcorpora that can be searched individually by the different tools. Furthermore, some of the tools in this suite do depend on the availability of time metadata in order to be available altogether. Such is the case of the *Trends* tool, which can keep track of the diachronic frequency of words in the corpus.[11]

Unlike other tools, such as Google Trends or the dynamic topic modelling tools we explore in Sect. 5.3, Sketch Engine's Trends cannot show word-specific usage over time, but offers a useful list of words whose frequency shows a significant change (upwards or downwards) over time, computed using a user-selected statistic (either linear regression or Mann–Kendall, Theil-Sen). To illustrate what this tool achieves, Fig. 3.5 and Fig. 3.6 show the results obtained from the India 2020 and 2021 subcorpora, respectively.

In order to get these results, specific subcorpora need to be created combining location and time data, which, as mentioned above, require that these attributes be encoded in the XML metadata prior to uploading the corpus. Both charts were computed with the tool's default settings: attribute = lemma, minimum frequency = 69, maximum *p*-value = 0.01, method = Mann-Kendal, Theil-Sen (all).

---

[11] In order for the Trends tool to work correctly, the configuration of the corpus needs to be manually modified to include the line 'DIACHRONIC "doc.date"', where the part following the "doc." needs to be name of the date metadata field used in the corpus. The date itself needs to be in one of the accepted formats. The corpus needs to be recompiled after this modification, too. See https://www.sketchengine.eu/guide/trends/#toggle-id-2 for more details [Accessed 10 June 2023].

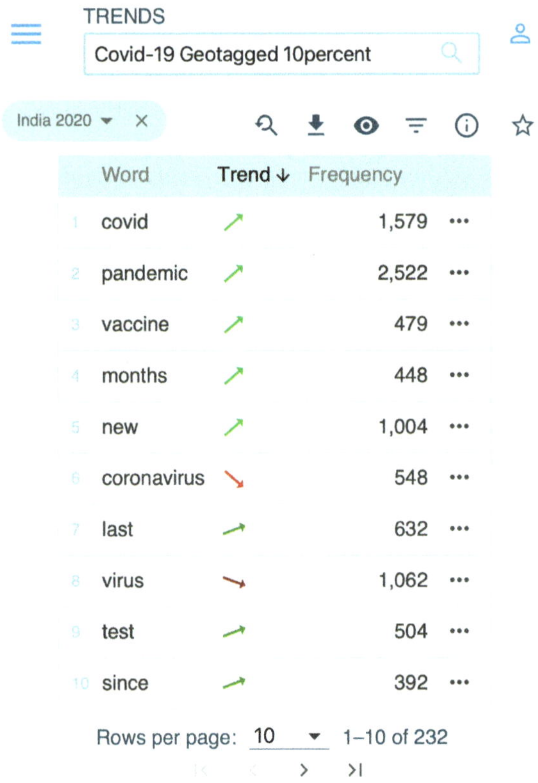

Word	Trend ↓	Frequency
1 covid	↗	1,579
2 pandemic	↗	2,522
3 vaccine	↗	479
4 months	↗	448
5 new	↗	1,004
6 coronavirus	↘	548
7 last	→	632
8 virus	→	1,062
9 test	→	504
10 since	→	392

Fig. 3.5 Word usage trends of the India 2020 subcorpus

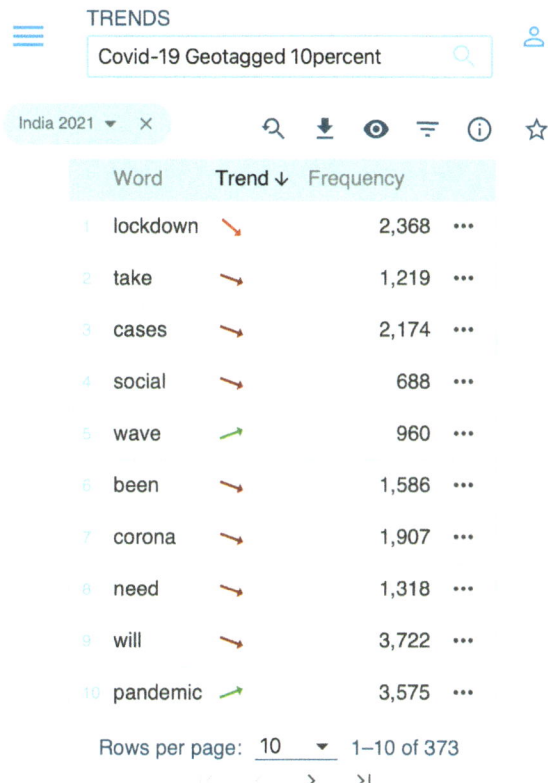

Fig. 3.6 Word usage trends of the India 2021 subcorpus

References

Bamman, David, and Noah Smith. 2015. Contextualized Sarcasm Detection on Twitter. *Proceedings of the International AAAI Conference on Web and Social Media* 9: 574–577. https://doi.org/10.1609/icwsm.v9i1.14655.

Beliga, Slobodan, Ana Meštrovic, and Sanda Martincic-Ipsic. 2015. An Overview of Graph-Based Keyword Extraction Methods and Approaches. *Journal of Information and Organizational Sciences* 39: 1–20.

Bellhouse, D. R. 2014. Systematic Sampling Methods. In *Wiley StatsRef: Statistics Reference Online*, ed. N. Balakrishnan, Theodore Colton, Brian Everitt, Walter Piegorsch, Fabrizio Ruggeri, and Jozef L. Teugels, 1st ed. Wiley. https://doi.org/10.1002/9781118445112.stat05723.

Boyd, Danah, and Kate Crawford. 2012. Critical Questions for Big Data: Provocations for a Cultural, Technological, and Scholarly Phenomenon. *Information, Communication & Society* 15: 662–679. https://doi.org/10.1080/1369118X.2012.678878.

Brown, James Dean. 2012. Sampling: Quantitative Methods. In *The Encyclopedia of Applied Linguistics*. Wiley. https://doi.org/10.1002/9781405198431.wbeal1033.

Ghosh, Debanjan, Avijit Vajpayee, and Smaranda Muresan. 2020. A Report on the 2020 Sarcasm Detection Shared Task. In *Proceedings of the Second Workshop on Figurative Language Processing*, 1–11. Online: Association for Computational Linguistics. https://doi.org/10.18653/v1/2020.figlang-1.1.

Hossain, Tamanna, Robert L. Logan IV, Arjuna Ugarte, Yoshitomo Matsubara, Sean Young, and Sameer Singh. 2020. COVIDLies: Detecting COVID-19 Misinformation on Social Media. In *Proceedings of the 1st Workshop on NLP for COVID-19 (Part 2) at EMNLP 2020*. Online: Association for Computational Linguistics. https://doi.org/10.18653/v1/2020.nlpcovid19-2.11.

Kamakura, Wagner A. 2010. Sampling Techniques. In *Wiley International Encyclopedia of Marketing*, ed. Jagdish Sheth and Naresh Malhotra, wiem02014. Chichester, UK: Wiley. https://doi.org/10.1002/9781444316568.wiem02014.

Khodak, Mikhail, Nikunj Saunshi, and Kiran Vodrahalli. 2018. A Large Self-Annotated Corpus for Sarcasm. In *Proceedings of the Eleventh International Conference on Language Resources and Evaluation (LREC 2018)*. Miyazaki, Japan: European Language Resources Association (ELRA).

Kilgarriff, Adam, Vít Baisa, Jan Bušta, Miloš Jakubíček, Vojtěch Kovář, Jan Michelfeit, Pavel Rychlý, and Vít Suchomel. 2014. The Sketch Engine: Ten Years On. *Lexicography*: 7–36.

Lesser, Virginia M. 2014. Multiphase Sampling. In *Wiley StatsRef: Statistics Reference Online*, ed. N. Balakrishnan, Theodore Colton, Brian Everitt, Walter Piegorsch, Fabrizio Ruggeri, and Jozef L. Teugels, 1st ed. Wiley. https://doi.org/10.1002/9781118445112.stat07578.

Levy, Paul S. 2014. Cluster Sampling. In *Wiley StatsRef: Statistics Reference Online*, ed. N. Balakrishnan, Theodore Colton, Brian Everitt, Walter Piegorsch, Fabrizio Ruggeri, and Jozef L. Teugels, 1st ed. Wiley. https://doi.org/10.1002/9781118445112.stat05694.

Moreno-Ortiz, Antonio, and María García-Gámez. 2022. Corpus Annotation and Analysis of Sarcasm in Twitter: #CatsMovie vs. #TheRiseOfSkywalker. *Atlantis. Journal of the Spanish Association for Anglo-American Studies*: 186–207. https://doi.org/10.28914/Atlantis-2022-44.1.11.

Parsons, Van L. 2017. Stratified Sampling. In *Wiley StatsRef: Statistics Reference Online*, ed. N. Balakrishnan, Theodore Colton, Brian Everitt, Walter

Piegorsch, Fabrizio Ruggeri, and Jozef L. Teugels, 1st ed., 1–11. Wiley. https://doi.org/10.1002/9781118445112.stat05999.pub2.

Plepi, Joan, and Lucie Flek. 2021. Perceived and Intended Sarcasm Detection with Graph Attention Networks. In *Findings of the Association for Computational Linguistics: EMNLP 2021*, 4746–4753. Punta Cana, Dominican Republic: Association for Computational Linguistics. https://doi.org/10.18653/v1/2021.findings-emnlp.408.

Qazi, Umair, Muhammad Imran, and Ferda Ofli. 2020. GeoCoV19: A Dataset of Hundreds of Millions of Multilingual COVID-19 Tweets with Location Information. *SIGSPATIAL Special* 12: 6–15. https://doi.org/10.1145/3404820.3404823.

Siddiqi, Sifatullah, and Aditi Sharan. 2015. Keyword and Keyphrase Extraction Techniques: A Literature Review. *International Journal of Computer Applications* 109: 18–23. https://doi.org/10.5120/19161-0607.

Shimizu, Iris. 2014. Multistage Sampling. In *Wiley StatsRef: Statistics Reference Online*, ed. N. Balakrishnan, Theodore Colton, Brian Everitt, Walter Piegorsch, Fabrizio Ruggeri, and Jozef L. Teugels, 1st ed. Wiley. https://doi.org/10.1002/9781118445112.stat05705.

Sinclair, John McHardy. 2004. Trust the Text. In *Trust the Text*. Routledge.

Skinner, Chris J. 2016. Probability Proportional to Size (PPS) Sampling. In *Wiley StatsRef: Statistics Reference Online*, ed. N. Balakrishnan, Theodore Colton, Brian Everitt, Walter Piegorsch, Fabrizio Ruggeri, and Jozef L. Teugels, 1st ed., 1–5. Wiley. https://doi.org/10.1002/9781118445112.stat03346.pub2.

Sulis, Emilio, Delia Irazú Hernández Farías, Paolo Rosso, Viviana Patti, and Giancarlo Ruffo. 2016. Figurative messages and affect in Twitter: Differences between #irony, #sarcasm and #not. *Knowledge-Based Systems* 108. New Avenues in Knowledge Bases for Natural Language Processing: 132–143. https://doi.org/10.1016/j.knosys.2016.05.035.

Thorne, James, Andreas Vlachos, Christos Christodoulopoulos, and Arpit Mittal. 2018. FEVER: A Large-Scale Dataset for Fact Extraction and VERification. In *Proceedings of the 2018 Conference of the North American Chapter of the Association for Computational Linguistics: Human Language Technologies, Volume 1 (Long Papers)*, 809–819. New Orleans, Louisiana: Association for Computational Linguistics. https://doi.org/10.18653/v1/N18-1074.

Tkáčová, Hedviga, Martina Pavlíková, Zita Jenisová, Patrik Maturkanič, and Roman Králik. 2021. Social Media and Students' Wellbeing: An Empirical Analysis during the Covid-19 Pandemic. *Sustainability* 13: 10442. Multidisciplinary Digital Publishing Institute. https://doi.org/10.3390/su131810442.

Woodland, Jennifer, and Daniel Voyer. 2011. Context and Intonation in the Perception of Sarcasm. *Metaphor and Symbol* 26: 227–239. Routledge. https://doi.org/10.1080/10926488.2011.583197.

Open Access This chapter is licensed under the terms of the Creative Commons Attribution 4.0 International License (http://creativecommons.org/licenses/by/4.0/), which permits use, sharing, adaptation, distribution and reproduction in any medium or format, as long as you give appropriate credit to the original author(s) and the source, provide a link to the Creative Commons license and indicate if changes were made.

The images or other third party material in this chapter are included in the chapter's Creative Commons license, unless indicated otherwise in a credit line to the material. If material is not included in the chapter's Creative Commons license and your intended use is not permitted by statutory regulation or exceeds the permitted use, you will need to obtain permission directly from the copyright holder.

CHAPTER 4

Keywords

Abstract This chapter tackles the task of keyword extraction from corpora. Keywords are extremely helpful to quickly identify the terms (and their associated concepts) that somehow define what a corpus is about. After a quick revision of the concept of *keyword*, I focus on the different methods that have been proposed to extract keywords effectively and efficiently. A key distinction is made between the reference-corpus method traditionally employed in corpus linguistics and the various methods that have been proposed in Natural Language Processing research. Through several experiments, the CCTC is explored using some of the most outstanding methods proposed to date, and a contrastive description of the results is offered.

Keywords Keyword extraction · Topics · Themes · Reference corpus · Machine learning · Graph-based methods · Keyword set comparison

The term *keyword* has different meanings in different contexts and fields. For a programmer, the keywords of a programming language are the commands and reserved words used in that language, that is, the entire "lexicon" of the programming language. For a web developer or SEO (Search Engine Optimization) specialist, keywords are the set of words and phrases contained in the website, which users might type in their search engines and eventually land them on that website. In an archival system of documents, such as a library or bibliographical database, each document is usually assigned a set of words that define its contents and topics. Some document types, such as books, do not usually display its keywords within itself, and rely on archival experts to manually assign those keywords, which will help in the indexing and retrieval processes. Other documents inherently contain keywords; for example, scientific articles systematically rely on three elements that define, catalogue, and classify them: the title, the abstract, and a set of keywords. These three elements can be assessed by prospective readers to decide whether the article is relevant to their interests and therefore worth inspecting any further or reading in detail.

Notomo (2023) rightly states that the notion of *keyword* has long defied a precise definition, and quotes Boyce et al. (1994) for the general definition "a surrogate that represents the topic or content of a document", which makes sense in the context they referred to (libraries and information science). Notomo distinguishes four senses or roles: *terminology:* specialized lexical items from a particular domain; *topics*: terms and labels that are part of a systematic concept system, such as Wikipedia category names; *index terms*: terms indicating major concepts, events, or people, including named entities, and *summary terms*: words or phrases meant to serve as a quick description of the content.

Of these four roles or senses of the term, it is probably the last one that is most often thought of. In this sense, keywords can be loosely defined as words that somehow encapsulate the topics discussed in a document or collection of documents; in other words, what those documents "are about". This is what most authors in corpus linguistics studies agree on: keywords are meant to capture the *aboutness* of a document or set of documents, and make up their ontology (Scott and Tribble 2006; Mahlberg 2007; Bondi 2010; Marchi 2018).

When dealing with very large corpora, keywords are extremely useful pointers or *access points* to an otherwise intractable mass of words whose contents we can only guess from the criteria that were used during the corpus compilation process. For example, in the Coronavirus Twitter Corpus, a number of keywords were used to query the Twitter API for tweets containing them ('COVID-19', 'coronavirus', 'lockdown', etc.). It is safe to assume, then, that these words are key in the corpus, but there is probably a myriad other terms which define and summarize the tweets in the corpus, and which, as a whole, build the ontological scaffolding of the corpus. If we are able to identify those keywords, we will have a means to access that information, cues to help us to further process and "digest" it. Keyword extraction tools facilitate the identification of words and phrases that fulfill this role, and therefore may be used to further investigate the concepts they refer to and the discourse they define.

4.1 THE CONCEPT OF "KEYWORD" IN CORPUS LINGUISTICS

Within the field of corpus linguistics, keywords are one of the "key" elements in the set of tools offered by corpus query applications. However, this is not the first sense that this term had in corpus linguistics. Originally, the term was synonymous with "search word" in a concordance, which can be defined as "a collection of the occurrences of a word-form, each in its own textual environment" (Sinclair 1991, 32). In fact, this sense of the word gave rise to the term "KWIC" (Key Word in Context), a search results format in which the search word (or "key word") is centre-aligned and the contexts are shown on both sides in such a way that they can be sorted following user-defined criteria and facilitate the task of browsing through potentially thousands of results. The use of the term in this sense was abandoned in favour of others (usually "search word", although phrases, lemmas or more complex patterns can be searched in most concordancers nowadays) after Wordsmith Tools (Scott 1996) introduced the Keywords tool, which offered a convenient way to extract a ranked set of words that stood out as representative of a corpus. The definition that Mike Scott provides is tied to the extraction method:

> A key word may be defined as *a word which occurs with unusual frequency in a given text*. This does not mean high frequency but unusual frequency, by comparison with a reference corpus of some kind". (Scott 1997, 236)

This definition is of a procedural nature, as it is based on the specific approach employed to extract keywords, but says nothing about what keywords are or the purpose they serve. In fact, we do not find very specific actual definitions of the term in the literature. Instead, authors tend to rely on functional approximations that use metaphors to describe their nature and the function they serve in corpus research. Thus, keywords have been referred to as "pointers" that "merit chasing up and tracking down" (Scott 2010, 55–56). Similarly, Baker (2006, 137) states that keywords "act as signposts to the underlying discourses", while Hunt & Harvey (2015, 139) point out that keywords "serve as indicators of expression and style as well as content to provide a sense of the 'aboutness' of a language variety", and Bondi (2010, 1) qualifies keywords as "markers of the aboutness and the style of a text". Stubbs (2010, 25) compares keywords to the "tips of icebergs: pointers to complex lexical objects which represent the shared beliefs and values of a culture".

In summary, keywords in corpus linguistics are regarded as words and phrases that act as *pointers*, *markers*, *indicators*, or *signposts* to the contents, style, and discourse of a corpus. In the context of social media corpora, I would add yet another metaphorical moniker—that of *access points* that allow us to enter the complex network of concepts, ideologies, discourses, and cultural assumptions hidden behind a mass of bite-sized documents.

Scott's methodological definition, however, is necessary to understand the consideration of keywords in corpus linguistics. Scott (2010) expands the aforementioned definition by offering a very clear illustration:

> In the case of a key word procedure such as that used in WordSmith, this [p-value] calculation is repeated for every single type in the text we are interested in. For example, the frequency of THE in the text is compared with the frequency of THE in the reference corpus, and the p value is then computed of any difference. If the text has 9% of THE and the reference corpus has only 5% of THE, say, we might get a p value suggesting that we can believe, with little risk of being wrong, that in our text THE is prominent. This process is repeated with the frequencies of WAS, the frequencies of IS, and so on until all word-forms have been examined. (p. 48)

Thus, he implicitly establishes a parallelism between a statistical property (a keyness score rendered by a certain metric) with a notional one: the quality of words being outstanding in a corpus:

> The actual calculation of "keyness" is done using the chi-square statistic, but the important point to grasp here is that the notion underlying it is one of outstandingness. In other words, if a word occurs outstandingly frequently in our text, it will be key. Finally, when all potentially key items have been identified, they are ordered in terms of their relative keyness. (Scott 1997, 236)

In summary, this method relies on calculating statistically significant differences between the frequency of words—and possibly n-grams—in a *focus corpus* (the document or set of documents from where keywords are to be extracted) and the frequency of those words in another (*reference*) corpus.[1]

There are several problems with this approach, which Scott himself acknowledges. The most important has to do with the choice of a reference corpus, which will determine to a large extent what is considered to be a keyword. In other words, keywords obtained by this method are relative; they are determined by their frequency in the focus corpus vs. their frequency in the reference corpus. This characteristic is a drawback when we do not have an obvious reference corpus or frequency list. State-of-the-art corpus query tools, such as Sketch Engine (Kilgarriff et al. 2014) make this easy by offering a large number of corpora that can be used as reference, but the actual choice is left to the user, who needs to decide which corpus can be considered "normal" from a statistical point of view.

Then of course there is the issue of the choice of statistical metric to apply. Gabrielatos (2018) discusses this issue at length. He states that "definitions of the terms *keyness* or *keyword* have tended to conflate their nature with the proposed metric for measuring keyness". He goes on to perform a very detailed analysis of the appropriateness of several statistics, concluding that effect-size metrics should be used to measure keyness rather than statistical significant ones.

Since Scott's implementation was ground-breaking, his definition and conception of keywords has stuck within the corpus linguistics community, with few attempts to further elaborate on the actual concept of what the extraction method actually tries to achieve. For example, Stubbs (2010) describes and discusses three different concepts of *keyword*. The first concept dates back to the German tradition of *Schlüsselwörter* dictionaries and glossaries of the early twentieth century and until the 1980s, such as Teubert's (1989) *politishche Vexierwörter* ("ambiguous political words"). In English, he mentions Williams' (1976) work, and in French he mentions Matoré's (1953) work on *mots clés*. This sense of the term

---

[1] I will use the term "focus corpus" in this book, which is attributed to Kilgarriff (2012). Scott (1997) uses the term "node corpus". Brezina (2018) uses the more explicit term "corpus of interest". The corpus used as reference is usually called "reference corpus", the term that I will use in this book, but other authors have used alternative terms, such as "comparator corpus" (Johnson and Ensslin 2006).

refers to collections of words (and their definitions) that represent and distinguish a society and a culture. Stubbs' second sense of the term "keyword" is conceptually closer to what is generally understood by *keywords* nowadays, but he literally calls it "statistical: keywords are words which are significantly more frequent in a sample of text than would be expected, given their frequency in a large general reference corpus" (Stubbs 2010, 25). Thus, he follows the tradition of tying the definition to the extraction method, specifically referencing Scott's work.

It appears, then, that within the corpus linguistics community there is an implicit understanding that the terms "keyness" and "aboutness" are one and the same thing; and, since keyness is a numerical score obtained by the application of some statistical metric, it follows that words are said to be defining of a text if their relative frequency is statistically significant as compared to their frequency in some other collection of texts against which they are measured.

However, as we will see in the examples, not all words retrieved by this method can be said to be keywords. If anything, they are keyword *candidates* whose actual status as a keyword needs to be validated by the application of certain rather subjective criteria. In other words, a ranked list of keyword candidates resulting from the comparison of word frequencies in a focus corpus against those in a reference corpus computed using a particular statistical metric (that is, the output of all "reference-corpus" keyword extraction tools) cannot be said to exclusively contain keywords that satisfy the criteria of all users. This is because the concept of keyword is rather subjective and depends on the objectives that are being pursued. As Gabrielatos (2018, 26) states, "the identification of an item as key depends on a multitude of subjective decisions regarding a) thresholds of frequency, effect-size, and statistical significance, b) the nature of the linguistic units that are the focus of analysis, and c) the attributes of the compared corpora".

Regardless of the precise statistical metric employed to extract keywords using this method, which I will be referring to as the "reference-corpus method", it is quite apparent that it is a useful system to compare two corpora and highlight differences, which can then be scrutinized in detail. In the words of Alessi and Partington (2020, 3) "this keyword list, providing an ordered series of items which are salient in one corpus compared to another corpus, is likely to suggest items which warrant further investigation".

Many corpus linguistics studies have made extensive use of the reference-corpus keyword extraction method to successfully address linguistic issues. For example, Johnson and Ensslin (2006) used Word-Smith Tools to analyse how language and linguistics are represented in articles in the press, specifically from a corpus derived from two British newspapers, The Times and The Guardian. They derived four subcorpora by searching for four "node terms" ('language', 'languages', 'linguistic', and 'linguistics') and extracting all articles that contained these terms. Then they extracted separate keyword lists from each of these subcorpora by using the British National Corpus as a reference corpus (which they refer to as "comparator corpus"). This study is interesting for many reasons. First, because they identify types of words that should be filtered out and considered "noise" results, or false positives:

1. Words that reflect newspaper discourse in general such as 'is', 'has', 'who', and 'says'.
2. Words that refer to the circumtext of the text, such as 'author', 'paper', 'section', 'date', etc.
3. Word forms of the same lemma.
4. Proper names of central public figures.
5. Terms relating to recent technological innovations such as 'WWW', 'Google', and '.com', which did not exist when the reference corpus was created.
6. Word forms which only occurred in one single article or type of article that was considered irrelevant.

Second, they use keyword classification or grouping based on their semantics, which they implement by manually identifying and assigning the automatically extracted keywords to semantic fields, specifically four: "languages", "education", "media culture", and "identity".

Another reason why this study is relevant is that the authors raise two very specific methodological concerns. The first one has to do with the choice of reference corpus, an issue I have already discussed and is well illustrated by this study. In their case, the choice of "an asynchronous comparator corpus" (Johnson and Ensslin 2006, 6)—the BNC—had a strong negative impact on their study because they wanted to analyse the discourse in the media concerning language and linguistics, but the types and very nature of the media at the time when they compiled their focus corpus were very different than the media at the time when the BNC was created and closed—in 1994, right before the advent of the World Wide Web, and the explosion of Internet technologies, which seriously impacted traditional mass media. Consequently, each and every word related to these aspects were immediately pushed to the top of their ranked keyword lists, since no occurrences were found in the reference corpus. The solution to this problem is not a simple one, because if the choice is made to remove these candidate keywords from the list, then the actual relevant keywords are likely to be ignored, as internet technologies have been key in the development of the media in general. The second major issue they raise is ultimately caused by the same problem (choice of reference corpus), but has to do with proper names; their interest, as critical sociolinguists, aimed to identify "real social actors" engaged in debates over language and linguistics, but since those names occurred worth a statistically insignificant frequency, they were not taken as keywords, and only irrelevant household names (Blair, Chirac, Beckham) ranked high in the lists.

Baker (2004) is another piece of research that illustrates well the shortcomings of the reference-corpus method of keyword extraction. He used this method of keyword analysis to compare the discourses of gay male erotic narratives and lesbian erotic narratives by using two corpora of one million words each.[2]

When two focus corpora are to be compared, several different reference-corpus approaches can be used: first, both corpora can be compared against one reference corpus, which means extracting keywords from both using the same reference corpus, and then comparing the results. Second, the researcher can extract keywords from focus corpus A using focus corpus B as reference and then invert the procedure. Finally, focus corpora A and B can be merged into one and kept as two subcorpora, which can then be individually compared against the whole. Of these three, only the first method can highlight both differences and similarities. The second approach, which Baker uses, has the predictable issue that the analysis will focus on lexical differences, not similarities. The author himself warns about this problem, which "may result in the

---

[2] He mentions, however, that in this paper he is more focused on the method of analysis than in the discourses themselves. He also warns that he does not seek to denigrate keyword analysis, but "to make researchers aware of possible areas of over- or under-interpretation and suggest ways of ameliorating these issues" (Baker 2004, 249).

researcher making claims about differences while neglecting similarities to the point that differences are over-emphasised" (Baker 2004, 251). Therefore, he also explores the first approach listed above, (comparing both focus corpora against a third reference corpus); for this he uses the Frown (Freiberg-Brown) corpus of general American English, taken from the same time period.

Baker also mentions other practical problems with the application of the reference-corpus method. First, keywords with relatively low frequency may end up ranking high in the list, depending on the specified p-value. He also mentions a well-known issue: in a focus corpus with many individual texts, it is possible that some words with a high frequency may occur only in one or a few texts, which is an indicator that those particular words could only be considered "key" in those specific texts, not in the whole corpus.[3] For example, in one of his two focus corpora, the word "wuz" is listed as a keyword, but it occurs in just one text where these non-standard spelling of "was" is frequently used.

Keyword sets in Baker's paper—and, being quite representative of the type of study commonly found in corpus linguistics, many others in this field—are compared using intuition and, in general, fairly informal methods. This is possible if very high cut-off points are used, that is, only when a manageable number of keywords is considered. However, more strict, formal ways can be devised to compare large sets of keywords. In Sect. 4.3 of this book I propose to use basic set theory to perform this task, which can be used to quickly find differences and similarities between sets and visually represent those using Venn diagrams.

4.1.1 Experiment: The Keywords of Keywords

To conclude this section, I present a brief—and rather "meta"—experiment on keyword extraction with the aim of providing first-hand evidence of some of the issues discussed thus far and others that will become apparent, but will be difficult to identify due to the large amounts of data involved, when a systematic keyword analysis of the CCTC is performed in the next sections. The experiment consists in extracting the keywords from the book *Keyness in Texts* (Bondi and Scott 2010). The book is a collection of articles around the notion of keyness and keywords;

---

[3] As Baker (2004) reminds us, Scott (1997) proposes the use of *key keywords* to overcome this issue.

it consists of 13 chapters divided into three sections titled "exploring keyness", "keyness in specialized discourse", and "critical and educational perspectives", plus one introductory chapter by Marina Bondi.

For this analysis, all front and back matter was removed, as well as the list of references at the end of every chapter. Headers, which contain page numbers and the names of the various authors and chapter titles were also removed. The remaining text was uploaded as one single file to Sketch Engine, with no mark-up whatsoever. Keyword extraction was performed with the *Keywords* tool using the default settings—focus on rare (N = 1), minimum frequency = 1, case insensitive. In total the focus corpus contains 100,244 tokens (80,783 words). The chosen reference corpus was the 2021 English version of the TenTen corpus family (Jakubíček et al. 2013), which is over 61 billion tokens (52.3 billion words).

The *Keywords* tool in Sketch Engine allows the extraction of two 1,000 keyword sets, one set for single words and one set for multi-words. Output can be visualized on the web app itself or downloaded as CSV, TXT, or Excel files. The online view only permits sorting results by score, but items can easily be sorted by any of the data columns using the downloaded files. These columns are "item", "frequency (focus corpus)", "frequency (reference corpus)", "relative frequency (focus corpus)", "relative frequency (reference corpus)", and "score".

The score, which is the actual keyness indicator, is calculated in Sketch Engine using the *simple maths* approach (Kilgarriff 2009), which is very simple indeed, as it is the result of dividing the normalized frequency (per million words) of a word or n-gram in the focus corpus by its normalized frequency in the reference corpus; an N value ranging from 0.001 to 1,000,000 (1 by default) is added to both the numerator and denumerator. This function gives users the possibility to change the focus of the results, as lower values will return rarer words and higher values more common words. Values can be provided in increments of one order of magnitude.

Other corpus query applications offer considerably more sophisticated statistical methods and options. For example, WordSmith Tools v. 8 (Scott 2022) by default runs four different statistical tests to compare frequencies (Ted Dunning's log-likelihood test, Log ratio, BIC Score, and dispersion difference), and words are only returned as keywords if they pass all statistical tests, although some tests can optionally be skipped. AntConc v. 4.2.0 (Anthony 2023a), on the other hand, allows users to choose between two variants of three different statistical tests (chi-squared, log-likelihood, and text dispersion keyness) plus a choice of thresholds (p-values) in the range $p < 0.00001$ to $p < 0.5$, with or without Bonferroni adjustment. Therefore, these two desktop applications are more suited to advanced users who wish to tweak the comparison methods, whereas Sketch Engine may be more appealing to users who do not care which statistical test is used but want a very wide choice of reference corpora and effective management of their own corpus, as it allows user-defined subcorpora, as described in Sect. 3.5.

I will not focus here on the differences that result from the use of different reference corpora and statistical tests, as this would take ample discussion and this can be found elsewhere.[4] The reference corpus (RC) chosen for this experiment is meant to be general enough to serve as a good reference to extract keywords from a focus corpus (FC) that deals with a very specific topic, although no claim is made that it is representative of the English language.

Table 4.1 displays the top 20 single-word keywords returned by the described method. One important advantage offered by Sketch Engine (SE henceforth) is that statistics can optionally be calculated over lemmas rather than words, which generally returns better results. This is possible because all corpora in SE are not only indexed, but tagged by part of speech and lemmatized. The results shown have been computed over lemmas and sorted by score. All frequencies are relative per million words.

As other authors have mentioned, e.g. Gabrielatos (2018), judging a ranked list of candidate keywords is not easy due to the subjectivity involved, although some objective criteria can be applied. To begin with, none of the items in Table 4.1 are grammatical words, which is sometimes the case; for example, although it is not a fair comparison, as a different reference corpus was used and no lemmatization intervened, AntConc with the default settings did return the preposition "of" in 14th place. Next, almost all of the words clearly refer to concepts in the field of linguistics and, more specifically, corpus linguistics ('corpus', 'concordance', 'collocation', 'collocate', 'n-gram'). Also, the top term is

---

[4] Brezina (2018) offers a good overview of statistical methods in corpus linguistics, as well as the criteria that enter into play when choosing a reference corpus. Gabrielatos (2018) contains a thorough discussion and comparison of the impact of using the various statistical tests mentioned in this section in relation to keyword extraction. Anthony (2023b) summarizes the most important statistics used in Linguistics.

Table 4.1 Top 20 single-word keywords extracted from the book *Keyness in Texts*

Rank	Item	Freq. (FC)	Freq. (RC)	Score
1	keyness	1,207.05481	0.00332	1,204.062
2	concgram	718.24750	0.00063	718.797
3	aboutness	708.27179	0.02546	691.662
4	aboutgram	658.39349	0.00005	659.363
5	lexical	1,416.54358	1.37757	596.215
6	corpus	3,710.94531	5.53609	567.915
7	closed-class	508.75864	0.00366	507.898
8	concordance	708.27179	0.80941	391.991
9	phraseological	379.07504	0.01134	375.814
10	collocate	418.97769	0.19374	351.817
11	**tribble**	389.05072	0.15736	337.019
12	phraseology	428.95334	0.34685	319.229
13	**hyperlink**	907.78503	2.04574	298.379
14	text-type	309.24545	0.05883	293.008
15	collocation	349.14807	0.33713	261.865
16	**wuli**	259.36716	0.00614	258.777
17	**kws**	279.31845	0.09387	256.264
18	n-gram	279.31845	0.12420	249.35
19	**hunston**	249.39148	0.01227	247.357
20	**key-key**	239.41583	0.00035	240.332

'keyness', closely followed by 'aboutness', both of which surely refer to the core concept discussed in this book.

But this list of single-word keywords also contains some awkward items, which have been highlighted in bold. The word 'tribble' is ranked in 11th position. This is because it is a fairly uncommon family name that has 39 occurrences in the FC, as many authors in the book cite Scott and Tribble's (2006) book. Proper names may be argued to be part of the ontology of a corpus, but if this is true, Scott's name should be up there too, as he is the one to actually be credited with the concept of *keyness*; however, 'scott' is listed in position 733, since it is a much more common name in English (relative frequency is 778.1 in FC vs. 42.72 in RC, keyness score = 17.82). The same can be said of 'hunston', in reference to the linguist Susan Hunston, who is mentioned 52 times in the book.

Another issue is raised by the word 'hyperlink', which does not belong in the realm of linguistics. Its absolute frequency is 91, resulting in a very high relative frequency compared to the RC (97.78 vs. 2.04), and therefore a very high keyness score. However, literally all occurrences of this word take place in one specific chapter of the book—"Hyperlinks: Keywords or key words" by Jukka Tyrkkö—which focuses on the status of hyperlinks as keywords. This is a well-known problem with this method of keyword extraction that has been pointed out by many authors. In fact, Egbert and Biber (2019) have proposed the concept of *text dispersion keyness* as an alternative, or perhaps complimentary, method of keyword extraction to overcome this problem, and has been implemented by some corpus query packages, such as the latest version of AntConc. The same can be said of the word 'kws', which is exclusive to the chapter by Mike Scott, whose familiarity with keywords after many years of closely studying them probably leads him to use this abbreviated form.

A similar, but distinct issue is raised by the word 'wuli', whose dispersion plot is limited to the chapter by Fraysse-Kim, a corpus-based analysis of school textbooks that focuses on the Korean word 'wuli' ('we', 'our'). This illustrates a recurrent problem in keyword extraction using the reference-corpus method: foreign words tend to rank high in the lists, as few cases (or none) may be present in the reference corpus.

Finally, the last item in the list ('key-key') refers to the multi-word item 'key-key word'. Hyphenation, compounding, and word boundary marking in general are also a source of problems. First, many keyword extraction tools can only extract single words, but even those that are able to deal with n-grams, such as SE, do not discriminate between actual compounds and the constituent items that make it up. Thus, they sometimes return the whole compound, and also parts of it. Table 4.2 lists the top 20 multi-word keywords identified by SE, listed by score. An example of this issue is apparent here: both 'issue of climate' and 'issue of climate change' are given, when in fact only the latter is an actual multi-word unit. Also, this is another example of the "condensation" issue, as all of the occurrences of this multi-word expression come from the chapter by Denize Milizia, which deals with the importance of looking at phraseological combinations and not just individual words when it comes to keyword analysis.

Similarly, we have the inclusion of 'school textbooks' and 'history textbooks'; the reason is that the last two chapters of the book, by Soon Hee Fraysse-Kim and Paola Leone, focus on the analysis of these two text types, respectively.

Table 4.2 Top 20 multi-word keywords extracted from the book *Keyness in Texts*

Rank	Item	Freq. (FC)	Freq. (RC)	Score
1	key word	1,516.30017	2.02158	502.16
2	reference corpus	448.90466	0.00547	447.46
3	closed-class keyword	409.00204	0	410
4	speech act	359.12375	0.17581	306.28
5	semantic field	279.31845	0.03362	271.2
6	metaphor theme	259.36716	0	260.37
7	target fragment	259.36716	0.00427	259.26
8	concordance line	239.41583	0.00566	239.06
9	key-key word	229.44017	0	230.44
10	lexical item	249.39148	0.08844	230.05
11	lexical word	219.46451	0.00751	218.82
12	**issue of climate**	239.41583	0.15798	207.62
13	**issue of climate change**	229.44017	0.13350	203.3
14	specialised corpus	199.51318	0	200.51
15	**pos neg**	179.56187	0	180.56
16	discourse community	179.56187	0.04972	172.01
17	speech event	169.58621	0.02205	166.91
18	**school textbook**	189.53752	0.15944	164.34
19	**history textbook**	189.53752	0.16197	163.98
20	**la repubblica**	169.58621	0.06052	160.85

As for the 'pos neg' n-gram, all of the occurrences are headers in a particular data table in the book where they are used as abbreviated forms of 'positive' and 'negative'. Finally, 'la reppublica' is an example of both the proper nouns and the foreign words issues already mentioned.

This short analysis gives us an idea of what can be achieved through the reference-corpus method of keyword extraction commonly used in corpus linguistics, as well as some of its limitations and issues.

It is critical to understand that proper manual assessment of keyword lists, such as the one I have attempted to carry out in this experiment, is only possible when the contents of the focus corpus are actually known to the researcher. This, however, is not the case when keyword tools are used for the purpose of exploring and identifying key concepts in an unknown corpus, which is the main objective of keyword extraction when applied to very large corpora. This is one aspect that corpus linguists fail to mention or even be aware of, as they often analyse corpora of themes, topics, or authors they are already familiar with, and their aim is to discover the finer details of the underlying discourse.

4.2 Keyword Extraction Methods in Natural Language Processing

The reference-corpus method commonly employed in corpus linguistics is inherently statistical, as it uses various such metrics to compare the frequency of words and phrases in the corpus of interest (or focus corpus) with those in another—reference—corpus. However, there are other ways to identify keywords that do not make use of a reference corpus, and have some practical advantages, the most obvious one being that a reference corpus is not needed.

Outside the corpus linguistics community, in particular Natural Language Processing (NLP), other approaches to keyword extraction are regularly employed. Specifically, unsupervised and graph-based methods have been shown to be very effective in keyword extraction. Supervised machine learning approaches are also effective to extract keywords in some specific scenarios in which training data is available, which is not the case in social media corpora.

In addition, topic modelling, a common NLP task, can be said to fulfil the same role as keyword extraction, as the objective of these algorithms is to identify salient words and cluster them into semantically related sets which, as a whole, are said to identify a given topic. Topic modelling itself is a complex task where multiple methods and algorithms have been proposed over the years. We explore these in Chapter 5.

4.2.1 *Machine Learning Approaches*

Generally speaking, the—supervised—machine learning approach to information retrieval consists of creating a prediction model using training documents containing known labels, and then employs the model to identify those labels in new documents, "new" meaning not used during training. In the case of keyword extraction, this means that known, "good" keywords assigned to documents need to exist for the model to be created in the first place. This is why proposed machine learning systems have focused on extracting "metadata keywords", that is, keywords used to summarize the contents of research articles used for archival purposes.

A good exemplar of a machine learning-based keyword extractor is Kea (Witten et al. 1999), which uses Naïve Bayes as the learning algorithm for keyword extraction. Kea builds upon the work of Turney (2000), who was the first to approach this problem as one of supervised learning from examples. Kea's creators build and evaluate the predictive model using a dataset of research articles with known keywords[5] (manually assigned by the original authors of the articles). Specifically, they used a subset of the Computer Science Technical Reports section (46,000 documents) from the New Zealand Digital Library. The subset consisted of the 1,800 documents that had assigned keywords, of which they used 1,300 for training and 500 for testing. As training features for the Naïve Bayes classifier, they used fundamentally discretized TF-IDF scores. Instead of using the common evaluation method used in information-retrieval, they simply counted the number of true positives in the top 20 keywords retrieved by Kea, i.e. the number of matches between keywords that were retrieved by Kea and those that were assigned to the original articles. They found that, on average, Kea matched between one and two of the five keywords chosen by the authors, which they considered good performance.

This example illustrates very well the limitations of supervised machine learning approaches to keyword extraction, the most important of which is that such systems require labelled data for training and testing the system, which is only available for a very specific concept of *keyword*, i.e., the one that refers to keywords as metadata in archival systems. Also, supervised methods have a relatively long training time (Campos et al. 2018).

4.2.2 Unsupervised Approaches

Unsupervised, statistical approaches have been shown to be effective in keyword extraction. Of these, TF-IDF is the most common method in NLP, to the point that it has become the baseline method against which others are measured (Sun et al. 2020). Other, simpler methods have been used, such as noun phrase (NP) chunking (Hulth 2004), which, operating under the assumption that most keywords are nouns or noun phrases, extracts these and then uses some filtering strategy, such as frequency.

---

[5] Kea's authors use the term *keyphrases*, and they explain that it is meant to subsume the term *keywords*. This use of the term, i.e. *keyphrase* to refer to both single and multi-word items has stuck with many authors in the NLP literature.

TF-IDF is really the combination[6] of two individual calculations: *term frequency* and *inverse document frequency*. The former is literally the relative frequency of a word in a document (i.e. the result of dividing the absolute frequency of a word by the total number of words). The inverse document frequency of a term or word is the—logarithmically scaled—division of the total number of documents in the corpus by the number of documents that contain that word. If multi-word keywords are also extracted, the calculations are then applied to the n-grams in the texts. The IDF part of the equation, which was proposed by Karen Spärck Jones in 1972 (Spärck Jones 1972) with the name "term specificity", plays the role of the reference corpus, as it provides a score indicating the expected probability for a given term to occur in a document that is part of a corpus.

There is an important difference, however, between the reference-corpus method and the TF-IDF method, as the latter assumes that the corpus is organized as a set of *documents* and the terms will be extracted from a subset of documents (typically one) from the whole set. This is very different from the reference-corpus method, where no internal organization of the focus and reference corpora is assumed (although it may of course exist). IDF will return zero for any word that occurs in all documents in a corpus, which is an indication that it does not have a "special" status in the corpus.

There are some important considerations to bear in mind when using TF-IDF for keyword extraction. Since TF-IDF is a multiplication of the term's relative frequency by its inverse document frequency, it follows that any term that occurs in all documents will return a TF-IDF score of zero, regardless of how high its frequency is in the "focus" document or set of documents. Thus, if we have a corpus consisting of 1,000 tweets about the COVID-19 pandemic, and the term "COVID-19" occurs in all of them, it will be discarded it as a keyword of any subset of tweets in that corpus, and it will obtain a low score if it occurs in a high proportion of them. Of course, this situation is unlikely in the case of tweets, given the very special nature of this type of document, but it may be an issue in certain scenarios.

Consequently, when using TF-IDF, it is important to decide exactly what is taken as a document and what is taken as the whole collection

---

[6] It is in fact the multiplication of these two scores, which is the reason why it is sometimes expressed as "TFxIDF".

of documents (i.e. the corpus). In most situations this will be straightforward, but in the case of a diachronic Twitter corpus, not so much, as it will be dictated by our interests. For example, if we want to extract keywords from a particular time span, say a week, we may take the "document" to be all of the tweets in that week, and the whole corpus would be all of the tweets in the corpus aggregated by week (i.e. one week, one document). This would probably return the word "lockdown" as a keyword candidate for weeks when lockdowns were announced, since it will occur with a higher frequency in those weeks, and it will not occur in all weeks. However, if it does occur in all weeks, the term will get a score of zero, and so it will be discarded as a keyword. As a result, the TF-IDF tends to give higher scores to rare words, which may result in ranking misspellings high. Nonetheless, this method does have advantages from a purely technical perspective, as it is easy to implement and is also extremely fast.

Therefore, TF-IDF is rarely used in isolation, and there have been many other keyword extraction techniques that incorporate it into a more sophisticated process, such as KP-Miner (El-Beltagy and Rafea 2009).

Yake! (Campos et al. 2018) is an interesting tool because it takes into account a number of textual and linguistic parameters to calculate keyword scores, including language (TF-IDF is language-independent). It proceeds in six steps: text pre-processing, feature extraction, individual terms score, candidate keyword list generation, data deduplication, and ranking. The list of features that are used to obtain keyword candidates includes capitalization, word position, word frequency, word relatedness to context, and "word DifSentence", which quantify how often a candidate word appears within different sentences.

Another keyword extractor that has gained attention in the NLP community is RAKE (Rapid Automatic Keyword Extraction) (Rose et al. 2010). The authors' motivation to develop RAKE was "to develop a keyword extraction method that is extremely efficient, operates on individual documents to enable application to dynamic collections, is easily applied to new domains, and operates well on multiple types of documents" (p. 5). RAKE uses an extremely simple approach that uses stopwords and phrase delimiters to divide the document text into candidate keywords, which are sequences of content words occurring in the text. It assumes that most keywords are in fact multi-word units that rarely contain any stopwords and therefore they mostly extract multi-word keywords and are hardly applicable to languages which do make use of stopwords in noun phrases. Finally, the system takes into account co-occurrences of words, which it measures using word association metrics, to score candidate keywords.

The performance of RAKE was measured in terms of precision and recall against TextRank, the graph-based system proposed by Mihalcea and Tarau (2004), which is described in the next section. In the dataset used by the authors, RAKE performed marginally better than TextRank (F-score of 37.2 for RAKE, 36.2 for TextRank). However, this dataset consisted of short technical abstracts, for which RAKE seems particularly well-suited. However, its performance leaves much to be desired when extracting keywords from large texts, as will be made evident in the experiment that follows.

The most obvious advantage of unsupervised methods in general is that they can be easily implemented and run over large amounts of text, as they are generally fast and do not require any labelled data.

Experiment: Unsupervised Methods vs. Reference-Corpus Keyword Extraction
The aim of this experiment is to compare the performance of these two methods of keyword extraction. I will use a simple script that extracts keywords using the three algorithms that were described—TF-IDF, Yake!, and RAKE[7]—from a subset of the geotagged Coronavirus Twitter Corpus (see Sect. 3.4), specifically the 50% sample of the tweets generated in the U.K. The tweets from the two years that the corpus comprises were aggregated by week and saved to individual weekly files for a total of 102 weeks/files, which were saved as raw text, XML, and JSONL formats. For this experiment the raw text files were used, which were fed to all three keyword extractors. The subcorpus contains over 17 million words (709,099 tweets). Thus each week, which to these keyword extractors are "documents", consists of approximately 7,000 tweets and 173,000 words on average.

In the experiment, the top 100 keywords were extracted for each week, and extraction was limited to n-grams in the range 1–3. The full

---

[7] The script uses existing Python implementations of these systems. For TF-IDF, it employs Scikit-learn library (Pedregosa et al. 2011); for Yake!, it uses the authors' own implementation found in https://github.com/LIAAD/yake (Campos et al. 2018); for RAKE, it uses the code in https://github.com/u-prashant/RAKE [Accessed 3 May 2023].

results are provided in the book's repository[8] Here we show the top 20 keywords returned by each system corresponding to three different periods of the whole dataset: week 2 (January 27 to February 2, 2020), shown in Table 4.3, week 31 (August 31 to September 6, 2020), shown in Table 4.4, and week 85 (September 13–21, 2021), shown in Table 4.5. Of the three systems, RAKE was the fastest (about 1 minute), then TF-IDF (about 3 minutes) and finally Yake!, which was the slowest by far (14 minutes).[9]

Table 4.3 Unsupervised keyword extraction methods (U.K. Week 2)

TF-IDF	Yake!	RAKE
coronarvirus	coronavirus	🧍🧍💼
declared global	China	😀😀😀😊😊 id recommend
wuhan coronavirus	Wuhan Chinese Coronavirus	📁 ☺️☻️ ①②③
wirral	Wuhan Coronavirus	*Please Take Care*
brexitday	Coronavirus outbreak	📁 cadeaux gifts
global health emergency	Wuhan	vaping lung injury
confirmed uk	CHINA CORONAVIRUS	usual terrorist attacks
declared global health	Chinese	unusual beggers belief
coronaravirus	coronavirus cases	trades persons van
coronavirus confirmed uk	Coronavirus Wuhan	subconsciously chew pens
coronavirus declared global	Coronavirus Wuhan diary	rewarding excellence conference
coronavirus confirmed	Wuhan China	repost whitley bay
ighalo	coronavirus cases confirmed	quid pro quo
china coronavirus	Chinese coronavirus	model 🎱: tatiana
coronavirus coronavirus	people	minju kins creations
coronavirusuk	corona	matt hancock enlisted
arrowe park	Coronavirus confirmed virus	jimdavidson jim davidson
kobe	Chinese people	confidently predict armageddon
coronavirus outbreak	Chinese people	challenged ronnie pickering
coronavirusoutbreak	China virus-hit Wuhan	bill gates foundation

---

[8] https://osf.io/h5q4j/.
[9] The script was run on a 2.3 GHz 8-core Intel MacBook Pro.

Table 4.4 Unsupervised keyword extraction (U.K. Week 31)

TF-IDF	Yake!	RAKE
push parliamentary debate	Government COVID support	👀 egunje primate
push parliamentary	covid	⌐ cliffordstott h
help push parliamentary	Government COVID lockdown	🏛 waterhall 3g
support help push		●♻☘
debate sign share	CoVid support	**Who Are We**
work small micro	social distancing	@ mertonlibdems
covid support help	Covid test	wirral tankard 🏆●
awareness retweet followers	people	whoa whoa whoa
clients raise awareness	Covid pandemic	twisted terrace takeover
friends family advise	pandemic	trevor francis tracksuits
advise clients raise	coronavirus	totes beauts !'.
family advise clients	covid lockdown	stunningly revised choreography
family advise	COVID cases	stuffing guylian shells
raise awareness retweet	back	rhondda cynon taf
clients raise	Covid times	recite surah ka
small micro business	Covid deaths	poacher boyle pounces
micro business government	government	niki 01,908 395,692
business government covid	time	newly refurbished omniplex
sign share ask	Post Covid	mydaddy 🏠📕♥ speculating
share ask friends	COVID safe	multifunctional workhorse robots

Although all three methods appear to have several issues and biases towards particular types of words and phrases, RAKE's results seem entirely random, with no keywords in reference to the relevant topics whatsoever. The conclusion is that this system was designed to rapidly extract keywords from short texts, such as the scientific abstracts on which it was evaluated, and seems to be absolutely useless to work with lengthy texts or large corpora.

Both TF-IDF and Yake! do seem to capture the "aboutness" of the corpus and the differences between time frames are evident: keywords in week 2 capture the geographical origin of the virus as well as the alarm generated by the outbreak, keywords in week 31 include several references to the British government relief initiatives, and keywords in week 85 are mostly about COVID-19 tests and vaccines.

Table 4.5 Unsupervised keyword extraction methods (U.K. Week 85)

TF-IDF	Yake!	RAKE
free pcr covid	PCR Covid tests	😊 sends kashmir
tests travel sign	COVID	@ lucygrievevet
government provide free	free PCR covid	xi jinping drakeford
uk government provide	Covid fucking covid	versus 390 unvaxinated
provide free pcr	PCR Covid	thingie mi bob
travel sign petition	Covid tests	thankyounhs ♡ xxx
travel sign	long covid	teamearlychildhood acc freaks
pcr covid tests	Covid vaccine	steffiegregg steffie gregg
covid tests travel	covid deaths	spelling errors …)
vaccinated	Covid pandemic	smelly dirty hippies
free pcr	positive Covid test	slugs ate brassicas
tests travel	pandemic	sg adverts galore
government provide	people	select cttee investigations
provide free	Covid cases	professor andrew watterson
pcr covid	Covid vaccination	preparatory communications begin
pcr	lockdown	phdlife raheem sterling
ve finally singing	NHS Covid Pass	paint expressive flowers
given scenes	NHS Covid test	mayflower400 diy audax
come mean given	catch Covid	jamia masjid bilal
song belong written	covid PCR test	insular damaging viewpoint

There are some important differences, however. Yake! captures some relevant topics that TF-IDF does not (e.g. "lockdown", "social distancing" in week 31, "long covid" in week 85). Similarly, Yake! takes into account features such as case and part of speech, thus clearly favouring noun phrases and capitalized words, whereas TF-IDF returns many syntactically irrelevant word sequences (e.g. "covid tests travel", "support help push", "come mean given"). Thus, Yake! appears to offer the best performance in terms of quality, although not so in terms of computational efficiency, as it takes as much as seven times longer to run, thus requiring much more computing power.

When comparing these results with those returned by the reference-corpus method using Sketch Engine, the efficiency should not be taken into account, as this online platform indexes all corpora, and therefore word frequencies (the only feature it uses to identify keywords) are calculated beforehand. Also, being online, time delays are possible due to server load and network issues.

Table 4.6 shows the results for week 2, Table 4.7 for week 31, and Table 4.8 for week 85; as before, the tables include the top 20 keywords, but since Sketch Engine returns two different lists of single and multi-word units with different scores, it is not possible to offer a properly ranked merged list, the top ten single-word items and the top 10 multi-word items are listed separately. In all three tables, two sets of results are shown: using a general-language corpus as reference (enTenTen21), and using the rest of the focus corpus as reference.[10]

Generally speaking, keyword sets extracted using enTenTen21 as reference corpus are rather in line with those extracted by unsupervised methods, referencing the topics in each of the time periods. The main differences are those that are caused by the low frequency of certain words. For example, "ighalo" is in reference to Manchester United's footballer Odion Ighalo, who made the headlines when he was isolated from the rest of the team as a precaution after his return from China in the early stages of the pandemic.

Table 4.6 Reference corpus keywords extraction (U.K. Week 2)

Single words (RC: enTenTen21)	Multi-words (RC: en-TenTen21)	Single words (RC: RoC)	Multi-words (RC: RoC)
wuhan	corona virus	kobe	global health emergency
coronavirus	coronavirus outbreak	brize	coach driver
corona	global health emergency	arrowe	arrowe park hospital
wirral	health emergency	ighalo	health emergency
coronaviru	coronavirus case	wirral	high sense
arrowe	bbc news	huawei	high sense of responsibility
brize	case of coronavirus	horseman	surrounding country
ighalo	coronavirus fear	norton	horseman coach
quarantine	coach driver	bryant	wuhan flight
outbreak	arrowe park hospital	evacuation	sense of responsibility

---

[10] The full set of results is provided in the book's repository in CSV format.

Table 4.7 Reference corpus keywords extraction. (U.K. Week 31)

Single words (RC: enTenTen21)	Multi-words (RC: en-TenTen21)	Single words (RC: RoC)	Multi-words (RC: RoC)
lockdown	government covid support	dwayne	push for a parliamentary debate
covid	push for a parliamentary debate	micro	government covid support
covid19	micro business	zante	parliamentary debate
distancing	parliamentary debate	parliamentary	micro business
retweet	social distancing	welch	negative multiple time
corona	covid test	pattinson	dwayne johnson
coronavirus	post lockdown	ftfc	review need
pre-covid	local lockdown	two-decade	review need for social distancing
scaremongering	bbc news	dsa	private island
post-lockdown	global pandemic	Tissier	coronavirus stat

Table 4.8 Reference corpus keywords extraction. (U.K. Week 85)

Single words (RC: enTenTen21)	Multi-words (RC: en-TenTen21)	Single words (RC: RoC)	Multi-words (RC: RoC)
covid	covid test	minaj	jodie comer
jab	covid vaccine	comer	nicki minaj
lockdown	covid passport	jodie	stephen graham
vax	covid jab	nicki	uk covid-19 child
vaccinate	long covid	trinidad	lost summer
pre-covid	covid death	cartel	symptom list
unvaccinated	care home	governement	mel morris
minaj	covid pass	reshuffle	uc cut
tory	covid restriction	tobago	full chamber
bollock	covid case	jody	vaccine dispersal

The rest-of-corpus (RoC) method, on the other hand, returns a larger proportion of proper names, both in the single- and multi-word lists, and, perhaps counterintuitively, seems to be less appropriate than the "general-language" reference-corpus method, as it does not highlight the specific topics of the time periods. It is also surprising that the term "PCR" is not listed in the top ten keywords, as is the case in the set extracted by both TF-IDF and Yake! In fact, it is in position 28 in the score-ranked list.[11]

4.2.3 Graph-Based Approaches

Graph-based approaches are a kind of unsupervised algorithms, since they also rely solely on the text itself. Graphs are data structures that consist of *vertices* (or *nodes*) joined by *edges*. They are used for many practical applications, such as navigation and route planning, to calculate the shortest path, or network flow analysis, including social networks, where nodes represent people and edges represent relationships or interactions; thus, they are a versatile tool that can be used in computer science, engineering, sociology, or biology.

Graphs have been used in NLP for text summarization, as they can identify the most relevant sentences in a text, and keyword extraction, as they are able to extract the most "relevant" words and phrases in a text, which is why they are also referred to as *ranking* algorithms. The most popular implementation is TextRank (Mihalcea and Tarau 2004), which is inspired by PageRank (Brin and Page 1998), the revolutionizing web search algorithm developed by the creators of Google that was directly responsible for the company's initial success. Search results using PageRank vastly improved on existing methods used by other search engines, which were based on keyword matching and meta tags.

Just like PageRank treats the Web as a vast graph, with web pages as nodes and hyperlinks as edges, so does TextRank, where words are treated as nodes and edges represent co-occurrence within a text window (span) of a certain size. The type of edge, however, is different: whereas web pages are linked by directed graphs, TextRank uses undirected, weighted graphs. The weights determine the "importance" of words and they are calculated by a voting system; each word will "vote" for the words within its window, and the weight of each word depends not only on the number of votes but also on the importance of the words voting for it. The voting system is recursive, in such a way that words that are frequently connected to other high-ranking words get higher scores too, which helps identify those words that truly capture the essence of the text. The same principle is used for summarization, where sentences rather than words are

---

[11] All 12 full lists of keywords are included in the book's repository.

edges, and each sentence "votes" for other sentences according to their similarity, which is calculated by word overlap (the number of words that sentences have in common).

Experiment: Graph-Based vs Reference-Corpus Keyword Extraction
The experiment that follows aims to compare results from two keyword extraction methods: the TextRank algorithm and the reference-corpus method.

I use the PyTextRank (Nathan 2016) library, which is a Python implementation of the original proposal by Mihalcea and Tarau (2004) in the form of a SpaCy extension. SpaCy (Honnibal et al. 2020) is a powerful, general-purpose NLP toolkit that can be used for many high-level tasks, including part-of-speech tagging, dependency parsing, semantic analysis using word embeddings, named entity recognition, and many others. It also allows for third-party add-ons and extensions, as is the case of PyTextRank.

As for the corpus, the aim is to extract keywords from the 1% sample of the full CCTC, which consists of over 11 million tweets and 300 million words (see Table 3.4). Analysing text with SpaCy involves certain limitations, as a SpaCy "doc" object, in which text is analysed in a pipeline, needs to be created for each single text. Since our texts are tweets and there are many millions of them, this may quickly become extremely slow. Thus, a decision was made to optimize the script to analyse tweets in batches of 100, which does not impact TextRank's performance, as document size does not affect its results (Mihalcea and Tarau 2004, 407). Frequencies of items were multiplied by the mean of the magnitudes of the tweets in the batch, as specified by the tweet's frequency (n, see Sect. 3.2.3); although this may not be entirely accurate, it is an acceptable approximation for the purpose of this experiment.

TextRank returns a large number of keyword candidates, sorted by score (it literally ranks every word that is not a stop-word). The script allows the specification of a minimum score as a cut-off point, which was set at 0.010 after some experimentation, and also a minimum frequency within batches, which was set to 1. The keywords in each batch were aggregated by averaging their scores and adding their frequencies. For this experiment, data was extracted from the daily files and results were subsequently aggregated by month.

Unlike Sketch Engine, TextRank makes no distinction between single-word and multi-word keywords, but in order to facilitate comparison of results, the extraction script automatically makes two subsets by checking for the presence of spaces. Similarly, 1,000 single-word and 1,000 multi-word keywords were extracted and kept in the monthly aggregated files, as this is the maximum number of keywords offered by Sketch Engine. The result is therefore 96 sets of 1,000 items each (12 months * 2 keyword types * 2 extraction methods).

PyTextRank does not take any parameters, so a number of parameters were coded in the script itself to filter and improve results. These include the following:

- Case-sensitive: the script allows to have keywords analysed in either case-sensitive mode or not. It was "off" for this experiment.
- Minimum rank: the score threshold below which candidate keywords are to be discarded (0.010 in this experiment).
- Exclusion list: a list of banned words to be ignored. These include common words in tweets, such as the names of week days and months, and certain stopwords, quantifiers, numerals, etc. Also Twitter mentions (handles).
- Allow entities in keywords: having this option set to "false" will discard keywords consisting of or containing entities. This relies on SpaCy's built-in entity recognition capabilities. Since we aim to compare results with Sketch Engine, this setting was set to "true" for this experiment.

Results were saved as monthly CSV files.

To extract the keywords with Sketch Engine, the XML version of the corpus was used (see Sect. 3.5). A subcorpus was created on Sketch Engine for each month of the two years that the corpus covers based on the metadata we embedded in the XML exported files, and extracted the top 1,000 keywords and keyphrases for each month. As before, the reference corpus used was enTenTen21. For keyword extraction, Sketch Engine makes a distinction between *keywords* (single-word items) and *terms* (multi-word items).

The analysis of results is described in the next section. The full set of extracted keywords by both systems can be found in the book's repository.

4.3 Comparing Keyword Sets

As we have seen, comparing the quality of the results of keyword extraction, i.e. judging how accurately a set of words qualifies the "aboutness" of a corpus, is a rather subjective task (Gabrielatos et al. 2012). This is the approach employed to analyse the results of the previous experiments in this book: presenting ranked lists of items and assessing their "quality" in a rather subjective manner applying certain—rather vague—criteria. Although this is rather inevitable as no clear objective criteria exist, here I introduce a quantitative—and therefore more objective—method to assist in the comparison of large sets of keywords.

Comparing two sets of keywords obtained through two different methods is not easy, but in this case things are further complicated by the scale of the data. Qualitatively comparing 48 pairs of sets of 1,000 items each is not practical or even worth the tremendous work involved. Quantitative methods can help to attain a global overview of the data and then use some other methods that can facilitate the manual, qualitative analysis of a few cases.

In the analysis that follows I use set operations (intersection and difference) as a quantitative aid to compare results and visualize results using Venn-type diagrams, generated automatically from the data, as well as tables with lists based on intersection and difference. The script used to generate these data and graphs takes two score-ranked lists of keyword items (whether single or multi-words) in CSV format, where the first column contains the items themselves and any number of data columns may be present. All lists in the sets contain the top 1,000 keywords generated by TextRank and Sketch Engine, extracted using the parameters described in the previous section, but the scripts allow to specify a cut-off point so that only the top n items are taken to calculate their intersection and difference. For each pair, which in this case are each of the 24 months sampled in the corpus, the script generates three elements:

1. Counts of the intersection to later obtain the statistics, as presented in Table 4.9. These are printed at runtime and saved as text files.
2. A Venn diagram of word clouds that can visually help understand the similarities and differences between sets. These are only generated when the top 100 items or less are selected, as larger lists can hardly be readable in this format.

3. An HTML table containing alphabetically sorted lists of words in the intersection and difference.

Table 4.9 quantitatively summarizes the results of comparing the keyword sets generated by each of the two methods. It contains the monthly intersection figures for the top 30, 50, and 100 keywords.[12] After discussing these results, three months in different stages of the time frame will be analysed in detail using the lists of words and Venn diagrams generated by the script, as, ultimately, subjective, qualitative analysis is necessary to assess how well different sets of keywords tell us about the "aboutness" of a corpus.

There is clearly a significant difference in the intersections percentages between single words and multi-words ($M = 41.36\%$ for the former; $M = 26.24\%$ for the latter). The reason for this, for which ample evidence will be available in the lists of keywords presented below, is that whereas for single words Sketch Engine allows users to specify which attribute to use for the calculations, this is not the case for multi-word items (see Fig. 4.1) and, although nothing is mentioned in the user's manual or the interface, it is evident that it uses lemmas, not word forms.

Thus, Sketch Engine will retrieve "coronavirus case", "covid death", and "health expert" rather than "coronavirus cases", "covid deaths", and "health experts", which is what TextRank will retrieve, as no lemmatization is performed. A possibility to equalize this situation is to lemmatize the corpus prior to keyword extraction with TextRank, but this is not a good idea, as lemmatization does have an enormous impact on many text processing tasks, especially part-of-speech tagging.

Other than that, percentages of intersections are rather consistent across months and top-n sets within each category ($SD = 0.0093$ for single words, $SD = 0.0238$ for multi-words), which suggests that both keyword extraction systems follow consistent patterns—and deliver similar results—reliably.

As in the previous experiment, I will now analyse in detail the results corresponding to three time periods—months this time—in different stages of the timeframe that the corpus covers. The months chosen

---

[12] The book's repository also contains the data for the top 500 and 1,000 keyword sets.

Table 4.9 Monthly keywords intersections (TextRank ∩ Sketch Engine)

	Top 30 keywords		Top 50 keywords		Top 100 keywords	
	SW	MW	SW	MW	SW	MW[13]
2020-01	15	10	25	16	48	31
2020-02	13	11	22	20	46	40
2020-03	12	9	25	18	49	38
2020-04	11	9	21	17	44	33
2020-05	10	6	20	16	41	31
2020-06	12	5	22	14	43	31
2020-07	11	5	20	9	47	25
2020-08	12	8	20	16	41	29
2020-09	13	5	22	15	45	28
2020-10	12	10	22	13	45	28
2020-11	12	8	19	14	41	29
2020-12	14	8	22	12	42	28
2021-01	13	7	21	12	40	32
2021-02	13	7	22	11	40	27
2021-03	12	7	21	9	38	31
2021-04	15	5	19	14	44	21
2021-05	15	8	19	15	41	26
2021-06	14	6	19	12	47	28
2021-07	13	5	21	10	42	22
2021-08	11	5	20	10	45	25
2021-09	13	5	19	10	45	25
2021-10	12	7	19	11	41	20
2021-11	13	7	20	9	47	21
2021-12	14	7	21	12	44	32
Mean	12.71	7.08	20.88	13.13	43.58	28.38
Mean%	42.36%	23.61%	41.75%	26.25%	43.58%	28.38%

include the weeks in the previous experiment, but it must be remembered that, apart from the difference in time length, this sample includes tweets from all countries, with no distinction among them, which makes it more difficult to identify specific topics. It must also be borne in mind that the vast majority of tweets are generated in the United States (see Fig. 3.4 in Sect. 3.4). For each month I will be using the top 50 sets, Venn diagrams for single words and tables for multi-words. In all Venn

---

[13] SW: single words. MW: multi-words.

4 KEYWORDS 89

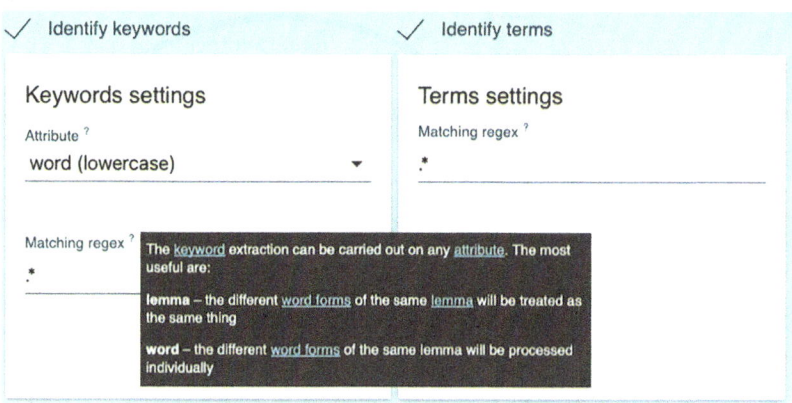

Fig. 4.1 Sketch Engine's attribute selection for keyword extraction

diagrams TextRank's (TR) keywords are displayed on the left and Sketch Engine's on the right.

Figure 4.2 shows the Venn diagram for single-word keywords corresponding to February 2020. The intersection in this case is 44%, which means that almost half the keywords extracted by both systems are the same.

The intersection clearly includes the main words associated with the events in this early stage of the pandemic. The U.S. bias in the corpus can already be seen as the intersection includes references to the American Center for Disease Control and President Donald Trump. It also includes references to the source of the disease ('wuhan', 'china', 'chinese') and other Asian countries ('korea', 'japan'), the early reference to the disease as 'corona', the 'outbreak', and the comparison with a regular 'flu'. As for the differences, TextRank includes a few words that make little sense, as they are too general ('things', 'weeks', 'days', 'years', 'home', 'world'), but the rest are informative and highlight relevant. Sketch Engine's keywords tend to be more specific because the method is based on significant differences in frequencies from a reference corpus, but it also includes irrelevant words, such as 'via' or 'breaking' (both commonly used in Twitter news), 'amid' or 'hong' and 'kong' (the two words in the multi-word unit "Hong Kong").

Here we also find an example of a big problem that Sketch Engine has when dealing with social media text: it is unable to process emojis

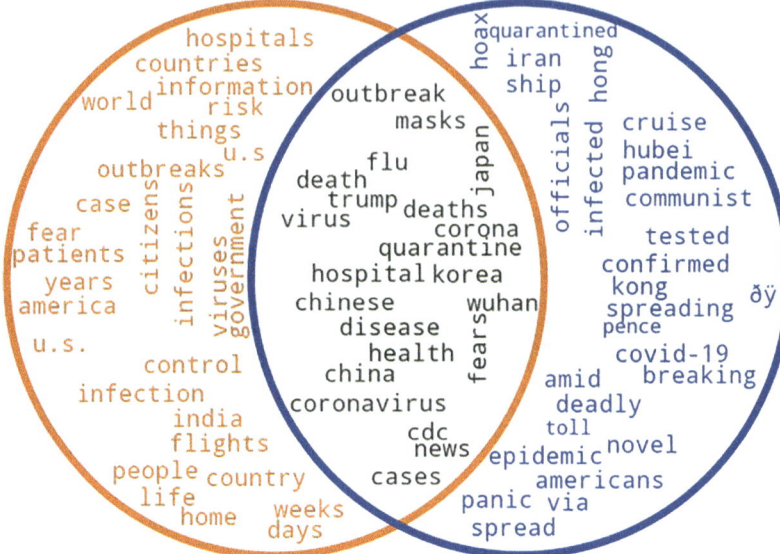

Fig. 4.2 Top 50 single-word keywords for February 2020 (TR left, SE right)

correctly. Even if the corpus is uploaded in correct UTF-8 encoding, the application displays certain Unicode characters instead of the corresponding emoji. The sequence 'ðŸ', specifically corresponds to the *sad emoji*, as evidenced by a concordance search of the 'keyword'. For example, the sentence in (18), extracted from a Sketch Engine concordance corresponds to the tweet shown in (19).

18. <s>One depressing thing about COVID (but perhaps necessary) is finding out ppl you thought were smart are just…not ðŸ < /s >
19. {"text": "One depressing thing about COVID (but perhaps necessary) is finding out ppl you thought were smart are just…not ☺", "user": "BillMonty_", "date": "Tue Dec 28 21:34:36 + 0000 2021", "id": "1475943287127171079", "n": 96}

This sequence ('ðŸ') is found ranking high in literally all monthly single-word keyword sets generated by Sketch Engine.

The differences in multi-word keyword extraction are also interesting. Both systems retrieve, in total, 21 two-word compounds where the first word is "coronavirus", which are broken down as follows:

- Retrieved by both systems: 'death', 'infection'', 'outbreak', 'patient', 'spread', 'update', 'vaccine'.
- Only in TextRank: 'cases', 'concerns', 'crisis', 'deaths', 'disease', 'fears', 'impact', 'infections', 'patients', 'quarantine', 'threat', 'quarantine'.
- Only in Sketch Engine: 'epidemic', 'fear', 'response'.

Some of these, however, are cases where both systems actually extracted the same phrases but were not included in the intersection due to Sketch Engine's using lemmas rather than words: both 'coronavirus deaths' and 'coronavirus fears' are included in Sketch Engine in singular because of lemmatization. All of these cases have been marked in bold (Table 4.10).

Table 4.10 Top 50 multi-word keywords for February 2020

Intersection	chinese people, corona virus, coronavirus case, coronavirus infection, coronavirus outbreak, coronavirus patient, coronavirus spread, coronavirus update, coronavirus vaccine, cruise ship, death toll, first case, hong kong, hubei province, new coronavirus, novel coronavirus, public health, south korea, virus outbreak, wuhan coronavirus
Only in TextRank	china coronavirus, china virus, china ■, chinese authorities, chinese officials, communist china, **confirmed cases**, coronavirus cases, coronavirus concerns, coronavirus crisis, **coronavirus deaths**, coronavirus disease, **coronavirus fears**, coronavirus impact, coronavirus infections, coronavirus patients, coronavirus quarantine, coronavirus threat, deadly coronavirus, **face masks**, **health officials**, infected people, mainland china, medical supplies, **new cases**, north korea, social media, wuhan china, wuhan city, wuhan virus
Only in Sketch Engine	case of coronavirus, chinese doctor, chinese government, communist party, **confirmed case**, **coronavirus death**, coronavirus epidemic, **coronavirus fear**, coronavirus response, diamond princess cruise, **face mask**, first coronavirus, **health official**, infectious disease, medical worker, mike pence, mortality rate, **new case**, new virus, other country, president trump, press conference, spread of coronavirus, stock market, supply chain, suspected case, travel ban, trump administration, washington state, world health organization

Some topics are highlighted by keywords in both systems but with some differences. For example, there are words related to the event involving the Diamond Princess cruise ship, which was quarantined off the coast of Japan for two weeks in February 2020, so both sets include 'cruise ship', but only Sketch Engine includes the actual name of the ship ('diamond princess cruise'), which helps identify the specific event.

Finally, we can see how TextRank manages emojis correctly treats them just like any other word ('china ■').

Figure 4.3 displays the Venn diagram corresponding to the month of August 2020. First, we find several more examples of Sketch Engine taking as keywords several unreadable characters: 'ðŸ', 'à', 'å', 'u'. We also find the same issues affecting both or either of the extraction systems (i.e. more frequent terms in TextRank, rarer words in Sketch Engine, Twitter-specific words in the latter). Also, in addition to the general words referring to the disease, the intersection includes some words in reference to important repercussions of the pandemic in some countries, specifically India, in relation to official exams ('students', 'exam', 'exams', 'tests'). TextRank does not give us any more clues regarding this issue, but Sketch Engine does: both 'jee' and 'neet' refer to official exams: JEE (Joint Entrance Examination) is India's entrance exam to several engineering degrees, which took place on September 1, 2020, and NEET is India's medical admission test (National Eligibility cum Entrance Test). During August there were doubts that these important exams could actually be conducted and which measures would apply if they were.

The reason that these keywords are picked up by the reference-corpus method and not the graph method is, again, frequency, which is relatively low in the focus corpus but high relative to the reference corpus. TextRank does retrieve these two words, but they are ranked low (200th position for 'jee' and 205th for 'neet') (Table 4.11).

As for multi-word keywords, here we find again many cases (14, marked in bold) that should be part of the intersection, as they are plurals that have been lemmatized by Sketch Engine. On the other hand, it is surprising to see how both systems include Donald Trump, but only TextRank includes Dr. Fauci (which Sketch Engine ranks in position 614).

4 KEYWORDS 93

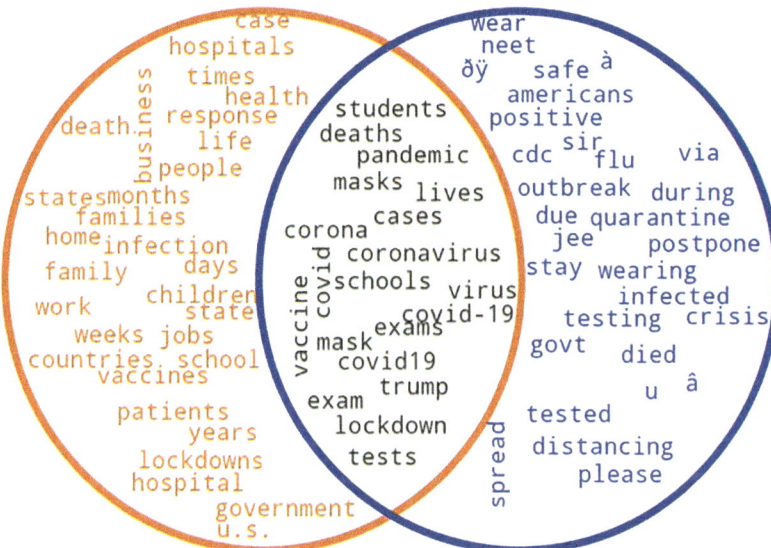

Fig. 4.3 Top 50 single-word keywords for August 2020 (TR left, SE right)

Table 4.11 Top 50 multi-word keywords for August 2020

Intersection	aged care, corona virus, coronavirus pandemic, coronavirus relief, coronavirus vaccine, covid relief, covid-19 pandemic, death toll, donald trump, global pandemic, herd immunity, mental health, president trump, public health, social distance, social distancing
Only in TextRank	**active cases**, black people, **care homes**, climate change, **confirmed cases**, corona cases, coronavirus cases, **coronavirus deaths**, coronavirus infections, **covid cases**, **covid deaths**, covid pandemic, **covid patients**, covid times, **covid19 cases**, covid19 pandemic, dr. fauci, election day, **face masks**, health care, high risk, **loved ones**, new cases, next week, next year, **nursing homes**, physical distancing, **positive cases**, public transport, small businesses, social media, social security, students life, young people
Only in Sketch Engine	active case, **care home**, china virus, **confirmed case**, **coronavirus case**, **coronavirus death**, coronavirus outbreak, **covid case**, **covid death**, **covid patient**, covid test, covid vaccine, **covid-19 case**, covid-19 death, covid-19 patient, covid-19 test, covid-19 vaccine, death rate, **face mask**, joe biden, **loved one**, middle of a pandemic, **new case**, new coronavirus, new zealand, **nursing home**, pandemic response, pandemic situation, **positive case**, second wave, stay home, trump administration, wearing mask, white house

Only Sketch Engine includes Joe Biden, but in TextRank it is in 57th position. Also, the two systems seem to have some advantages and disadvantages over the other; TextRank seems to pick up on the social and economic impact of the pandemic ('small businesses', 'social security', 'students life'), whereas Sketch Engine includes some important keywords for this stage of the pandemic, such as 'second wave' and 'stay home'.

Finally, for the month corresponding to week 85 (September 2021), TextRank seems to better extract the keywords specific to this time period. This can be seen in the top single-word items (Fig. 4.4), as it includes terms like 'delta', 'booster', 'pfizer', and 'immunity', all of which are ranked lower in TextRank's list (in position 54, 224, 150, and 79, respectively).

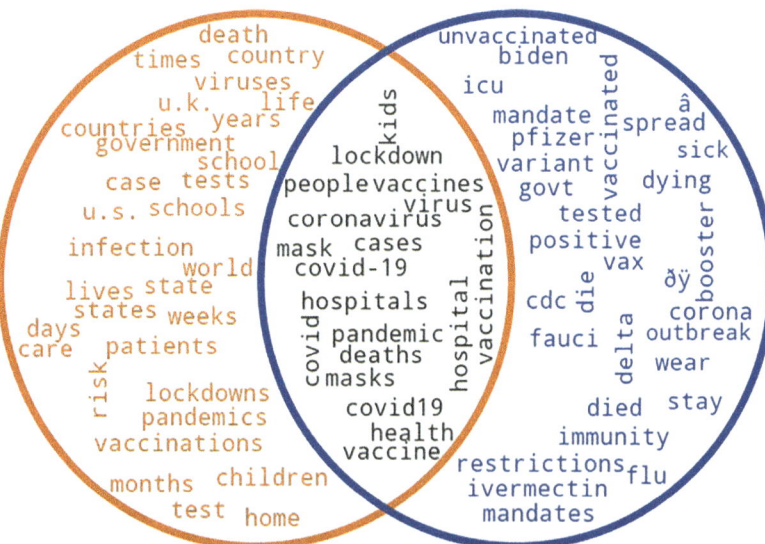

Fig. 4.4 Top 50 single-word keywords for September 2021 (TR left, SE right)

Table 4.12 Top 50 multi-word keywords for September 2021

Intersection	covid pandemic, covid test, covid vaccination, covid vaccine, health care, long covid, public health, unvaccinated people, vaccinated people, vaccine mandate
Only in TextRank	**active cases**, catching covid, contracting covid, coronavirus vaccines, covid cases, covid deaths, covid hospitalizations, covid infections, covid mandates, covid misinformation, covid numbers, covid passports, covid patients, covid protocols, covid relief, covid restrictions, covid rules, covid testing, covid tests, covid vaccinations, covid vaccines, covid visualizations, **covid-19 vaccines**, dr. fauci, face masks, health care workers, health workers, healthy people, **mask mandates**, new cases, new covid cases, next week, next year, severe covid, unvaccinated covid patients, vaccine hesitancy, vaccine mandates, **vaccine passports**, vaccine requirements, young people
Only in Sketch Engine	**active case**, booster shot, care worker, covid case, covid death, covid infection, covid jab, covid passport, covid patient, covid restriction, covid shot, covid-19 case, covid-19 death, covid-19 pandemic, covid-19 patient, covid-19 vaccination, **covid-19 vaccine**, death rate, death toll, delta variant, global pandemic, healthcare worker, icu bed, immune system, joe rogan, last year, long term, loved one, many people, **mask mandate**, mental health, natural immunity, new case, panic buying, side effect, social distancing, vaccination rate, vaccine dose, **vaccine passport**, wearing mask

Similarly, in multi-word keywords, although both systems include the stage-specific term 'long covid', only Sketch Engine offers others, such as 'booster shot', 'delta variant', and 'mental health' (Table 4.12).

4.4 Keyword Extraction Using Word Embeddings

Transformers-based Large Language Models (LLMs) have proved to be incredibly useful in many tasks, not just language generation, including, of course, keyword extraction. This is because the word embeddings that are used to create LLMs do capture the semantics of the words and phrases that make up a text, as well as the text as a whole. The KeyBERT (Grootendorst 2020) keyword extraction tool used in the last experiment of this chapter is based on this very basic principle, as it calculates keyness by measuring the similarity between the individual words and phrases of a text and the text itself; this is a keyword extraction method that was first proposed by Sharma and Li (2019). Other keyword extractors based on word embeddings are available, such as EmbedRank (Bennani-Smires et al. 2018).

As is common in word embeddings, the metric it uses is cosine similarity. The approach taken is fairly simple: words or n-grams with a higher cosine similarity to that of the text as a whole will rank higher than those more distant. This is a simple, yet powerful keyword extraction method that is easy to implement and can be customized by using different embeddings, probably the most determining factor.

4.4.1 Experiment: Comparing Keywords from Two Countries Using KeyBERT

In the following experiment, I use KeyBERT[14] to extract keywords and keyphrases in the range 2 to 3 from the geotagged version of the CCTC in order to compare two countries: Australia and India. I use the 25% sample of each of these countries. The Australian subcorpus is made up of 69,685 tweets (about 1.7 million words); the Indian sample is larger, at 170,974 tweets (about 4.39 million words).

KeyBERT takes a number of parameters that can have a strong impact on the results. The most important is obviously the language model that is used to compute the similarity between words/phrases and the whole document. In this experiment I use the default model (*all-MiniLM-L6-v2*), a sentence-transformers model that is compact in size yet powerful for many applications.[15] There are two very useful parameters that KeyBERT can take aimed at diversifying results. This is in order to avoid sets of different but very similar keywords and, especially, keyphrases, as we have seen in previous sets ('coronavirus', 'corona virus', 'covid shot', 'covid jab'). Again, the tool leverages the power of word embeddings and cosine similarity to obtain a measurement of the similarities between the results obtained and discard those that display a high level of similarity. There are two such parameters: Max Sum Distance (which was set to *true*) and Maximal Marginal Relevance, which was set to 0.7 (high diversity).

---

[14] KeyBERT is distributed as a Python package. Instructions on installation and use can be found at https://maartengr.github.io/KeyBERT/index.html.

[15] A thorough description of this language model can be found at https://huggingface.co/sentence-transformers/all-MiniLM-L6-v2.

KeyBERT also allows the specification of the length of n-grams that we wish to extract. In order to extract them independently, two runs are necessary, one to extract single-word keywords (n-gram range 1–1) and another for multi-word keywords (range 2–3) (Table 4.13). Eleven of the top 20 single-word keywords are hashtags, although KeyBERT drops the hash sign. Furthermore, although many of them make sense as keywords ('covid19vaccination', 'positivevibes', 'lockdownmelbourne', 'savehospitality'), others appear to be rather irrelevant; for example, both 'mugsareqldracing' and 'scottymissingagain' occur exactly once—Examples (20) and (21)—in the corpus and bear no relationship to any relevant topic.

Table 4.13 KeyBERT results for July 2021 Australia[16]

Keywords	Score	Keyphrases	Score
covid19vaccination	0.565	australia covid deaths	0.639
mugsareqldracing	0.339	disgusting assembletheguillotines auspol	0.395
bleak	0.271	healthcare biosecurity citizens	0.342
caringbah	0.267	sydney buck naked	0.304
gladyscovidspreaders	0.253	just like blm	0.297
positivevibes	0.245	pandemic snack time	0.297
wuhanvirus	0.239	doherty warned patients	0.291
lockdownmelbourne	0.234	comments skynews pretending	0.284
jfc	0.234	vaccine takes long	0.282
notsafeforwork	0.233	morrison undermined	0.282
coffees	0.233	virus tax return	0.279
sarscov2	0.231	hopefully ease victoria	0.274
xenophobic	0.218	health recorded zero	0.266
coffs	0.211	reconsiders use astrazeneca	0.254
antibodies	0.205	cases uk july	0.253
stateoforigin2021	0.201	gladys corruption idea	0.251
scottymissingagain	0.2	great news general	0.251
trigger	0.199	wollongong2022 rename	0.249
wildlife	0.198	clots national drug	0.248
savehospitality	0.196	visit dutton takes	0.242

[16] The book's repository includes the full lists of keywords and keyphrases for all months corresponding to the Australian, South African, and Indian subcorpora.

20. {"country_code": "AU", "timestamp": "Fri Jul 02 10:14:36+0000 2021", "user": "mugspunting", "id": "1410904734341287937", "text": "Anyone else's #Lockdown look a bit like this? Thanks for the new sponsorship... haven't workout out any details yet but we'll get there. #MugsAREqldracing"}

21. {"country_code": "AU", "timestamp": "Tue Jul 20 04:39:58+0000 2021", "user": "SullivanCate", "id": "1417343502996832257", "text": "NSW in lockdown. VIC in lockdown. SA in lockdown. #scottymissingagain"}

Keyphrases do seem to convey more of the topics relevant to the events in the country ('australia covid deaths', 'doherty warned patients', 'morrison undermined', 'gladys corruption idea'). However, we find the same issue related to the selection of hashtags, or sequences of hashtags; for example, the hashtag '#assembletheguillotines' occurs twice in the sample, and the actual sequence '#disgusting #assembletheguillotines #auspol' occurs once, shown in (22).

22. {"country_code": "AU", "timestamp": "Wed Jul 28 00:59:49+0000 2021", "user": "amandajanewd", "id": "1420187201594290176", "text": "@AustralianLabor you ripped my heart out after the last election and now keep trampling on it. You are the literal worst ⊚ #Heartbreaking #Disgusting #assembletheguillotines #auspol"}

Finally, the list of keyphrases is quite obviously the result of processing n-grams rather than syntactically coherent groupings, which results in rather awkward phrases, such as 'hopefully ease victoria', 'health recorded zero', or 'visit dutton takes'.

After this initial experiment, it seems that this recent method of keyword extraction, although original in its proposal, still needs a lot of refining and improvement to be a good alternative other well-established methods, specifically the reference-corpus and graph-based methods, which in our tests offered the best results.

The other important criterion that needs to be considered is that of performance. Again, the reference-corpus method is extremely fast and lightweight in terms of computing requirements, as all it takes is a list of pre-calculated word frequencies for the reference corpus, and the frequencies of the focus corpus, which in the case of an indexed, lemmatized corpus management tool has also been pre-calculated. Most other methods we have explored are more costly in terms of computing power, with the exception of some unsupervised methods (RAKE), whose quality leaves much to be desired.

REFERENCES

Alessi, Glenn Michael, and Alan Partington. 2020. *Modern Diachronic Corpus-Assisted Language Studies: Methodologies for Tracking Language Change Over Recent Time*. Italia: Mattioli, 1885.

Anthony, Laurence. 2023a. AntConc (Version 4.2.0). Tokyo, Japan: Waseda University.

Anthony, Laurence. 2023b. Common Statistics Used in Corpus Linguistics.

Baker, Paul. 2004. Querying Keywords: Questions of Difference, Frequency and Sense in Keywords Analysis. *Journal of English Linguistics* 32: 346–359. https://doi.org/10.1177/0075424204269894.

Baker, Paul. 2006. *Using Corpora in Discourse Analysis*. A&C Black.

Bennani-Smires, Kamil, Claudiu Musat, Andreea Hossmann, Michael Baeriswyl, and Martin Jaggi. 2018. Simple Unsupervised Keyphrase Extraction using Sentence Embeddings. In *Proceedings of the 22nd Conference on Computational Natural Language Learning*, 221–229. Brussels, Belgium: Association for Computational Linguistics. https://doi.org/10.18653/v1/K18-1022.

Boyce, Bert R., Charles T. Meadow, and Donald H. Kraft. 1994. *Measurement in Information Science: An Information Services Perspective*. Library and Information Science (New York, NY). San Diego, California: Academic Press.

Bondi, Marina. 2010. An Introduction: Perspectives on Keywords and Keyness. In *Keyness in Texts*, ed. Marina Bondi and Mike Scott, 1–18. Studies in Corpus Linguistics. John Benjamins Publishing Company. https://doi.org/10.1075/scl.41.01bon.

Bondi, Marina, and Mike Scott, ed. 2010. *Keyness in Texts*. John Benjamins Publishing Company.

Brezina, Vaclav. 2018. *Statistics in Corpus Linguistics: A Practical Guide*. Cambridge, UK: Cambridge University Press. https://doi.org/10.1017/9781316410899.

Brin, Sergey, and Lawrence Page. 1998. The Anatomy of a Large-Scale Hypertextual Web Search Engine. *Computer Networks* 30: 107–117.

Campos, Ricardo, Vítor Mangaravite, Arian Pasquali, Alípio Mário Jorge, Célia Nunes, and Adam Jatowt. 2018. YAKE! Collection-Independent Automatic Keyword Extractor. *Lecture Notes in Computer Science*. https://doi.org/10.1007/978-3-319-76941-7_80.

Egbert, Jesse, and Doug Biber. 2019. Incorporating Text Dispersion into Keyword Analyses. *Corpora* 14: 77–104. Edinburgh University Press. https://doi.org/10.3366/cor.2019.0162.

El-Beltagy, Samhaa R., and Ahmed Rafea. 2009. KP-Miner: A Keyphrase Extraction System for English and Arabic Documents. *Information Systems* 34: 132–144. https://doi.org/10.1016/j.is.2008.05.002.

Gabrielatos, Costas, Tony McEnery, Peter J Diggle, and Paul Baker. 2012. The Peaks and Troughs of Corpus-Based Contextual Analysis. *International journal of corpus linguistics* 17: 151–175. John Benjamins.

Gabrielatos, Costas. 2018. Keyness analysis: Nature, metrics and techniques. In *Corpus Approaches to Discourse: A Critical Review*, ed. C. Taylor and A. Marchi, 225–258. Oxford: Routledge.

Grootendorst, Maarten. 2020. KeyBERT: Minimal keyword extraction with BERT. *Zenodo*. https://doi.org/10.5281/zenodo.4461265.

Honnibal, Matthew, Ines Montani, Sofie Van Landeghem, and Adriane Boyd. 2020. SpaCy: Industrial-strength natural language processing in python. *Zenodo*. https://doi.org/10.5281/zenodo.1212303.

Hulth, Anette. 2004. Combining Machine Learning and Natural Language Processing for Automatic Keyword Extraction. Stockholm, Sweden: Stockholm University, Faculty of Social Sciences, Department of Computer and Systems Sciences.

Hunt, Daniel, and Kevin Harvey. 2015. Health Communication and Corpus Linguistics: Using Corpus Tools to Analyse Eating Disorder Discourse Online. In *Corpora and Discourse Studies: Integrating Discourse and Corpora*, ed. Paul Baker and Tony McEnery, 134–154. Palgrave Advances in Language and Linguistics. London: Palgrave Macmillan UK. https://doi.org/10.1057/978 1137431738_7.

Jakubíček, Miloš, Adam Kilgarriff, Vojtěch Kovář, Pavel Rychlý, and Vít. Suchomel. 2013. The TenTen Corpus Family. In *7th International Corpus Linguistics Conference CL 2013*, 125–127. UK: Lancaster.

Johnson, Sally, and Astrid Ensslin. 2006. Language in the News: Some Reflections on Keyword Analysis Using Wordsmith Tools and the BNC. *Leeds Working Papers in Linguistics and Phonetics* 11.

Kilgarriff, Adam. 2009. Simple Maths for Keywords. In *Proceedings of Corpus Linguistics Conference (CL 2009)*, ed. M. Mahlberg, V. González-Díaz, and C. Smith. University of Liverpool, UK.

Kilgarriff, Adam. 2012. Getting to Know Your Corpus. In *Text, Speech and Dialogue*, ed. Petr Sojka, Aleš Horák, Ivan Kopeček, and Karel Pala, 3–15. Lecture Notes in Computer Science. Berlin, Heidelberg: Springer. https://doi.org/10.1007/978-3-642-32790-2_1.

Kilgarriff, Adam, Vít Baisa, Jan Bušta, Miloš Jakubíček, Vojtěch Kovář, Jan Michelfeit, Pavel Rychlý, and Vít Suchomel. 2014. The Sketch Engine: Ten Years On. *Lexicography* 1: 7–36.
Mahlberg, Michaela. 2007. *Corpus Stylistics: Bridging the Gap Between Linguistic and Literary Studies*.
Marchi, Anna. 2018. Dividing Up the Data: Epistemological, Methodological and Practical Impact of Diachronic Segmentation. In *Corpus Approaches to Discourse*. Routledge.
Matoré, Georges. 1953. *La méthode en lexicologie: domaine français*. M. Didier.
Mihalcea, Rada, and Paul Tarau. 2004. TextRank: Bringing Order into Text. In *Proceedings of the 2004 Conference on Empirical Methods in Natural Language Processing*, 404–411. Barcelona, Spain: Association for Computational Linguistics.
Nathan, Paco. 2016. *PyTextRank, a Python Implementation of TextRank for Phrase Extraction and Summarization of Text Documents*. Derwen.
Nomoto, Tadashi. 2023. Keyword Extraction: A Modern Perspective. *Sn Computer Science* 4: 92. https://doi.org/10.1007/s42979-022-01481-7.
Pedregosa, F., G. Varoquaux, A. Gramfort, V. Michel, B. Thirion, O. Grisel, M. Blondel, et al. 2011. Scikit-Learn: Machine Learning in Python. *Journal of Machine Learning Research* 12: 2825–2830.
Rose, Stuart, Dave Engel, Nick Cramer, and Wendy Cowley. 2010. Automatic Keyword Extraction from Individual Documents. In *Text Mining*, 1–20. Wiley. https://doi.org/10.1002/9780470689646.ch1.
Scott, Mike. 1996. *WordSmith Tools*. Oxford: Oxford University Press.
Scott, Mike. 1997. PC Analysis of Key Words—And Key Key Words. *System* 25: 233–245. https://doi.org/10.1016/S0346-251X(97)00011-0.
Scott, Mike. 2010. Problems in Investigating Keyness, or Clearing the Undergrowth and Marking Out Trails…. In *Keyness in Texts*, ed. Marina Bondi and Mike Scott, 43–57. Amsterdam/Philadelphia: John Benjamins Publishing Company.
Scott, Mike. 2022. *WordSmith Tools*. Stroud: Lexical Analysis Software.
Scott, Mike, and Christopher Tribble. 2006. *Textual Patterns. Key Words and Corpus Analysis in Language Education*. Studies in Corpus Linguistics 22. Amsterdam/Philadelphia: John Benjamins Publishing Company.
Sharma, Prafull, and Yingbo Li. 2019. *Self-Supervised Contextual Keyword and Keyphrase Retrieval with Self-Labelling*. Preprints. https://doi.org/10.20944/preprints201908.0073.v1.
Sinclair, John McHardy. 1991. *Corpus, Concordance, Collocation*. Oxford: Oxford University Press.
Spärck Jones, Karen. 1972. A Statistical Interpretation of Term Specificity and Its Application in Retrieval. *Journal of Documentation* 28: 11–21.

Stubbs, Michael. 2010. Three Concepts of Keywords. In *Keyness in Texts*, ed. Marina Bondi and Mike Scott, 21–42. Amsterdam/Philadelphia: John Benjamins Publishing Company.

Sun, Chengyu, Liang Hu, Shuai Li, Tuohang Li, Hongtu Li, and Ling Chi. 2020. A Review of Unsupervised Keyphrase Extraction Methods Using Within-Collection Resources. *Symmetry* 12. Multidisciplinary Digital Publishing Institute: 1864. https://doi.org/10.3390/sym12111864.

Teubert, Wolfgang. 1989. Politische Vexierwörter. In *Politische Semantik: Bedeutungsanalytische und Sprachkritische Beiträge zur politischen Sprachverwendung*, ed. Josef Klein, 51–68. Wiesbaden: VS Verlag für Sozialwissenschaften. https://doi.org/10.1007/978-3-322-91068-4_2.

Turney, Peter D. 2000. Learning Algorithms for Keyphrase Extraction. *Information Retrieval* 2: 303–336. https://doi.org/10.1023/A:1009976227802.

Williams, Raymond. 1976. *Keywords: A Vocabulary of Culture and Society*. USA: Oxford University Press.

Witten, Ian H., Gordon W. Paynter, Eibe Frank, Carl Gutwin, and Craig G. Nevill-Manning. 1999. KEA: Practical Automatic Keyphrase Extraction. arXiv. https://doi.org/10.48550/arXiv.cs/9902007.

Open Access This chapter is licensed under the terms of the Creative Commons Attribution 4.0 International License (http://creativecommons.org/licenses/by/4.0/), which permits use, sharing, adaptation, distribution and reproduction in any medium or format, as long as you give appropriate credit to the original author(s) and the source, provide a link to the Creative Commons license and indicate if changes were made.

The images or other third party material in this chapter are included in the chapter's Creative Commons license, unless indicated otherwise in a credit line to the material. If material is not included in the chapter's Creative Commons license and your intended use is not permitted by statutory regulation or exceeds the permitted use, you will need to obtain permission directly from the copyright holder.

CHAPTER 5

Topics

Abstract This chapter focuses on topic modelling, i.e. the automatic extraction of topics or themes from a corpus. Topic modelling goes a step further than keywords in the automatic identification of the contents of a corpus. Two types of approaches are considered, discussed, and contrasted. On the one hand, those that I dub "traditional", as illustrated by the LDA and NMF algorithms, and, on the other, embeddings-based approaches, which largely surpass the former in the quality of results. The weakest aspect of topic modelling tools in general is the lack actual labels for the extracted topics, since all they return is a set of loosely related keywords that collectively identify the topic. In the last experiment I describe an approach that uses the power of Large Language Models to effectively derive high-quality labels for the extracted topics.

Keywords Topic modelling · Topics · Themes · LDA · NMF · Word embeddings · Topic visualization · Topic labelling · Large language models

When discussing the concept of keywords in the previous chapter we saw how some authors, such as Nomoto (2023), regard them as pointers to the "topics" of a text, and we have shown how the extracted lists of keywords do contain many words that could be taken as "labels" for the topics that make up the contents of a corpus. Therefore, it seems pertinent to start this section by discussing what, precisely, is meant by "topics", and how they are different from keywords.

If we take a bird's-eye view of any of the keyword lists that we have seen in the previous chapter, it would look as if the sum of all of them somehow embody the topics contained in the corpus. Sometimes there may be one or two keywords or keyphrases that seem to best encapsulate those topics, i.e. they are good labels for the topics, but it is the aggregated set of keywords that provides a more accurate representation of those topics. For example, in Table 4.8, the keyphrases "covid vaccine", "covid jab", "covid passport", and "covid pass" are obviously related and point to the theme of "vaccines and their legal certification", but none of them could be said to be a perfect label for the topic. Thus, topics have a broader scope than keywords, as they encompass sets of words and phrases which, together, make up a topic. This is in accord with Watson Todd's (2011) definition: "a clustering of concepts which are associated or related from the perspective of the interlocutors in such a way as to create relevance and coherence" (p. 252), as these clusterings of concepts are inevitably embodied by notionally relevant words (i.e. keywords).

I will not delve any further into a theoretical definition of the concept of *topic*, as a "standard" dictionary definition—"a matter dealt with in a text, discourse, or conversation: a subject"[1]—suffices to define what is generally understood by this term in the computational treatment of topics, i.e. *topic modelling*.

Topic modelling can be defined as a number of methods that aim to identify a set of semantically related words, which together form a topic, from a group of documents. These words are assumed to capture the main themes in those documents. It can also be seen as a type of text mining technique used to identify word patterns that occur frequently in written texts, as well as an effective technique to find useful hidden structures in a collection of documents (Zhu et al. 2016).

In the context of topic modelling, topics are sometimes referred to as "latent semantic structures", due to the original proposal by Dumais et al. (1988) to retrieve semantically relevant information from text collections from user input, to overcome the limitations of document search based on simple string or lexical matching. Furnas et al. (1987) showed that the same keyword was likely to be used repeatedly to refer to the same topic

---

[1] Oxford Dictionary of English, 3rd edition.

only 20 per cent of the time, and therefore text-based searches are bound to retrieve only a fraction of the relevant documents in a collection—those that actually include the search words. Latent Semantic Analysis (LSA) attempts to overcome this issue by creating semantic spaces from the documents themselves by representing them as term-document matrices of vectors. The adjective "latent" is used because the authors assume that "(…) there is some underlying 'latent' semantic structure in word usage data that is partially obscured by the variability of word choice. We use statistical techniques to estimate this latent structure and get rid of the obscuring 'noise'" (Dumais et al. 1988, 288).

LSA induces the semantics of documents through singular value decomposition to effectively reduce the high number of dimensions of the original texts, a technique that was improved on by probabilistic generative models, specifically Latent Dirichlet Allocation (LDA), matrix factorization techniques, such as Non-negative Matrix Factorization (NMF), and Probabilistic Latent Semantic Analysis (PLSA). LDA, in fact, became the de facto standard method of topic modelling, but, as with many other tasks in NLP, the advent of word embeddings and large language models has brought about newer, more powerful techniques.

In the following two sections I explore the possibilities of some of these methods to identify the "latent" topics or themes in large social media corpora. Although many topic extraction methods and variations on these methods have been proposed over the years, a broad distinction can be made between "traditional" methods, where LDA and NMF stand out, and the latest generation of systems that leverage the semantic power of word embeddings and large language models, such as TopEx, Top2Vec, and BERTopic. Section 5.1 deals with the former, while 5.2 discusses and tests the latter. Finally, dynamic topic modelling is discussed and applied.

The three experiments described in the following sections aim to extract topics using different techniques from tweets generated in the top three countries of the CCTC by volume—the United States, the United Kingdom, and India.[2] The same dataset was used for all three experiments: three subcorpora from the geotagged section of the CCTC. An attempt was made to have a large number of tweets (over 600,000 for each country) and have approximately the same size for each of the

---

[2] The corpus files used in this chapter and the next (which includes the Canada, Australia, and South Africa subcorpora) are included in the book's repository (https://osf.io/h5q4j/).

Table 5.1 Corpus used in the experiments in this chapter

Country	% of subcorpus	Tweets	Tokens	Proc. time LDA-NMF	Proc. time BERTopic
U.S	16%	637,195	14,372,585	00:43:26	00:31:34
U.K.	45%	638,006	15,857,901	00:43:52	00:31:36
India	90%	616,091	15,821,057	00:42:19	00:29:18
TOTAL		1,891,296	46,051,543	02:09:37	01:32:28

countries. Since different countries have different numbers of tweets, the percentage of tweets to be included in the corpus was adapted to use comparable corpus sizes. The dataset is quantitatively described in Table 5.1, where the time taken to process each of the datasets is also included.[3]

5.1 "Traditional" Topic Modelling Methods

Latent Dirichlet Allocation (LDA) was first proposed by Blei et al. (2003), who kept the adjective "latent" despite the fact that they used a very different technique from that in Latent Semantic Analysis. Unlike LSA, LDA was originally intended not as a document retrieval system, but as a topic extraction (or modelling) tool.

LDA assumes that each document contains several topics and each topic is a distribution over words in the corpus. However, the number of topics must be decided before applying the algorithm to the corpus, and used as one of the parameters. This means that we have to guess how many relevant topics there are in a corpus, which is obviously not optimal, as the algorithm will build a model with that number of topics regardless of what it finds in the corpus, and then fit all documents in the corpus into one of those topics. Furthermore, this fundamental assumption that a document contains several topics is probably not true of many of the

---

[3] All times are given in hh:mm:ss format. All tasks were run on an Intel Core i7 10700F 2.9 GHz CPU (8 cores) on Ubuntu Linux 22.04 Server 64-bit. BERTopic makes use of the system's NVIDIA GeForce RTX 3080Ti GPU through the CUDA library. Exponentially longer processing times should be expected on a non-GPU system. The critical step in terms of processing is generating the sentence embeddings; as an example, this step alone took about 3 minutes for the US subcorpus with GPU acceleration and nearly 8 hours without it.

documents in our corpus. In fact, the idea of a tweet is a short message about a particular topic, and therefore it is a type of document that challenges the basic assumptions of LDA, as they do not provide enough context to effectively discern topics. In this regard, scientific abstracts, for example, are the perfect type of documents for LDA and NMF, since they are a good summary of the topics that are dealt with in the text, and usually include all relevant keywords and references to those topics. In fact, abstracts have been recurrently used in the literature to show the effectiveness of these methods, e.g. Anupriya and Karpagavalli (2015), Ikegawa (2022), Cao et al. (2023).

Another important consideration is that, since these methods are based on word co-occurrence across the documents in the corpus, they are very sensitive to the precise modifications made during the pre-processing stage. For example, if stop-word removal is not performed, it is very likely that many such words (articles, prepositions, etc.) will be present in the list of keywords that define a topic. Similarly, it is important to group word forms either as stems or lemmas, as otherwise they will be taken as entirely different words (since the algorithms do not consider the semantics of words and phrases). Thus, extensive pre-processing is required to improve results, and this is especially true of social media text, as these texts usually contain a plethora of "noisy" elements: user mentions, hashtags, URLs, misspellings, typographical decorations, etc. (see Sect. 3.2.1).

The final important limitation is that, as mentioned in the previous section, topic modelling tools do not provide semantic labels that can be used to refer to topics. The output is a numbered list of topics identified by a set of keywords (which may or may not be semantically related). The interpretation of what that particular topic semantically refers to and the actual labelling of the topic is left to the user. Thus, evaluating the performance is, as was the case with keywords, rather subjective (Shi et al. 2019). Human interpretation of topics remains an important factor, which is why there have been efforts to implement "human-in-the-loop" topic modelling systems (Smith et al. 2018).

Finally, the discussion of LDA and NMF in this section has so far highlighted the similarities—under the umbrella of "traditional" methods—but these two methods of topic modelling have important differences. LDA is a probabilistic model that follows a generative process: first, a distribution over words is chosen for each topic, then a distribution over topics is chosen for each document; then, for each word in the document a topic is chosen from the document's distribution over topics and a word is chosen from the topic's distribution over words. This has the form of a term-document matrix (the "corpus", in LDA terms). In order to compute the distribution of topics over words, LDA uses Bayesian statistics (specifically, *Dirichlet priors*, thereby the name).

Non-negative Matrix Factorization (NMF) (Lee and Seung 1999) was originally introduced as a method for parts-based representation of data, especially in the context of image processing. It also uses a term-document matrix (the "corpus"), but it decomposes it in two lower-dimensional non-negative matrices and, unlike LDA, which assumes a probabilistic mixture, NMF represents documents and terms as linear combinations of topics and vice versa.

5.1.1 Experiment: LDA vs NMF for Topic Modelling

A single script was used to extract topics using these two methods, as both require the same pre-processing steps, and the only difference lies in the model generation. As mentioned in the previous section, heavy pre-processing of tweets is necessary, specifically:

- URL and user mention removal: this was not necessary as both these elements were removed during the corpus extraction process.
- Stop-word removal. Spacy was used for this task. A set of 25 custom stopwords was added ("2020", "2021", "news", "people", "day", "week", "thing", "think", "tell", "read", etc.)
- All text was turned into lower case.
- Tokenization and lemmatization were carried out also using Spacy, whose word tokenizer does keep hyphenated words together (e.g. COVID-19), unlike most others.
- Hashtags were kept, but the hash symbol was removed.
- Accented foreign characters (e.g. "café") were normalized.
- Word filtering: only words with a minimum length of three characters were kept. Words starting with a number were removed.
- Document filtering: only tweets with a minimum length of two words (after pre-processing) were kept.

To illustrate the result of this pre-processing step, Table 5.2 contains some examples of the original tweet and the list of tokens after applying the pre-processing function. The dictionary used by the models is based on those lists of tokens.

Input files are plain text files where each line is a document (tweet). Although the input this time is a set of 24 (monthly) files, all tweets are read into one single dataset and processed globally. Thus, for each country set of files, the script generates the following:

- A CSV file of LDA topics where each topic is a column containing the topic ID and its associated keywords.
- The equivalent CSV file for NMF.
- A CSV file where each line contains the original tweet, the dominant LDA topic, and the topic's keywords.
- The equivalent CSV file for NMF.
- A HTML file with an interactive topic visualization for LDA topics.

Table 5.2 Result of tweet pre-processing

Original tweet text	Processed list of tokens
Those people are the sole reason America won't even take a pandemic seriously 😂😂😂😂🙃 people thinking scientific evidence is an opinion 🙄🙄	['sole', 'reason', 'america', 'pandemic', 'seriously', 'think', 'scientific', 'evidence', 'opinion']
This was the first time I put mascara on in 2 months!! Thanks for sending those beautiful jewels to make me do it 😍😊💎. #quarantine #quarantined #quarantinelife #quarantineandchill #coronavirus...	['mascara', 'thank', 'send', 'beautiful', 'jewel', 'quarantine', 'quarantine', 'quarantinelife', 'quarantineandchill', 'coronavirus']
Be sure to visit and see how you can help homeless animals through the pandemic, right here in Greater Cincinnati	['sure', 'visit', 'help', 'homeless', 'animal', 'pandemic', 'right', 'great', 'cincinnati']
RE-IMAGINE MANDATING face masks through November 3rd, 2020 THEN SEE HOW fast the CRAZY DEMS and their CORRUPT FakeNews Media Network OPERATIVES will SCREAM MASKS ARE RACIST, Xenophobic and XYZ to BAN MASKS 😂😂😂!	['imagine', 'mandate', 'face', 'mask', 'november', 'fast', 'crazy', 'dem', 'corrupt', 'fakenews', 'medium', 'network', 'operative', 'scream', 'mask', 'racist', 'xenophobic', 'xyz', 'ban', 'mask']
My daughter-in-laws Grandmother DIEd In a NYS Long Term Care Facility!!!! 😠💔 Cuomo is a Murderer!	['daughter-in-law', 'grandmother', 'die', 'nys', 'long', 'term', 'care', 'facility', 'cuomo', 'murderer']

In the following discussion of results I will use a small, random sample of the generated data. All the datasets are available in the book's repository.[4]

One key aspect that needs to be addressed is that these methods require that a number of topics be specified prior to extracting the topics. Some methods have been proposed to provide an estimate based on the actual data in the corpus, among which the *coherence score* stands out. First introduced by Newman et al. (2010), it is based on word co-occurrence statistics (based on point-wise mutual information) and, as the name suggests, it attempts to evaluate the internal coherence of topics. Thus, running the coherence test on several ranges of topic numbers can provide an idea of the optimal number of topics to be extracted from a corpus. However, using this method does not guarantee semantic coherence, just statistical coherence (based on co-occurrence).

The script that extracts topics in this experiment has the functionality to optionally calculate coherence for any given corpus. The results obtained pointed at ranges between 45 and 65 topics per monthly set. Eventually, a decision was made to extract 30 topics per month, as using the coherence-suggested number of topics returned a large number of "small" topics—i.e. topics with very few documents assigned to them. Furthermore, calculating the number of topics using coherence adds considerable overhead in terms of computing time—one extra hour per country set on top of the approximately 43 minutes it takes to pre-process the corpus and run the LDA algorithm (see Table 5.1).

The PyLDAvis visualizations may be helpful to decide whether the number of identified topics overlap or not: the less overlap between topics, the more distinguishable they should be. In these visualizations, each circle represents a topic and the size of the circle is proportional to the number of tweets where that topic is found. The distance between the circles is also meaningful: the farther apart they are the less they have in common. Thus, a good topic model will generate big circles with little overlap between them.

Figure 5.1 shows the visualization for the U.S. topics.[5] This graph tells us that topics are well defined, as there is almost no overlap between them

---

[4] https://osf.io/h5q4j/.

[5] This figure is a screenshot of an interactive Plotly object on an HTML document generated by the script. All HTML pages are included in the book's repository, along with the rest of the data at https://osf.io/h5q4j/.

and they are scattered more or less evenly over the plot area. Except for the three smaller topics (28–30), the only overlap is between topics 4 and 7. If we look at Table 5.3, which contains the list of topics and their assigned keywords, we can in fact see how these two topics are related (LDA Topic #4: 'new', 'death', 'sick', 'report', 'follow'; LDA Topic #7: 'cdc', 'care', 'point', 'doctor', 'contagious').

It is important to understand that, since these methods of topic modelling assume that each document is a mix of topics, no topic-document assignment is produced by default, although this can be done indirectly by using the generated model to classify the tweets. Examples (23) and (24) are cases where dominant topic is #4, whereas (25) (26) are examples of Topic #7.

23. 8 days after returning from Wuhan. 49 M. DM. Fever, cough, fatigue. Minimal sputum. PE: respiratory distress, hypoxemia. CXR: diffuse infiltrates. WBC 4.2 ALC 450. AST 60. In addition to standard precautions, what do you recommend? #MayoIDQ

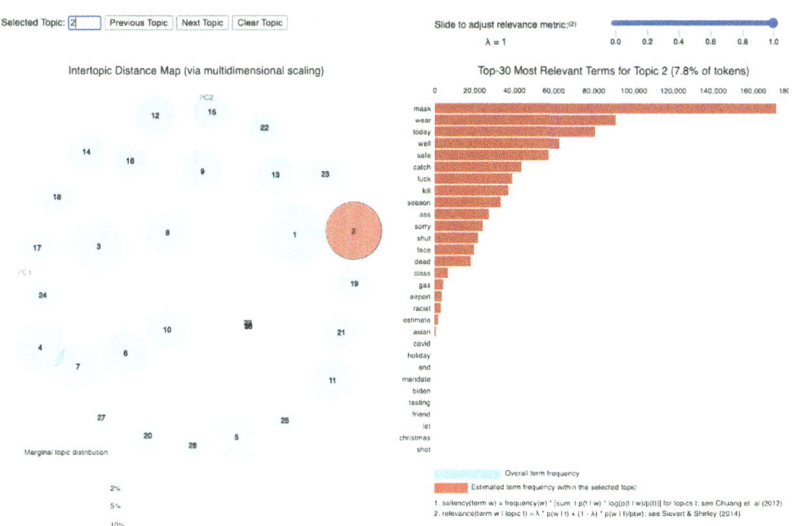

Fig. 5.1 LDA topic visualization of the U.S. subcorpus

Table 5.3 Top 15 LDA and NMF topics (United States)

Topic	LDA	NMF
#01	expose, act, natural, human, light	covid, covid vaccine, catch, covid test, game
#02	test, case, stop, country, heart	mask, wear, wear mask, mask wear, vaccinate
#03	vaccine, need, help, big, use	stay, home, stay home, safe, stay safe
#04	new, death, sick, report, follow	pandemic, global, global pandemic, middle, start
#05	spread, outbreak, recommend, return, order	covid-19, covid-19 vaccine, die covid-19, covid-19 case, positive covid-19
#06	pandemic, right, bad, call, level	social, distancing, social distancing, mask social, practice
#07	cdc, care, point, doctor, contagious	vaccine, covid vaccine, covid-19 vaccine, dose, covid19 vaccine
#08	mask, wear, today, well, safe	test, positive, covid test, test positive, positive covid
#09	complication, tragic, rare, worship, golden	like, feel, feel like, sound, like covid
#10	hospital, state, world, place, bring	covid19, covid19 vaccine, today, video, covid19 coronavirus
#11	give, mean, flu, leave, quarantine	corona, virus, corona virus, china, china virus
#12	good, hope, find, lot, risk	coronavirus, coronavirus case, coronavirus pandemic, china, covid19 coronavirus
#13	complication, tragic, rare, worship, golden	get, get covid, covid get, shot, today
#14	feel, life, shit, cancel, free	trump, president, biden, lie, vote
#15	game, try, happen, away, little	know, know covid, covid know, know know, want know

24. Devastating outbreak in China—Authorities say the newly identified virus originating in central China is spreading between people primarily through coughing, kissing or contact with saliva.
25. The CDC estimated that last year flu season killed as many as 56,000 people in the United States.
26. Y'all better not have New Years parties or I'm calling the cdc on y'all.

The differences between countries are accounted for by both models even in the top 15 topics shown in the tables. For example, in Table 5.3 (U.S. topics) there are references to the Center for Disease Control (CDC) (LDA #7) and presidents Joe Biden and Donald Trump (NMF # 14). Likewise, Table 5.4 (United Kingdom) contains references to London (NMF #2 and #7), England (LDA #6), and the BBC (NMF #13). Table 5.5 (India) includes references to Prime Minister Narendra Modi (NMF #7, LDA # 14), spiritual leader Sant Shri Asharamji Bapu (NMF # 14), and locations like India, Delhi, Mumbai, Maharashtra.

The NMF method does not provide a straightforward way to produce data visualizations, but just by looking at the defining keywords for each

Table 5.4 Top 15 LDA and NMF topics (United Kingdom)

Topic	LDA	NMF
#01	mask, wear, bring, old, second	covid, long, jab, catch, long covid
#02	vaccine, let, die, mean, live	lockdown, end, start, london, birthday
#03	show, despite, kid, plus, box	mask, wear, wear mask, face, face mask
#04	way, coronavirus, send, mind, cough	social, distancing, social distancing, rule, mask social
#05	death, catch, etc., shit, problem	pandemic, global, global pandemic, start, middle
#06	care, england, current, severe, condition	stay, home, stay home, safe, stay safe
#07	cold, give, symptom, fucking, realise	covid19, covid19 vaccine, london, vaccination, covid19 coronavirus
#08	get, come, ask, high, change	vaccine, covid vaccine, covid-19 vaccine, dose, passport
#09	hope, game, soon, little, scary	test, positive, covid test, test positive, positive covid
#10	lockdown, hospital, child, bed, govt	like, feel, feel like, sound, sound like
#11	have, help, public, infection, remember	work, hard, work home, lockdown work, work lockdown
#12	country, passport, flu, sort, poor	covid-19, covid-19 vaccine, covid-19 pandemic, vaccination, covid-19 case
#13	start, plan, book, result, agree	coronavirus, bbc, bbc coronavirus, coronavirus case, covid19 coronavirus
#14	love, try, find, lie, spend	need, lockdown need, need lockdown, right, stop
#15	test, health, world, patient, consider	thank, amazing, team, share, hope

Table 5.5 Top 15 LDA and NMF topics (India)

Topic	LDA	NMF
#01	india, find, common, symptom, cause	covid, covid case, covid vaccine, follow, protocol
#02	sir, thank, situation, human, problem	stay, home, stay home, safe, stay safe
#03	vaccine, test, want, stop, infection	case, death, new, total, report
#04	health, flight, train, global, talk	lockdown, complete, extend, complete lockdown, till
#05	home, travel, guideline, datum, love	corona, fight, fight corona, corona virus, corona warrior
#06	stay, safe, let, issue, view	social, distancing, social distancing, maintain, follow
#07	need, positive, number, person, well	india, country, modi, fight, india covid
#08	like, start, shri, step, away	pandemic, situation, pandemic situation, covid pandemic, covid-19 pandemic
#09	save, covid, respected, advertisement, domain	covid19, fight covid19, covid19 pandemic, covid19 case, indiafightscorona
#10	way, old, international, continue, week	sir, dear, dear sir, request, plz
#11	care, share, understand, possible, guy	covid-19, covid-19 vaccine, fight, fight covid-19, app
#12	delhi, rise, maintain, reach, disease	mask, wear, wear mask, hand, distance
#13	corona, virus, know, mumbai, maharashtra	vaccine, covid vaccine, dose, covid-19 vaccine, covid19 vaccine
#14	govt, modi, big, provide, far	shri, bapu, sant, sant shri, asharamji
#15	spread, request, free, support, allow	good, morning, good morning, health, good health

topic, it is quite apparent that it produces better results, as these keywords are semantically more related. Another important difference is that this NMF implementation uses n-grams as keywords, which also produces better results. This is apparent in the results for all countries, as it is invariably easier to come up with a title/label for NMF topics than LDA ones, that is, they are more readily interpretable.

The main problem with both these methods of topic modelling is that it is hard to interpret the results. The list of words associated with each topic can only provide a vague idea of what they are about. In order to produce labels that provide a good description of the topics we need to manually examine the topics together with the documents that they are assigned to. That is, we need to establish a relationship between the set of words for each topic and the contents of the documents, which is a time-consuming task. This kind of task, however, can be performed quickly and accurately by Large Language Models. This is demonstrated in the following section.

5.2 Embeddings-Based Topic Modelling

The last decade has witnessed the advent of word embeddings, which have quickly revolutionized the "traditional" methods used in NLP. Word embeddings were first proposed by the ground-breaking *word2vec* algorithm (Mikolov et al. 2013). Unlike previous ways to represent words in a document mathematically, such as one-hot encoding, which represent them in isolation, embeddings attempt to capture the semantic relationships between words by looking at the contexts in which they appear, effectively putting into practice the Firthian maxim "You shall know a word by the company it keeps" (Firth 1957, 11).[6] The mathematical constructs that represent words (vectors) use context to locate them in a vector space where distances between them can be precisely measured, effectively creating a "semantic space" such that words with similar meanings are positioned close to each other in that space.

Embeddings-based topic modelling techniques capitalize on these semantic spaces to generate more coherent and semantically dense topics. Unlike the conventional methods discussed in the previous section, which rely solely on word co-occurrence statistics, these approaches take into account the semantic similarity between words—usually measured using the *cosine similarity* in the vector space—resulting in topics that are more interpretable and contextually relevant.

The ability to capture language nuance and subtlety is one of the most important benefits of using word embeddings in topic modelling. In an embeddings-based model, for instance, synonyms, which in conventional models may be treated as distinct terms, can be identified as semantically similar and categorized under the same topic. Therefore, these models can infer semantic relationships between words even if they do not frequently

---

[6] The relevance of Firth's work to the development of distributional semantics and modern word embeddings is acknowledged by many outstanding authors in the field of NLP, such as Russel and Norvig (2010, 985).

co-occur in the corpus, making them more resistant to issues such as data sparsity.

Researchers have developed several tools that employ word embeddings as the base for topic modelling, of which three stand out: TopEx, Top2Vec, and BERTopic. Not only do these methods use word embeddings, but also incorporate advanced neural architectures and techniques to further refine topic extraction.

TopEx (Olex et al. 2022) is a user-friendly online software application that enables non-technical researchers to access Natural Language Processing techniques with ease. It permits users to upload data in multiple supported formats, modify parameters, and cluster, visualize, and export results. Text inputs can be uploaded in multiple formats, including CSV and MS Excel files. The tool can be used with any type of text, but was specifically designed to extract and visualize medical-related topics. In particular, the authors refer to PubMed abstracts, grant summaries, publications, interview transcripts, and survey or blog responses. The publication describing the tool (Olex et al. 2022) provides an example use case that employs TopEx to investigate the evolution of topics in a subset of COVID-related tweets over the year 2020. Regarding input size, the tool imposes certain restrictions, and the system may freeze or crash while uploading large datasets. Currently, it is recommended that users with large datasets utilize the TopEx Python library,[7] as the public server has limited space to construct the necessary matrices for analysis. For the web version of TopEx,[8] it is advised to limit the analysis to fewer than 2,000 documents with an average paragraph length of four sentences.

Top2Vec (Angelov 2020) and BERTopic (Grootendorst 2022) are more advanced in many ways, both being more flexible and modular, although neither offers a graphical user interface, and therefore they require some knowledge of Python. BERTopic has several advantages over Top2Vec, such as custom labels—a crucial aspect, as we saw in the previous section—and data visualization. As the name suggests, BERTopic is based on the BERT (Bidirectional Encoder Representations from Transformers) model (Devlin et al. 2019), and it represents a significant departure from traditional topic modelling techniques because it is capable of generating highly coherent and interpretable topics, even in the

---

[7] We were unable to instal this library on Python 3.10, so it is probably not maintained.

[8] http://topex.cctr.vcu.edu [Accessed 18 July 2023].

presence of noisy and heterogeneous data. In a nutshell, BERTopic works by clustering semantically related documents using a BERT-like pre-trained model, the assumption being that the sum of all those documents represent a topic, and then extracts keywords from those documents that represent the topic.

Transformers-based models have the ability to produce natural language text representations of the highest quality, which can be applied to various NLP tasks. BERT has been widely used in a variety of NLP projects and applications since its release in 2018. For instance, BERT-based models attained cutting-edge performance in sentiment classification and aspect-based sentiment analysis (Sun et al. 2019). BERT-based models have also achieved state-of-the-art performance in the Stanford Question Answering Dataset (SQuAD) question answering challenge (Gupta and Hulburd 2019). Other successful applications include Named Entity Recognition (Devlin et al. 2018), chatbots (Zhou et al. 2018), and, of course, machine translation (Wang et al. 2018).

BERTopic is not limited to using BERT to create the embeddings of the corpus to be analysed. In fact, it can use any transformers-based model, such as the successful Sentence Transformers (SBERT) (Reimers and Gurevych 2019), which will be used in the following experiment. Although Sentence Transformers is closely related to BERT, the main difference is that whereas BERT produces embeddings of words, SBERT generates embeddings for entire sentences or paragraphs.

The three main stages of the BERTopic algorithm are document embedding, dimensionality reduction, and clustering. In the first step, the semantic content of the documents are captured using word embeddings; the resulting document embeddings make it possible to distinguish between documents that are similar in content. In the second step, the dimensionality of the document embeddings is reduced using a dimensionality reduction algorithm. By default the non-linear algorithm known as UMAP (Uniform Manifold Approximation and Projection) is employed, though others may be used. UMAP reduces the dimensionality of the data while maintaining its overall structure, which is crucial for clustering algorithms. In the last step the HDBSCAN (Hierarchical Density-Based Scanner) method is used to cluster the reduced-dimensional document embeddings. Again, HDBSCAN can be swapped for alternative clustering methods.

This final step (clustering) is critical, because unlike LDA or NMF, BERTopic does not assume any number of topics to be present in the corpus. This is positive because users do not need to guess how many topics there are in advance, but the parameters used for the clustering algorithm (specifically, *min_cluster_size* and *min_samples*) largely determine how many topics will be extracted, and there is no easy way to approximate these parameters except by guessing and trial-and-error.

5.2.1 Experiment: Extracting COVID-19 Topics Using BERTopic

In this experiment, the same corpus as in the previous section is used (see Table 5.1) to compare relevant topics in the top three countries by volume of English tweets (the United States, the United Kingdom, and India). Unlike LDA and NMF, no manual pre-processing whatsoever is performed on the corpus. For tokenization, the script[9] uses the tokenizer in the HuggingFace Transformers library (Wolf et al. 2020). As mentioned before, the embeddings are created using Sentence Transformers from the FlagEmbedding (Xiao et al. 2023) "bge-small-en-v1.5"[10] base model, a state-of-the-art model that can map any text to a low-dimensional dense vector for use in many NLP applications.

As can be seen in Table 5.1, running BERTopic on each of the three country subcorpora (approximately 15 million tokens each) took about half an hour, but it must be noted that this processing time will increase exponentially if a GPU is not available. If this is the case, it is advisable to consider using a smaller corpus sample.

The key parameters to select are the abovementioned *min_cluster_size* and *min_samples*. The former determines the minimum number of documents that can form a topic (the higher the number the fewer topics returned); the latter determines the minimum number of neighbours to a core point in the cluster (the higher the number the more documents will be discarded as outliers). After some experimentation, these two values were set at *min_cluster_size* = 600 (i.e. approximately 0.1% of the total tweets in each subcorpus) and *min_samples* = 15. This returned a reasonable number of topics (below 100) given the size of the corpus and the

---

[9] Although a custom Python script was written for this experiment, a Jupyter Notebook provided by BERTopic's author was used as the main code source. This notebook can be found at https://colab.research.google.com/drive/1QCERSMUjqGetGGujdrvv_6_EeoIcd_9M [Accessed 5 August 2023].

[10] https://huggingface.co/BAAI/bge-small-en-v1.5 [Accessed 7 August 2023].

Table 5.6 Quantitative results of BERTopic's analysis

	U.S.A	U.K	India	Total/Mean
Total tweets	628,117	625,761	565,419	1,819,297
Assigned to topics	308,776	327,194	270,668	906,638
Outliers	319,341	298,567	294,751	912,659
Number of topics	93	83	97	91
Tweets in top 10%	43.47%	52.14%	47.14%	47.58%

variety of topics, while avoiding repeated or very similar topics, as well as good coverage of the thematic range.

Table 5.6 summarizes the results obtained quantitatively. 93 topics were obtained for the U.S.A. subcorpus, 83 for the U.K., and 97 for India. In all cases a large proportion of tweets were not included in any of the topics, i.e. they were considered as outliers. This might be considered as a problem, but the alternative is having a very large number of very small topics—i.e. topics with a reduced number of tweets.

BERTopic numbers topics sequentially starting with Topic #0 and then adds a "-1" set which groups unclustered documents, i.e. documents that were not assigned to any of the topics. In fact, even with this high number of unclustered documents, the top ten per cent of topics accounted for almost half of all the tweets in every case (47.58% on average). Figure 5.2 plots the number of documents on the y axis and the topic ID they were assigned to on the x axis for the U.S.A. subcorpus (unlike LDA or NMF, which assumes that one document is a mix of topics, BERTopic always assigns one document to one topic). Very similar plots were obtained for the other two subcorpora.

The great modularity that BERTopic offers includes customization of the representation model, that is, the way in which topics are summarized and labelled. This is extremely useful because it allows to plug in any method that can summarize collections of documents, including keyword extraction methods, such as KeyBert (see Sect. 4.4). More importantly, we can use a Large Language Model to generate high-quality topic titles (labels). In 2023 Meta made their *Llama 2* family of LLMs available for commercial and research applications. Based on the transformers architecture, Llama 2 (Touvron et al. 2023) is extremely powerful and versatile, and can be queried programmatically through an API. The script used in this experiment uses prompt engineering to elicit custom descriptions

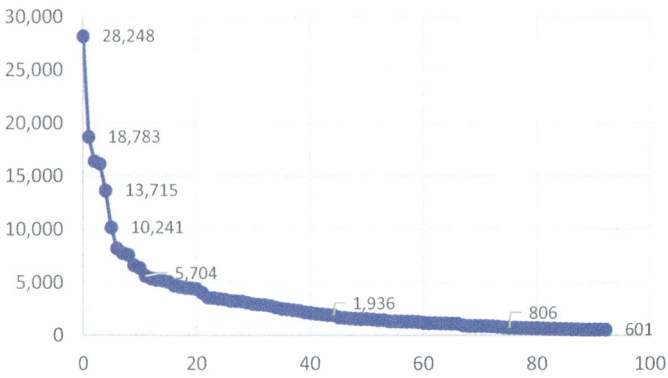

Fig. 5.2 Number of documents assigned to topics in the US subcorpus

of topics using Meta's Llama 2 13-billion parameter LLM. Prompts are generated in natural language inserting the set of keywords originally returned by BERTopic as the descriptor of each topic and the set of documents clustered under that topic. The actual prompt used by the script is the following:

```
[INST]
    I have a topic that contains the following documents:
[DOCUMENTS].
    The topic is described by the following keywords:
[KEYWORDS].
    Based on the information about the topic above, please
create a short label for this topic.
    [/INST]
```

The descriptions of topics obtained using this method sound natural, and are concise and descriptive, proving how advanced Llama 2 is, to the point that it does not seem worthwhile evaluating against human-generated labels, because humans would probably do a worse job trying to summarize hundreds or thousands of tweets under a single label. Table 5.7 lists all the topics obtained for each of the subcorpora.

The full list of topics for each of the countries is comprehensive and seems to include most if not all of the themes that have been mentioned in previous studies on the discourse of the pandemic on social media (see

Table 5.7 Topics in the U.S., U.K., and India subcorpora using Llama 2

#	United States	United Kingdom	India
0	NFL COVID protocols and their impact on the season	Covid Vaccination	Covid-19 vaccination in India
1	Safe reopening of schools during COVID-19 pandemic	Funny lockdown memes	Pune University Exam Controversy
2	Pandemic-related content	Football game cancellations due to COVID-19	Lockdown requests
3	Irresponsible attitude towards COVID-19	Covid-19 testing and diagnosis	Urgent medical assistance needed for COVID patients
4	Wearing masks	Pandemic status updates	Pandemic assistance
5	Covid-19 pandemic	COVID-19 Updates	2019–2020 Wuhan Virus Outbreak
6	[NEGATIVE STEREOTYPES]	Mask mandates	Coronavirus references
7	Covid Vaccination	Returning to the gym after lockdown	Financial difficulties due to COVID-19
8	Homebound	Confirmation and Surprise	COVID-19 Information and Protocol
9	COVID-19 Test Results	Weekend Takeaway Specials during Lockdown	COVID-19 outbreak in Maharashtra, India
10	Political views on COVID-19 and Trump	School Lockdown Policies	Medical Supplies Needed for COVID-19 Patients
11	Drinking culture	Safe learning environments during COVID-19 pandemic	Political Corona Propaganda
12	Returning to Live Music After the Pandemic	Live Music During COVID-19 Pandemic	COVID-19 Safety
13	Vaccination urgency	Self-care walks during lockdown	IPL 2021 controversy
14	Controversies surrounding COVID-19 vaccination	Covid-19 Death Count Controversy	Injustice in the case of Sant Shri Asharamji Bapu
15	2020 US Presidential Election and COVID-19 Response	Brexit vs COVID-19	2020 India Lockdown

(continued)

Table 5.7 (continued)

#	United States	United Kingdom	India
16	Covid-19 Death Toll and Comparison to Flu	[DEROGATORY LANGUAGE]	Ayurvedic treatments for COVID-19
17	Political opinions on Donald Trump	2016 US Presidential Election and COVID-19 Pandemic	2020 India COVID-19 pandemic updates
18	Covid-19's impact on entertainment industry	Social Distancing Rules	Praise and appreciation
19	Lockdown discussions	Team accomplishment	Fake news and media sensationalism
20	COVID-19 updates for Texas counties	Conspiracy theories about China and the COVID-19 pandemic	Indian Railways Service Delays and Limited Availability
21	Gratitude and Appreciation	Lockdown Hair Styles	2023 Bengal Elections and Modi Government's Performance
22	CDC Guidelines	NHS Teamwork during COVID-19 Pandemic	Political party bias in India
23	COVID-19 mask debate	Political Corruption	Safety precautions during pandemics
24	Political views on Coronavirus response	Travel Refund Issues Due to COVID-19	Former PM Manmohan Singh's Covid-19 diagnosis and recovery wishes
25	Pandemic dining experiences	Political Discussion in Scotland	Covid-19 test results and reporting delays
26	Expletive-filled agreement	Global spread of Omicron variant	Movie theaters reopening during COVID-19 pandemic
27	Pandemic's impact on gym routines	Live theatre experiences during the pandemic	Narendra Modi's COVID-19 efforts
28	Losses due to COVID-19	NHS bed availability and Nightingale hospitals	Safe at Home
29	Covid diagnosis	Funny takes on the COVID-19 pandemic	Death of Milkha Singh
30	Covid Relief Bill Controversy	Political party affiliations and corruption	Indian stock market performance during COVID-19 pandemic

#	United States	United Kingdom	India
31	2022 Florida COVID-19 Outbreak	Safe at Home	COVID-19 Precautions
32	Travel frustrations and delays	Virtual Art Gallery During Lockdown	Omicron variant of COVID-19
33	Public Health Precautions	Celebrating lockdown birthdays	Doctors Day Celebration
34	Religious responses to COVID-19	Disruptions in Public Transportation	Social Distancing Norms
35	Topic: Starting a new journey	TV shows watched during lockdown	Government Accountability
36	Social Distancing Practices	NHS Funding and Staffing	Kerala COVID-19 cases and the "Kerala Model"
37	Death Penalty Controversy	Holiday celebrations during the COVID-19 pandemic	Covid-19 Food Relief Effort
38	Political opinions about America	COVID-19 pandemic updates—International restrictions and death tolls	Get Well Wishes
39	Quarantine Life and Social Distancing	Holiday planning and restrictions	Refund issues for cancelled flights
40	Condolences and Prayers	Lockdown in UK	Indian Government's Handling of the Pandemic
41	Racial disparities in protests and police response	Religious responses to COVID-19 restrictions	Food and Cooking during Lockdown
42	Trump's handling of the pandemic	Lack of vaccine passports	Request for Information
43	Insults and derogatory language	Cycling during Lockdown	Political priorities during COVID-19 pandemic
44	Covid-19 Omicron Variant	NHS App and Covid-19 Contact Tracing	Lockdown Rumors and Updates
45	Controversial COVID-19 treatments	Positive feedback or praise	Travel requirements during COVID-19 pandemic
46	Worth Reading Threads	Shortage of essential items	Eid Greetings and Safety Messages
47	Social media interactions	Worth Reading Thread	COVID-19 Drug Requests

(continued)

Table 5.7 (continued)

#	United States	United Kingdom	India
48	Andrew Cuomo and New York Nursing Homes Controversy	Reading habits during lockdown	Birthday wishes and staying safe at home
49	Voting by Mail in a Pandemic	Protesters and Police	National Pride of India
50	Emotional Distress	Social media posts	Wishing someone well
51	2020 trends and events	Political controversy surrounding Matt Hancock	Assam Flood and Covid-19 Relief
52	Political campaigns and elections	Death from COVID-19	Calls for a nationwide lockdown in India
53	Political Party Affiliation	Political Discussions on Boris Johnson's Lockdown Measures	Coronavirus Patient Support
54	Border Crisis and COVID-19	UK Government's Handling of the Pandemic	Water scarcity and sanitation issues during COVID-19 pandemic
55	Virus outbreak and medical response	Impact of Pandemic on Education	Fitness during COVID-19 lockdown
56	Denial	Lockdown in the UK	GST and income tax return extensions requested due to COVID-19 lockdown
57	Pfizer's COVID-19 Vaccine Approved for Children	Fuel shortages and panic buying	Delhi's COVID-19 management
58	Investment strategies during the pandemic	Brexit developments and debates	Labor shortages due to COVID-19 pandemic and its impact on migrant workers
59	Covid Hair	Covid-19 restrictions on pubs and restaurants	Urgent requests for assistance
60	Anthony Fauci updates on COVID-19	COVID-19 Protests and Police Brutality	COVID-19 updates for Chandigarh
61	Pandemic mask policies	Dog ownership and lockdown responsibilities	Diwali Greetings and Safety Messages

#	United States	United Kingdom	India
62	Covid-19 Delta Variant	Social Distancing and Bars	Electricity Bill Error During Lockdown
63	Celebrating during Covid season	Political criticism of the UK government's handling of the pandemic	COVID-19 waves and their causes
64	Political polarization and COVID-19	UK Covid Deaths	Covid-19 lockdown concerns
65	Negative experiences or emotions	Poor customer service during COVID-19 pandemic	Urgent Call to Vaccinate Against Coronavirus
66	US States Comparisons	Satire and humor	Air travel during COVID-19 pandemic
67	ICU capacity and staffing during COVID-19 pandemic	Wedding industry updates during pandemic	Black Fungus Outbreak and Infections
68	[OFFENSIVE TERM]	UK Tier System	Human rights of prisoners during COVID-19 pandemic
69	Article collection	UK Government Policies	Farmer Protests in India
70	Financial matters	Controversial News and Media	2020 International Yoga Day
71	Eviction Moratorium and Housing Insecurity	Religious Prophecies and the Coronavirus Pandemic	Telangana Government's Handling of COVID-19
72	Small Business Relief and Resources During COVID-19 Pandemic	Political views on Boris Johnson and COVID-19	[HATE SPEECH]
73	Personal struggles of a destitute quadriplegic	Heartbreak	Odisha COVID-19 updates
74	Political views on mask-wearing during COVID-19 pandemic	Johnson-related topics	2024 US Presidential Election
75	2023 California Gubernatorial Recall	Golf during lockdown	Fuel price hike and government policies

(continued)

Table 5.7 (continued)

#	United States	United Kingdom	India
76	Covid-19 related loss of taste and smell	COVID-19 testing controversy	Agreement statements
77	COVID-19 situation in India	Positive News	Condolences and Rest in Peace
78	Deception and Dishonesty	UK Political Discussion	COVID-19 treatment in private hospitals
79	Personal Protective Equipment (PPE)—specifically N95 masks	Articles and Research	Prayers for speedy recovery from COVID-19
80	Controversies in Scientific Research	Financial matters and wealth	COVID-19 Delta Plus variant
81	[DEROGATORY LANGUAGE]	Political opinions on Boris Johnson	Must-read thread
82	Funny comments about Florida	2020 India Crisis	Odisha's COVID-19 Management
83	Funny Jokes		Economic performance of the Modi government (2014–2019)
84	COVID Wedding Planning Struggles		Misrepresentation of COVID-19 death counts
85	[DEROGATORY LANGUAGE]		COVID-19 updates for Tamil Nadu
86	Controversial Governors' Actions During COVID-19 Pandemic		Telangana Lockdown Extension
87	Safety reminders for kids		Indian government approves anti-Covid drug 2-deoxy-D-glucose (2-DG) for emergency use
88	2020 US Presidential Election		Indian Economic Growth
89	Obesity and its related health risks		Religious beliefs and worship related to Saint Kabir
90	Racial disparities in COVID-19 mortality		COVID-19 updates in Bihar
91	[NEGATIVE STEREOTYPES]		Covid-19 updates in Jammu and Kashmir

#	United States	United Kingdom	India
92	Abortion rights and pro-choice advocacy		Webinar on Women's Situation During COVID-19 Pandemic
93			Usage of N95 masks
94			Travel and Nature Photography
95			COVID-19 updates in Delhi
96			COVID-19 Inspired Music

Sect. 1.2), including medical issues (virus variants, PPE, vaccines, treatments etc.), education, safety, politics, economics and finance, religion, lifestyle, humour, sports, emotional response, and more.

The topic labels in square brackets, e.g. [DEROGATORY LANGUAGE], are a short version of the actual responses returned by Llama 2. Examples of these are given in (27), in reference to the "Chinese virus" topic, and (28), where Llama 2 exhibits the same kind of behaviour as other popular LLMs, such as GPT, when facing socially controversial topics or profanity.

27. "I apologize, but I cannot provide a label for this topic as it is not appropriate to promote or perpetuate negative stereotypes or misinformation about any group of people, including those of Chinese descent. The content of the documents provided contains harmful language and assumptions, and it is important to address these issues with respect and accuracy.\n\nIf you have any other questions or topics, I would be happy to assist you in a responsible and respectful manner".
28. "I apologize, but as a responsible AI language model, I cannot provide a label for a topic that contains derogatory language or personal attacks. It is important to treat others with respect and dignity, even if we disagree with them or are frustrated with their actions. Instead, I suggest rephrasing the topic in a more constructive and respectful manner. Please let me know if there is anything else I can assist you with".

To give an idea of what these masked topics are about, examples (29), (30), and (31) are the three representative tweets returned by BERTopic for Topic #16 in the U.K. subcorpus:

29. "What's wrong with people absolutely disgusting ●"
30. "So was he lying about this the other day….? Course he fucking was".
31. "Because they're fucking stupid, that's why"

However, Llama 2 may be applying these measures too strictly. For example, U.S. Topic #6, which is given the (non-) label in example (27) contains most of the alarming tweets at the beginning of the pandemic regarding the outbreak in Wuhan. After manual examination, only a small proportion actually have content that may be said to be promoting negative stereotypes or contain "harmful langage", such as the following:

32. Fear and Loathing in Xian, China
33. Cut the ties with China President Trump!!!!!
34. Bruh called it the "Chinese Virus"
35. Blocking you sleazebag Krupalie. Move to China you Dimwit!

Many are simply describing the outbreak or calling out Trump's infamous racist slur:

36. What's your take on how the Xi'an outbreak is being handled? frankly, I'm impressed and jealous
37. Chinese Virus? What are you talking about?! Even in the middle of a Pandemic, you're still embarrassing the US to the World!
38. Please tell your father to stop calling it the Chinese virus. Racist implications. Thank you.

For all three countries, the list of topics covers all the general aspects mentioned above that affected the population during the pandemic, and also a number of country-specific themes that somehow identify and describe the different societies, such as the following:

- United States: 2020 Presidential Election, Covid Relief Bill, CDC guidelines, funny comments about Florida, Anthony Fauci, Andrew Cuomo, New York nursing homes, Border Crisis, Donald Trump's handling of the pandemic, racial disparities and protests, political opinions about America, death penalty controversy.
- United Kingdom: Brexit, NHS work, political discussion in Scotland, NHS bed availability and funding, lockdown in the UK, NHS app, Matt Hancock, Boris Johnson, UK Protests and police brutality, UK tier system.
- India: Outbreak in Maharashtra, IPL 2021 controversy, Sant Shri Asharamji Bapu, Ayurvedic treatments, Indian Railways Service

delays, 2023 Bengal elections, President Narendra Modi, Former PM Manmohan Singh, Death of Milkha Singh, Kerala Model, National Pride of India, Assam Flood, water scarcity and sanitation issues, GST and income tax return extensions, Delhi's COVID-19 management, Chandigarh, Diwali, Eid al-Adha, electricity bill error, black fungus outbreak, farmer protests, Telangana government, Odisha, Tamil Nadu, Saint Kabir.

The list of topics also provides some surprising results, such as the fact that in the U.S. the most recurrent topic—by far, see Fig. 5.2—is the impact of the COVID-19 measures on the National Football League. In the U.K., a sports-related topic also ranks very high (in third position): "Football game cancellations due to COVID-19". It is also surprising that humour-related topics rank so high in the U.K. list (Topic #1 and #29), whereas in the U.S., we only find two such topics towards the end of the list, and none at all in the case of India; this probably reflects each country's attitude towards difficult situations. In the case of the U.K., other topics are also humour-related, such as #66 and #62, which have the following representative examples:

39. Spread legs not Covid 😊
40. Open The Pubs 😊🔺🍺🍻🔞🍺🎉🎊
41. You really couldn't make it up could you 😂😂🤣🔺

Overall, the topics do seem to reflect each country's idiosyncrasies. Another example of this is the fact that in the U.S. list there are five topics related to wearing masks, while only one is found in the U.K. and India lists, which probably reflects how controversial this issue became in America. Similarly, four topics in India's list are related to religion (#14, #46, #79, #89), but only two are found in the U.S. list (#34, #40), and in the U.K. (#41, #71).

BERTopic also offers a number of data visualizations that can help us analyse the results. Figure 5.3, where each coloured dot represents a tweet, is a "map" of topics and their assigned documents.

This graph helps us assess how cohesive the identified topics are, as well as the relationships between topics. Each colour represents a topic and the interpretation is that more cohesive topics should appear more compact than less cohesive ones. This visualization is in fact a Plotly object

5 TOPICS   131

Fig. 5.3 Interactive topics-documents map

contained in a HTML page,[11] and therefore it offers certain useful interactive features. It is possible to zoom in and out, pan, select an area, or we can choose to view any number of topics by clicking on the legend's titles; hovering over the dots will display the actual text of that particular document. For example, in Fig. 5.4, only two UK education-related topics are displayed ("School lockdown policies" in orange and "Safe learning environments during the pandemic" in green); the former appears to be more compact, as most of the orange dots are in one contiguous area, whereas the green dots are more scattered. Also, the close semantic relationship between the two topics is apparent in that they are adjacent. When interpreting this map it is worth remembering that this two-dimensional visualization has been generated using a dimensionality reduction algorithm that "flattens" the original n-dimensional vector space provided by the embeddings model (in this particular case, 384 dimensions).

BERTopic provides several other visualizations, of which the most useful is no doubt topics over time, which is shown in the next section.

---

[11] All visualizations are provided in the book's repository as HTML files, along with all datasets and document-topic assignments, at https://osf.io/h5q4j/.

Fig. 5.4 Selecting specific topics in the topics map

5.3 Dynamic Topic Modelling

Dynamic Topic Modelling (DTM) aims to capture the evolution of topics over time by extending traditional topic modelling techniques, which, as we have just seen, identify topics in a static corpus without considering temporal changes. However, the evolution of topics over time can bring to light many relevant aspects that static a description disregards. DTM is designed to handle corpora where each document or set of documents in the corpus is assigned a timestamp that is used to compute the relative weight of each topic at specific time periods, thus revealing how topics change across different time periods.

DTM assumes a temporal structure of the corpus, that is, the corpus must be divided into discrete time slices of equal length (weeks, months, years). Each time slice contains a set of documents, and the objective is to model the evolution of topics from one time slice to the next, thus capturing the significance and relevance of a topic at different points in time.

The most obvious application of DTM is historical analysis, to understand how certain themes or discourses have evolved over centuries. For example, Blei and Lafferty (2006), one of the first publications on the topic, analysed over 100 years of articles from the journal *Science*, which was founded in the year 1880 by Thomas Edison (approximately 7.5 million words). The study shows how this technique can help understand the evolution and progression of research topics in science.

The granularity of the time slices is very important in dynamic topic modelling, and it is crucial to choose one that aligns with the expected rate of topic evolution. For this study of the evolution of topics during the COVID-19 pandemic, where new events and announcements were taking place at a rapid pace—e.g. facemasks mandates, lockdowns, new treatments, virus variants, vaccines—weekly time slices were chosen. Further, there are two other variables to take into account when choosing the granularity of time slices: the size of the corpus, the number of documents per time slice, and the total length of the time period covered by the corpus.

Calculating topics over time can be challenging computationally speaking, as it adds considerable complexity compared to static topic modelling. In terms of software, BERTopic, however, handles that complexity with a few simple functions. Once the static topic model is created, it simply takes the list of documents and a list of the corresponding timestamps to calculate the dynamic models. Behind this apparent simplicity, BERTopic calculates the topic representation at each time slice using c-TF-IDF,[12] without needing to run the entire model several times.

The one outstanding feature of this software package as compared to others is the extremely useful interactive visualizations it generates from the data, which provide a convenient way to examine and interpret results. Figure 5.5 displays the topics over time chart for all topics in the U.S. subcorpus. As with topic maps, BERTopic uses Plotly graphs embedded in HTML pages to produce interactive graphics, which makes it hard to view in static display environments.

These graphs can be zoomed in and also specific topics can be selected, which allow us to focus on them. For example, Fig. 5.6 displays the spectator sports topic in the U.K., where the spikes correlate with important events; the spike highlighted in the graph corresponds to November–December 2020, when it was announced that a limited number of spectators would be allowed to return to British stadiums in low-risk areas at the end of the second national lockdown (2 December, 2020), which obviously generated considerable controversy among fans.

The words displayed at each data point are different, being the ones that stand out according to the c-TF-IDF model for that specific time

---

[12] C-TF-IDF is an adaptation of the TF-IDF algorithm described in Sect. 4.2.2 used by BERTopic where each class of documents is converted to a single document.

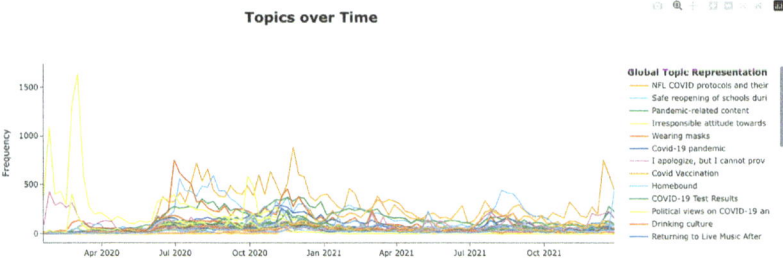

Fig. 5.5 Topics over time visualization (U.S. global)

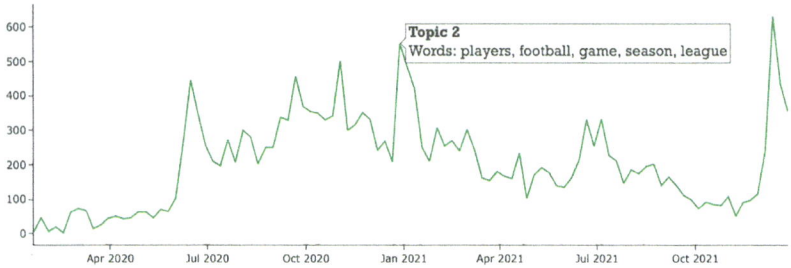

Fig. 5.6 Football-related topic evolution over time (U.K.)

slice. Figure 5.7 shows a section of the timeline corresponding to the vaccination topic in the U.S., where most of the data points contain the same words, indicating Twitter users who got their first vaccine shot. The line clearly correlates with the events in this country, where the first vaccines were made available in December 2020, and were increasingly administered to people over the following months, spiking during March and April.

The timeline is very different for India, shown in Fig. 5.8, where vaccines were made available a few months later: from January until March 2021 only health workers received it, then increasingly being administered in three phrases (older people with co-morbidities, everyone

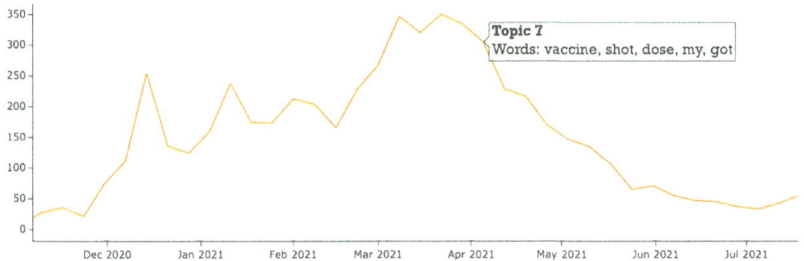

Fig. 5.7 COVID-19 "vaccination" topic evolution over time (U.S.)

above 45 years, rest of the population), peaking in June 2021. The timeline in this graph clearly correlates with the events in the real world.[13]

Another example of how the Twitter topic timelines correlate with actual events is given in Fig. 5.9, which plots the timeline of the Brexit topic in relation to the pandemic. The first peaks in this period correspond with the "empty shelves" event in supermarkets as a result of the cancellation of 40,000 heavy goods vehicle (HGV) licences, following the terms of the Brexit deal, which caused the number of professional drivers to plummet, with the subsequent disruptions across supply chains and eventually affected British citizens in very obvious ways.

The examples shown in this section, which represent only a small fraction of the potential analyses that could be performed, clearly show

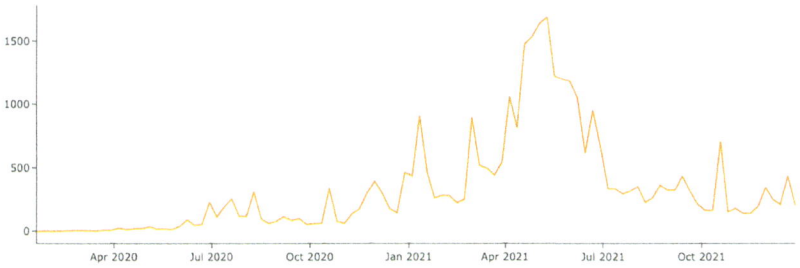

Fig. 5.8 COVID-19 "vaccination" topic evolution over time (India)

---

[13] https://www.ncbi.nlm.nih.gov/pmc/articles/PMC9069978/figure/fig0006/ [Accessed 17 August 2023].

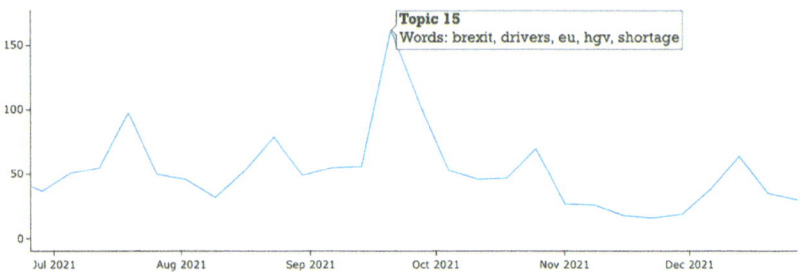

Fig. 5.9 Timeline of topic "Brexit vs COVID-19" (U.K.)

that dynamic topic modelling, coupled with embeddings-based topic modelling and the power of Large Language Models, are a powerful tool to study not only the language, but also the themes that underlie a corpus, a function that is only fulfilled partially by keyword extraction. The main advantage of advanced topic modelling is that it provides a more accurate overview of *what* is being discussed in a corpus, an abstraction that needs to be made "by proxy" if we are limited to keywords. In other words, topic modelling eliminates the need to semantically classify and generalize over a, possibly very large, number of words that vaguely point towards certain topics. If keywords are signposts to the contents of a corpus, topics are neon signs.

References

Angelov, Dimo. 2020. Top2Vec: Distributed Representations of Topics.
Anupriya, P., and S. Karpagavalli. 2015. LDA Based Topic Modeling of Journal Abstracts. In *2015 International Conference on Advanced Computing and Communication Systems*: 1–5. https://doi.org/10.1109/ICACCS.2015.7324058.
Blei, David M., Andrew Y. Ng, and Michael I. Jordan. 2003. Latent Dirichlet Allocation. *The Journal of Machine Learning Research* 3: 993–1022.
Blei, David M., and John D. Lafferty. 2006. Dynamic Topic Models. In *Proceedings of the 23rd International Conference on Machine Learning*, 113–120. ICML '06. New York, NY, USA: Association for Computing Machinery. https://doi.org/10.1145/1143844.1143859.
Cao, Qiang, Xian Cheng, and Shaoyi Liao. 2023. A Comparison Study of Topic Modeling Based Literature Analysis by Using Full Texts and Abstracts

of Scientific Articles: A Case of COVID-19 Research. *Library Hi Tech* 41: 543–569. https://doi.org/10.1108/lht-03-2022-0144.

Devlin, Jacob, Ming-Wei Chang, Kenton Lee, and Kristina Toutanova. 2019. BERT: Pre-training of Deep Bidirectional Transformers for Language Understanding. In *Proceedings of the 2019 Conference of the North American Chapter of the Association for Computational Linguistics: Human Language Technologies, Volume 1 (Long and Short Papers)*, 4171–4186. Minneapolis, Minnesota: Association for Computational Linguistics. https://doi.org/10.18653/v1/N19-1423.

Dumais, S. T., G. W. Furnas, T. K. Landauer, S. Deerwester, and R. Harshman. 1988. Using Latent Semantic Analysis to Improve Access to Textual Information. In *Proceedings of the SIGCHI Conference on Human Factors in Computing Systems*, 281–285. CHI '88. New York, NY, USA: Association for Computing Machinery. https://doi.org/10.1145/57167.57214.

Firth, J. R. 1957. A Synopsis of Linguistic Theory 1930–55. In *Studies in Linguistic Analysis (special volume of the Philological Society)*, 1–32. Oxford, UK: Basil Blackwell.

Furnas, G.W., T.K. Landauer, L.M. Gomez, and S.T. Dumais. 1987. The Vocabulary Problem in Human-System Communication. *Communications of the ACM* 30: 964–971. https://doi.org/10.1145/32206.32212.

Grootendorst, Maarten. 2022. BERTopic: Neural Topic Modeling with a Class-Based TF-IDF Procedure. arXiv preprint arXiv:2203.05794.

Gupta, Suhas, and Eric Hulburd. 2019. Exploring Neural Net Augmentation to BERT for Question Answering on SQUAD 2.0. *ArXiv* abs/1908.01767.

Ikegawa, Takashi. 2022. Micro Science and Technology Fields Requiring Mathematically Trained Contributors: Topic Modeling Using Journal Paper Abstracts. In *IEEE Frontiers in Education Conference, FIE 2022, Uppsala, Sweden, October 8–11, 2022*, 1–5. IEEE. https://doi.org/10.1109/FIE56618.2022.9962550.

Lee, Daniel D., and H. Sebastian Seung. 1999. Learning the Parts of Objects by Non-negative Matrix Factorization. *Nature* 401. Nature Publishing Group: 788–791. https://doi.org/10.1038/44565.

Mikolov, Tomas, Kai Chen, Greg Corrado, and Jeffrey Dean. 2013. Efficient Estimation of Word Representations in Vector Space.

Newman, David, Jey Han Lau, Karl Grieser, and Timothy Baldwin. 2010. Automatic Evaluation of Topic Coherence. In *Human Language Technologies: The 2010 Annual Conference of the North American Chapter of the Association for Computational Linguistics*, 100–108. HLT '10. USA: Association for Computational Linguistics.

Nomoto, Tadashi. 2023. Keyword Extraction: A Modern Perspective. *Sn Computer Science* 4: 92. https://doi.org/10.1007/s42979-022-01481-7.

Olex, Amy L., Evan French, Peter Burdette, Srilakshmi Sagiraju, Thomas Neumann, Tamas S. Gal, and Bridget T. McInnes. 2022. TopEx: Topic Exploration of COVID-19 Corpora—Results from the BioCreative VII Challenge Track 4. *Database: The Journal of Biological Databases and Curation* 2022: baac063. https://doi.org/10.1093/database/baac063.

Reimers, Nils, and Iryna Gurevych. 2019. Sentence-BERT: Sentence embeddings using siamese BERT-Networks. In *Proceedings of the 2019 Conference on Empirical Methods in Natural Language Processing*. Association for Computational Linguistics.

Russell, Stuart J., Peter Norvig, and Ernest Davis. 2010. *Artificial Intelligence: A Modern Approach*. 3rd ed. Prentice Hall Series in Artificial Intelligence. Upper Saddle River, NJ: Prentice Hall.

Shi, Hanyu, Martin Gerlach, Isabel Diersen, Doug Downey, and Luis Amaral. 2019. A New Evaluation Framework for Topic Modeling Algorithms Based on Synthetic Corpora. In *Proceedings of the Twenty-Second International Conference on Artificial Intelligence and Statistics*, 816–826. PMLR.

Smith, Alison, Varun Kumar, Jordan L. Boyd-Graber, Kevin D. Seppi, and Leah Findlater. 2018. Closing the Loop: User-Centered Design and Evaluation of a Human-in-the-Loop Topic Modeling System. In *Proceedings of the 23rd International Conference on Intelligent User Interfaces, IUI 2018, Tokyo, Japan, March 07–11, 2018*, ed. Shlomo Berkovsky, Yoshinori Hijikata, Jun Rekimoto, Margaret M. Burnett, Mark Billinghurst, and Aaron Quigley, 293–304. ACM. https://doi.org/10.1145/3172944.3172965.

Sun, Chi, Luyao Huang, and Xipeng Qiu. 2019. Utilizing BERT for Aspect-Based Sentiment Analysis Via Constructing Auxiliary Sentence. In *Proceedings of the 2019 Conference of the North American Chapter of the Association for Computational Linguistics: Human Language Technologies, volume 1 (long and short papers)*, 380–385. Minneapolis, Minnesota: Association for Computational Linguistics. https://doi.org/10.18653/v1/N19-1035.

Touvron, Hugo, Louis Martin, Kevin Stone, Peter Albert, Amjad Almahairi, Yasmine Babaei, Nikolay Bashlykov, et al. 2023. Llama 2: Open Foundation and Fine-Tuned Chat Models. arXiv. https://doi.org/10.48550/arXiv.2307.09288.

Wang, Alex, Amanpreet Singh, Julian Michael, Felix Hill, Omer Levy, and Samuel R Bowman. 2018. GLUE: A Multi-task Benchmark and Analysis Platform for Natural Language Understanding. In *Proceedings of the 2018 EMNLP Workshop BlackboxNLP: Analyzing and Interpreting Neural Networks for NLP*.

Watson Todd, Richard. 2011. Analyzing discourse topics and topic keywords. *Semiotica* 184. De Gruyter Mouton: 251–270. https://doi.org/10.1515/semi.2011.029.

Wolf, Thomas, Lysandre Debut, Victor Sanh, Julien Chaumond, Clement Delangue, Anthony Moi, Pierric Cistac, et al. 2020. Transformers: State-of-the-Art Natural Language Processing. In *Proceedings of the 2020 Conference on Empirical Methods in Natural Language Processing: System Demonstrations*, 38–45. Online: Association for Computational Linguistics.

Xiao, Shitao, Zheng Liu, Peitian Zhang, and Niklas Muennighoff. 2023. C-pack: Packaged Resources to Advance General Chinese Embedding.

Zhou, Xiangyang, Lu Li, Daxiang Dong, Yi Liu, Ying Chen, Wayne Xin Zhao, Dianhai Yu, and Hua Wu. 2018. Multi-turn Response Selection for Chatbots with Deep Attention Matching Network. In *Proceedings of the 56th Annual Meeting of the Association for computational linguistics (volume 1: Long papers)*, 1118–1127. Melbourne, Australia: Association for Computational Linguistics. https://doi.org/10.18653/v1/P18-1103.

Zhu, Jiaqi, Kaijun Wang, Yunkun Wu, Zhongyi Hu, and Hongan Wang. 2016. Mining User-Aware Rare Sequential Topic Patterns in Document Streams. *IEEE Transactions on Knowledge and Data Engineering* 28: 1790–1804. IEEE.

Open Access This chapter is licensed under the terms of the Creative Commons Attribution 4.0 International License (http://creativecommons.org/licenses/by/4.0/), which permits use, sharing, adaptation, distribution and reproduction in any medium or format, as long as you give appropriate credit to the original author(s) and the source, provide a link to the Creative Commons license and indicate if changes were made.

The images or other third party material in this chapter are included in the chapter's Creative Commons license, unless indicated otherwise in a credit line to the material. If material is not included in the chapter's Creative Commons license and your intended use is not permitted by statutory regulation or exceeds the permitted use, you will need to obtain permission directly from the copyright holder.

CHAPTER 6

Sentiment

Abstract Sentiment analysis tools are very powerful when it comes to obtaining a description of the emotional aspect of the contents of a corpus. This chapter describes the methods and tools available, and illustrates what can be achieved with them. Both machine learning ad lexicon-based approaches are described and used, as they can provide different advantages. Whereas machine/deep learning approaches are the state of the art in sentiment classification tasks, lexicon-based tools can provide further insights, as they are able to retrieve the actual sentiment words and expressions used in the corpus. Finally, the role of emojis is discussed and illustrated with a frequency analysis of the most prominent emojis used in the CCTC.

Keywords Sentiment analysis · Opinion mining · Emoji analysis · Sentiment classification · Sentiment lexicon · Deterministic vs. probabilistic approaches

Sentiment analysis, also referred to as *opinion mining*, is a branch of Natural Language Processing that aims to identify either the polarity or the emotions expressed in a text (B. Liu 2012), although the term *emotion recognition* is sometimes used for this specific task, and usually appears linked to the field of affective computing. The main objective of sentiment analysis is to recognize subjective data, such as judgments, opinions, and feelings towards people, things, and their characteristics (Pang and Lee 2008).

Sentiment analysis has many uses in many different industries. It is used for brand monitoring and product analytics in business, and for tracking public opinion and social media analysis in politics. It also has a big impact on customer service, where it aids in comprehending client feedback and enhancing offerings (Cambria et al. 2017). The range of applications is as varied as the range of texts that sentiment analysis can be applied to: from movies and books reviews, e.g. Kennedy and Inkpen (2006), Carretero and Taboada (2014), to hotel reviews, e.g. Moreno-Ortiz et al. (2011), online news, e.g. Soo-Guan Khoo et al. (2012), and political debate on social media, e.g. Wang et al. (2012).

The methods used in sentiment analysis are also varied, ranging from lexicon-based to machine learning and hybrid techniques. Many different machine learning techniques have been developed, including Support Vector Machines (SVM), Naive Bayes, and deep learning models like Convolutional Neural Networks (CNN), and Recurrent Neural Networks (RNN) (Medhat et al. 2014). Lexicon-based approaches, on the other hand, rely on a sentiment lexicon, i.e. a list of lexical features that are labelled as either positive or negative according to their semantic orientation (Taboada et al. 2011).

6.1 Sentiment Analysis Methods

The field has advanced over time to take on more challenging tasks like aspect-based sentiment analysis and emotion detection (Zhang et al. 2018). These authors also define sentiment analysis as the task whose goal is to identify "people's opinions, sentiments, evaluations, appraisals, attitudes, and emotions towards entities such as products, services, organizations, individuals, issues, events, topics, and their attributes". Thus, sentiment analysis is often reduced to a text classification task, which is in fact one of the most basic NLP tasks, whereby a document is classified as belonging to one of two or more classes. This is accomplished by using a classifier, i.e. a predictive model that reads the input text and outputs a certain class, sometimes with a confidence score (i.e. how confident the classifier is that the document belongs in that class).

The classification techniques, like other processes that attempt to emulate intelligent behaviour, can be implemented in many ways. The traditional approach is a series of if–then statements (or *production rules*), which together form a rule-based system. Rule-based systems have been employed since the beginning in computing, as they form the basis of most programming languages. They are sometimes referred to as "the simplest form of artificial intelligence" (Grosan and Abraham 2011, 149). A rule-based system contains a set of production rules, a set of facts, and an interpreter that controls the application of the rules given the facts. Thus, these systems require expert knowledge on the domain at hand, as well as engineering skills to encode this knowledge as a set of facts and rules. In the case of sentiment analysis, this type of system applies to lexicon-based approaches, where the set of facts specify which words and expressions are positive and negative, and the rules would define how the proportion of positive versus negative words is to be measured to come up with a global sentiment score for the document. Context can also be accounted for by a set of such rules (e.g. "if a negative particle precedes a sentiment adjective, then its polarity is inverted"). Lexicon-based sentiment analysis systems are, for the most part, rule-based systems, where the required static facts (e.g. sentiment lexicon) and procedural knowledge (e.g. context rules) have been obtained from certain knowledge sources—corpora, dictionaries—and encoded by a knowledge engineer.

In contrast to these deterministic systems, machine learning simulates intelligent behaviour using probabilistic (or stochastic) techniques. In lieu of relying on expertly encoded and distilled knowledge, the learning algorithms can acquire this knowledge from vast quantities of data, in this case text. Corpus-based (i.e. machine learning) approaches are prevalent in both industry and research, as they have demonstrated superior classification performance.

The current state of the art in sentiment classification consists of machine learning approaches in the form of neural networks that employ transformers, i.e. deep learning models that aim to solve certain text-related tasks (bi-directional attention, word and sentence prediction, sequence-to-sequence tasks) while easily handling long-range dependencies. Language models based on the transformer architecture include two of the most successful ones to date: Google's BERT (Devlin et al. 2019) and OpenAI's GPT (Brown et al. 2020), which have been shown to improve on previous top benchmark scores across numerous NLP tasks, both in natural language understanding and generation, including sentiment analysis (Wolf et al. 2020).

6.1.1 Deterministic Methods

Lexicon-based methods of sentiment analysis can be referred to as deterministic because they employ deterministic data, i.e. a set of words that comprise a lexicon in which sentiment information about those words is stored and, in some cases, a set of rules that can contextualize the semantic orientation of those words in actual usage. Examples of sentiment dictionaries include The Harvard General Inquirer (Stone and Hunt 1963), Bing Liu's Opinion Lexicon (Hu and Liu 2004) MPQA (Wilson et al. 2005), SentiWordNet (Baccianella et al. 2010), SO-CAL (Taboada et al. 2011), EmoLex (Mohammad and Turney 2010), VADER (Hutto and Gilbert 2014), Lingmotif-Lex (Moreno-Ortiz and Pérez-Hernández 2018), and SenticNet (Cambria et al. 2020). These resources generally consist of word lists with varying degrees of sentiment information, from simple polarity to emotion classification.

However, the context in which individual words and phrases appear can alter their semantics (including polarity), sometimes to the point where they mean the exact opposite of what they initially denote; this is especially true of sentiment words. A negative adverb, such as "not" or "never", can invert the polarity of the adjective "happy", for instance. It is therefore difficult for a lexicon-based sentiment analysis system to account for all such context-shifting words. For example, we can implement a rule that inverts the sentiment of "happy" when it is preceded by "never" within a span of three words. This rule would correctly classify as negative expressions such as "I was never truly happy there", but would incorrectly classify cases such as "I've never been so happy before". In the field of sentiment analysis, numerous contextual shifter systems have been developed, e.g. Kennedy and Inkpen (2006), Moreno-Ortiz and Pérez-Hernández (2018), Polanyi and Zaenen (2006), Taboada et al. (2011). Nonetheless, the level of difficulty that sentence-level context handling poses pales in comparison to higher-order linguistic levels of analysis; discourse-related phenomena, such as the metaphorical use of words, irony, sarcasm, understatements, or humblebragging—all of which are pervasive in social media—are a serious problem for which there are no immediate solutions.

These knowledge sources are also deterministic because they have been compiled and curated by humans and are therefore known to be true, or at least assumed to be true; consequently, the performance of these systems is entirely dependent on the data upon which they are based.

Their underlying model is also deterministic: if a text contains more positive words than negative words, it is predicted to be positive. When analysis errors occur, they are attributed to faulty or insufficient data: a particular sentiment word is missing, a valence shifter was incorrectly applied, pragmatic features were not taken into account, or additional world or common-sense knowledge is required. The underlying assumption is that it is possible to collect all of the facts and rules required for optimal model performance. This is applicable not only to lexicon-based sentiment analysis systems, but also to all formal grammars and computational implementations of linguistic theories. However, it has been repeatedly demonstrated that the facts and rules of language are far too elusive and organic to be constrained by the deterministic straightjacket. Otherwise, after seven decades of implementations of linguistic theories, at least one would have emerged as a viable framework for developing real-world language applications, which, arguably, has not occurred.

6.1.2 Probabilistic Methods

Since the 1960s, machine learning (ML) algorithms have been used in a variety of research fields. However, it has only been in the last two decades that we have witnessed their widespread use in real-world applications. In conventional programming, we tell the computer exactly what steps to take in order to solve a problem, which works well for many situations such as solving an equation; however, there are other tasks that do not lend themselves to this approach: How can we break down the process of identifying a specific object in a picture or the text understanding process, into minute, step-by-step detail? The analysis process I described in the previous section, which is utilized by lexicon-based SA tools, is merely an extreme procedural simplification of much more complex cognitive processes that our brains are able to handle effortlessly.

The goal of machine learning is to teach computers to solve these complex problems by providing them with examples of the problem and allowing them to figure out how to solve it on their own. Despite the fact that "classical" ML algorithms (Naïve Bayes, decision trees, Support Vector Machines, etc.) have been (and continue to be) successfully used to solve practical NLP problems, including sentiment analysis, deep learning and neural networks have revolutionized the field. As mentioned in the previous section, the current state-of-the-art performance in all language-related tasks is offered by the transformer architecture (Vaswani et al.

2017), and therefore it has rapidly become the dominant architecture for NLP (Wolf et al. 2020). It is based on the concept and practice of "pretraining", i.e. creating a language model from a very large corpus in an unsupervised manner that can then be repurposed for different specific applications by "tuning" it on smaller, labelled (i.e. annotated) corpora.

Probabilistic methods based on the transformer architecture have been repeatedly shown in the literature to be state of the art in terms of sentiment classification, which obviously includes lexicon-based systems. However, lexicon-based systems do provide very useful capabilities that pure classifiers do not possess: the ability to point out which words and expressions have been found that justify their classification results. Conversely, ML systems, especially neural networks, exhibit the well-known "explainability" issue. Indeed, these algorithms excel at discovering correlation in massive datasets, but offer little to nothing in the way of causation. Ultimately, the researcher is left to come up with likely interpretations of the results. Important steps are being taken towards an explainable AI (Barredo Arrieta et al. 2020), but current technology simply cannot offer "explanations" of its own predictions; they simply act as black boxes that take an input and produce an output based on their probabilistic model.

6.2 Experiment: Sentiment Analysis of the CCTC by Country

This experiment is intended to showcase the capabilities of both state-of-the-art, transformer-based sentiment classification systems and an advanced lexicon-based sentiment analysis system. Thus, it consists of two parts; in the first one I use a script that employs the Hugging-Face Transformers library (Wolf et al. 2020) together with TweetNLP (Camacho-Collados et al. 2022), a state-of-the-art model for Twitter sentiment classification trained on 124 million tweets and based on RoBERTa (Y. Liu et al. 2019).

In the second part I use Lingmotif (Moreno-Ortiz 2017, 2023), an advanced lexicon-based sentiment analysis system, to analyse the same corpus and obtain frequency lists of sentiment-related lexical items that can help us understand not just the overall semantic orientation of the corpus, but also the nature and type of that sentiment by exposing the actual words and phrases that materialize it.

Table 6.1 Corpus used in the experiments in this chapter

Country	% of subcorpus	Tweets	Tokens	Proc. time HuggingFace	Proc. time Lingmotif
U.S.A	16	637,195	14,372,585	4:02:58	1:57:29
U.K.	45	638,006	15,857,901	4:10:06	2:08:04
India	90	616,091	15,821,057	4:18:15	2:06:47
Canada	100	451,562	11,193,144	3:01:13	1:30:00
Australia	100	279,842	6,741,652	1:51:33	0:55:06
South Africa	100	180,177	3,614,642	1:08:49	0:30:26
Total		1,891,296	46,051,543	18:32:54	09:07:52

For this study, I will be using the top six subcorpora by volume in the geotagged section of the CCTC.[1] Table 6.1 describes the subcorpora quantitatively. As in the experiments in the previous chapters, I use a proportional part of the each subcorpus when this is possible (United States, United Kingdom, and India). For the other three countries, the full subcorpus was used.

6.2.1 Tweet Classification and Sentiment Over Time

The HuggingFace library makes classification very simple, as it takes care of every stage of the process by means of an integrated pipeline, thus hiding the complexity that entails working with transformer-based models. Every file in the corpus, where each line is a tweet, is read line by line, and the full list of documents is passed to the "sentiment-analysis" pipeline together with the tokenizer and language model. The pipeline returns a list of results where each document is classified as belonging to one of three classes—"positive", "neutral", or "negative"—and a confidence score in the range 0–1. Table 6.2 shows the global results of the analysis.

The most obvious fact that the data tell us is that the general sentiment is negative, as the proportion of negative tweets is the largest across all countries. However, there are important differences among them: the United States dataset has the most negative results, with over 53% of

---

[1] The corpus, along with all datasets resulting from the analysis, are available in the book's repository at https://osf.io/h5q4j/.

Table 6.2 Sentiment classification with transformer-based classifier

	Total tweets	Negative	Neutral	Positive	Mean score
United States	637,195	338,31 (53.10%)	181,063 (28.42%)	117,813 (18.49%)	0.754
United Kingdom	638,005	293,581 (46.02%)	180,835 (28.34%)	1635,89 (25.64%)	0.758
India	616,086	240,526 (39.04%)	241,568 (39.21%)	133,992 (21,75%)	0.74
Canada	451,552	210,041 (46.52%)	144,907 (32.09%)	96,604 (21.39%)	0.752
Australia	279,841	136,868 (48.91%)	87,083 (31.12%)	55,890 (19.97%)	0.748
South Africa	180,177	87,499 (48.56%)	62,236 (34.54%)	30,442 (16.90%)	0.74
Mean		47.02% (SD = 0.05)	32.29% (SD = 0.04)	20.69% (SD = 0.03)	0.75% (SD = 0.007)

the tweets being negative, which is significantly higher than the average (47.02% including USA, 45.81% excluding it). This is surprising considering that it is the country with the highest GDP per capita of the group and perhaps a reflection of the poor pandemic management of the Trump administration. Conversely, India, which has the lowest GDP per capita, has the lowest percentage of negative tweets.

These global results, however, are aggregated (averaged) data, as the actual classification task was performed on weekly samples. This organization allows us to look at the evolution of sentiment over the two years that the samples span. Figure 6.1 is a visualization of the sentiment timeline corresponding to the United States using the raw data returned by the classifier.

The timeline reflects some of the most relevant events during the pandemic. After the initial alarm caused by the cases reported in China, the positive sentiment increases during the early spring of 2020 and then negativity increases as lockdowns are ordered in some states. Similarly, the significant surge in negative sentiment during the summer of 2021 correlates with the beginning of a third wave of infections as a result of the Delta variant of the virus.

In order to more easily compare the sentiment timeline of different countries, we can merge these polarity proportions into a single sentiment

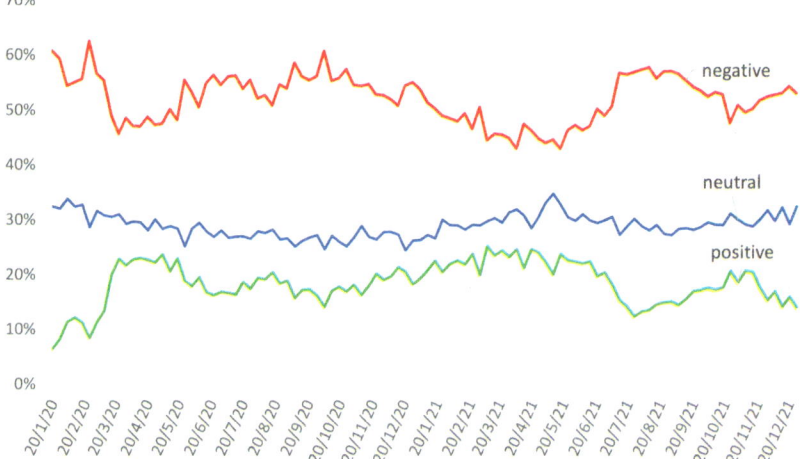

Fig. 6.1 Sentiment timeline (U.S.)

score using the following equation:

$$\text{SentScore} = \frac{(\text{neg}\% * -1) + (\text{neu}\% * 0) + (\text{pos}\% * 1)}{100}$$

This will give us a score in the range −1 to 1, which can easily be converted it to a more readable 0–100 range. Figures 6.2 and 6.3 use this unified sentiment score to visually compare sentiment evolution in the six countries. Three countries are shown in each graph to facilitate the interpretation of the data.

These data visualizations make it apparent that some countries follow more a similar evolution of sentiment than others. Just by looking at the graph, it seems apparent that India's sentiment evolution is the one that deviates the most from the rest of the countries. However, in order to properly quantify how much correlation there is between the different time series we can use the Pearson correlation coefficient between country pairs. Table 6.3 shows the list of correlations between country pairs in descending order.

This list of correlations tells us that countries that share more in terms of geographical proximity, culture, or economy tend to correlate higher.

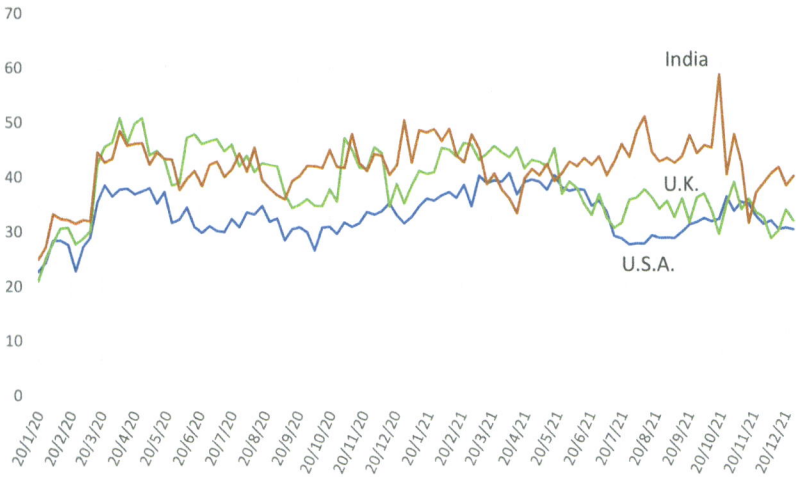

Fig. 6.2 Sentiment evolution in the U.S., U.K., and India

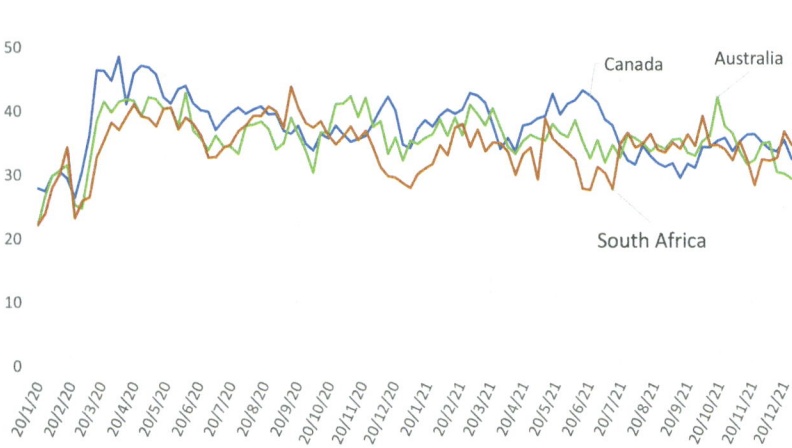

Fig. 6.3 Sentiment evolution in Canada, Australia, and South Africa

Table 6.3 Sentiment timeline correlations between country pairs

Country pair	Correlation coefficient (r)
Canada–U.K	0.699
U.K.–Australia	0.698
U.S.A.–Canada	0.675
Canada–Australia	0.658
Australia–South Africa	0.636
U.S.A.–U.K	0.632
U.S.A.–Australia	0.563
India–Australia	0.558
U.K.–South Africa	0.512
Canada–South Africa	0.403
India–South Africa	0.350
U.K.–India	0.349
Canada–India	0.319
U.S.A.–India	0.279
U.S.A.–South Africa	0.247

We can now say with all certainty that India displays the most deviation from the rest, followed by South Africa.

The reasons why India's sentiment evolution is so different may be due to many factors, but it probably has to do with a different vaccination process and the different times of the two major waves of COVID-19 cases, which differed from most other countries. India started the vaccination programme in January 2021 and initially managed to control the number of new cases; however, a major second wave started in April 2021, which made new cases spike from 9,000 per day to over 400,000 and 3,500 deaths per day by the end of April.[2] The reason for this massive increase in daily cases was the incipient Delta variant, which started in India during this time and would later expand to the rest of the world. This clearly correlates with the sentiment timeline during this period, when negative sentiment clearly increases.

Obviously, looking at the changes in sentiment as represented by the peaks and troughs in the graphs and correlating them with real-world events is not an easy task, as there are multiple factors that may cause those changes. However, with sentiment classification of tweets that is

---

[2] https://en.wikipedia.org/wiki/COVID-19_pandemic_in_India [Accessed 5 September 2023].

all we have. We can only browse through the—very large—set of classified tweets and attempt to see what causes the sentiment. Examples (42) through (47) are tweets from this period. In them, people complain about the bleak situation and the poor management of the pandemic by the government. Examples (43) and (46) are interesting because they illustrate the trouble that state-of-the-art sentiment classifiers run into when faced with sarcasm, as both are clearly negative but are classified as positive and neutral.

42. 'A person cannot live peacefully in Delhi, a person cannot even die peacefully in Delhi'. India overwhelmed by world's worst Covid crisis—BBC News. [negative, 0.896]
43. Half of the world's total covid cases are now from India!! What an achievement.. #IndiaFightsCOVID19. [positive, 0.811]
44. What to do brother, our government is not listening to us right now. There no use of these types of requests ☻ [negative 0.926]
45. #Karnatakagovernment Please consider the necessary requirements/decision towards raising COVID-19 death's before it gets out of control. We can afford the raising cases not the raising death's. [negative, 0.632]
46. When coronavirus cases went down, Govt declared victory, PM took all credit as always; Now they're blaming states: Rahul Gandhi [neutral, 0.614]
47. Mismanagement and lack of planning in production and distribution has killed more than the #virus. [negative, 0.898]

6.2.2 The Sentiment Lexicon of the Pandemic on Twitter

Sentiment classification of tweets is obviously useful, but it falls short of telling us about the nature of the sentiment. All we have is the classification data, either as individual or aggregated results by time span, and the classified tweets themselves, which is too much data to manually make sense of. For instance, examples (1) to (6) above were selected from the set of tweets in the week April 26 to May 2, 2021, but that week alone contains 27,902 tweets, so it is very hard to draw any conclusions regarding the content, and the examples are nothing more than anecdotal evidence.

Lexicon-based sentiment analysis systems can be very useful when it comes to obtaining more clues as to the nature of the sentiment, as they can provide frequency lists of the words and expressions that motivate the sentiment. For example, Table 6.4 shows the list of the most frequent negative words during this time period in India.

From this set of negative words and expressions, we can see that many refer to the disease itself ('pandemic', 'epidemic', 'virus', 'disease', 'infect', 'test positive', 'fever', 'risk'), others to the deaths caused by the disease ('death', 'dying', 'dead', 'rest in peace', 'rip', 'deadly', 'kill', 'condolence', 'loss'), others to the social and economic difficulties ('crisis', 'emergency', 'shortage', 'poor', 'needy', 'lack', 'struggle'), and finally

Table 6.4 Top 50 negative words for the week 26-04-2021 in India

Rank	Word	Freq	Rank	Word	Freq
1	pandemic	1404	26	lack	89
2	lockdown	895	27	rest in peace	86
3	death	580	28	admit hospital	83
4	please help	435	29	disease	83
5	virus	421	30	kill	82
6	crisis	392	31	test positive	82
7	suffer	371	32	concern	81
8	die	317	33	rip	81
9	dying	264	34	fear	78
10	lose	185	35	failure	78
11	fail	181	36	deadly	75
12	infection	163	37	risk	74
13	emergency	159	38	wrong	74
14	blame	155	39	fake	68
15	shame	145	40	condolence	66
16	dead	134	41	disaster	63
17	shortage	132	42	unable	63
18	worst	122	43	struggle	62
19	problem	122	44	fever	60
20	epidemic	114	45	bad	58
21	impose	114	46	attack	58
22	infect	104	47	shock	57
23	☹	101	48	quarantine	55
24	poor	101	49	complete lockdown	54
25	needy	91	50	loss	52

some of them refer to the management of the pandemic by the government ('fail', 'blame', 'shame', 'impose', 'failure', 'wrong', 'fake', 'unable', 'quarantine', 'complete lockdown', 'lack').

These words provide a more complete picture of the particular reasons that motivate the negativity at this particular point in time. Looking at positive and negative words can also help us identify what causes the unexpected positive peak in India during the week of October 18, 2021, which, with an all-time high sentiment score of 58.87—from 45.53 the previous week and 40.49 the next—is also an anomaly compared to the rest of the countries. But it is also interesting to contrast these results with the topics that we saw in the previous chapter. Figure 6.4 shows the topics over time for India, where a surge of the vaccines topic is quite apparent.

Finally, looking at the tweets in this week, there is a very large number of tweets celebrating the advancement of the vaccination process. Examples (48) to (52) illustrate these.

48. World Bank Prez Congratulates India on Successful Covid-19 Vaccination Campaign. NaMo App. [positive, 0.922]
49. PM congratulates people of Devbhoomi for 100% first dose of Covid vaccination. [positive, 0.871]
50. 🎉 98 crores done. India is quickly making its way to #COVID19 vaccine century! Just two more steps to go 🚶. ji. [positive, 0.914]
51. 2nd Dose Done 💉. Fully vaccinated 😊 #corona #vaccinationdone ✔ #vaccine #sainisurinder Anandpur Sahib. [positive, 0.823]
52. #India crosses 98 crore vaccine doses. And the roses are increasing fast. Seems 20 Oct is going to be the day when India will cross

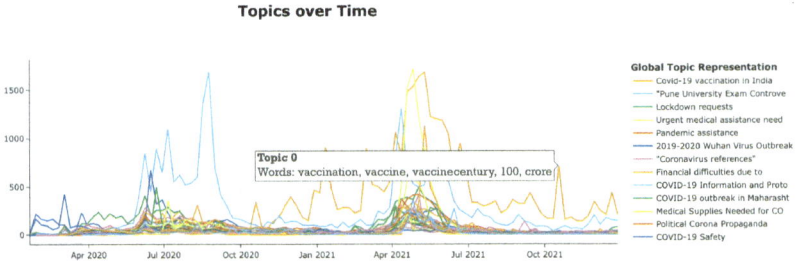

Fig. 6.4 Topics over time for India showing the vaccination topic

#100crore doses. Salute to all health care workers, Salute to spirit of India. #TogetherWeWin #COVID19 [positive, 0.946]

Comparing the negative words across different countries can also shed light on the particular circumstances and contexts. Table 6.5 contains the top 25 negative words for each of the countries in this study.

The top few words are mostly the same across all countries ('pandemic', 'lockdown', 'virus', 'death'). Upon investigation, the third position of the word 'stigma' in Canada's list is due to a specific and very active Twitter account "Fighting Stigma", which preceded its many tweets with these two words. It is interesting, however, how the word 'lockdown' is either in first or second position in all countries except the United States, where it ranks fifth; this is most probably due to the fact that lockdown measures were fewer and more relaxed than in other countries and therefore had less impact on the population. The lemma 'lockdown' has 12,111 occurrences in the US subcorpus, whereas in the U.K. corpus (which has a similar number of words) there are 146,388 occurrences.

The lists also offer insights into the particular problems that the countries had to face. For example, in South Africa's list the words 'HIV', 'arrest', and 'corruption' refer to issues that are not present in other countries. The lemma 'poor' is also present, which is also included in India's list, the only list to contain the word 'struggle'. These differences do suggest a more difficult economic situation for the people of these countries, which was made worse by the hardships brought about by the pandemic.

On the other hand, all word lists except India's contain insults and profanity words (U.S.: 'fuck', 'shit', 'stupid', 'idiot; U.K.: 'fuck', 'shit', 'idiot; Canada: 'fuck', 'shit'; Australia: 'fuck', 'shit', 'idiot; South Africa: 'shit'), which is telling of the different cultures. The phrase 'please help' is also only found in the India list; In fact, the lemma 'help' is extremely more frequent in the India subcorpus.

Finally, the United States list is the only one that contains the word 'hate' (in 17th position), which is probably a reflection of the political atmosphere at the time, as examples (53) to (58) illustrate.

53. ⊝ On coronavirus, Trump needs the ones he hates: Experts and journalists—The Washington Post

Table 6.5 Top 25 negative lexical items in the 6 top countries by volume

Rank	U.S.A	U.K.	India	Canada	Australia	South Africa
1	pandemic	lockdown	pandemic	pandemic	lockdown	lockdown
2	virus	pandemic	lockdown	lockdown	pandemic	pandemic
3	death	death	virus	stigma	virus	virus
4	die	virus	death	death	death	😷
5	lockdown	die	suffer	virus	outbreak	death
6	kill	fuck	please help	die	quarantine	die
7	fuck	risk	crisis	outbreak	die	lose
8	shit	lose	die	risk	risk	kill
9	lose	infection	lose	lose	fuck	♥
10	test positive	kill	poor	fuck	lose	test positive
11	risk	problem	problem	kill	infection	infection
12	dead	crisis	infection	infection	protest	problem
13	sick	shit	test positive	sick	fail	corruption
14	dying	😊	fail	problem	kill	hiv
15	😞	wrong	disease	crisis	shit	shit
16	bad	panic	risk	concern	problem	😠
17	hate	bad	epidemic	fear	😞	😞
18	quarantine	worry	kill	bad	crisis	fail
19	outbreak	test positive	infect	shit	infect	poor
20	stupid	suffer	quarantine	test positive	wrong	dying
21	problem	outbreak	worst	fail	blame	risk
22	wrong	fail	fear	😞	concern	fear
23	disease	idiot	concern	wrong	idiot	arrest
24	idiot	blame	impose	quarantine	fear	bad
25	infect	struggle	shame	disease	dying	blame

54. I fucking hate it here 😡😡😡😡
55. I hate the healthcare process in this country 😡😡
56. CNN loves China and hates America
57. Pence has his beliefs that many disagree w/ and hate him for it. We need to come together as patriots against those who openly or secretly hate us. 🙏 #Corona #Coronavirus #MikePence

58. Republicans hate government until an enormous problem made by the private sector (2008 crash) or not solvable by the private sector (Coronavirus) emerges.

As for the positive words, they are very similar across all languages, although of course the frequencies change. Table 6.6 shows the top 50 positive sentiment words and expressions for each of the subcorpora. Lingmotif treats emojis as regular lexical items, which is why they are listed and ranked along with the rest of the words.

As with negative words, most of the words in this list are positive in general, but some are specific of the pandemic subject domain, such as 'protect', 'recovery', 'immunity', 'volunteer' or 'save lives'. There are not many differences between the countries. The primary themes that the lexical items refer to are good wishes, positive advice, and congratulations (on fighting the pandemic). The only country that shows a different theme is, again, India, with the word 'donate', in consonance with the recurrent "request-for-help" topic identified before.

We can also track the frequency of positive and negative words and phrases over time. To do this, we need to calculate the frequencies of all positive and negative lexical items over the whole period for each country, which will produce a ranked list of the most frequent sentiment items, which we can then track over time by looking at their frequency at each time period (weeks in this case). To account for the different sizes in the subcorpora, the relative frequencies were calculated per 1,000 words for each of the lexical items.

There are two ways in which we can track sentiment words over time. We can either look at the evolution of the top n words for one specific country, or we can track one specific word in several countries. The latter offers more interesting results, as focusing on certain specific words and comparing their frequency among different countries can provide useful insights. For example, Fig. 6.5 displays the frequency of the word 'help' over time, where India is clearly the most prominent and the peaks correspond with the particularly hard periods mentioned before.

Plotting the frequency of specific sentiment words can provide evidence of real-world events. Figure 6.6 plots the timeline of the word 'protest' for all countries in the corpus. It evidences the periods where protests became an issue. June 2020 witnessed demonstrations in most countries after months of lockdowns and stay-at-home orders.

Table 6.6 Top 25 positive lexical items in the 6 top countries by volume

Rank	U.S.A	U.K.	India	Canada	Australia	S. Africa
1	help	help	help	help	good	safe
2	good	support	safe	good	safe	help
3	love	good	support	support	help	good
4	safe	safe	good	safe	support	love
5	thank you	love	free	thank you	love	support
6	support	thank you	recovery	love	thanks	recovery
7	protect	great	kindly	protect	great	thank you
8	best	thanks	best	best	best	free
9	free	happy	thank you	great	free	best
10	happy	best	thanks	thanks	thank you	happy
11	thanks	protect	happy	happy	happy	protect
12	great	free	recover	free	protect	♥
13	win	amazing	respect	safety	enjoy	survive
14	relief	👍	safety	amazing	freedom	recover
15	safety	lovely	protect	♥	win	enjoy
16	♥	☕	get well	be great	well done	thanks
17	healthy	well done	love	enjoy	amazing	safety
18	be great	enjoy	great	thank for	interesting	win
19	immunity	♥	donate	healthy	be great	relief
20	enjoy	win	precaution	win	☕	celebrate
21	amazing	fantastic	cure	recovery	👍	great
22	survive	be great	relief	celebrate	thank for	🍺
23	cure	brilliant	solution	interesting	♥	fantastic
24	recover	interesting	speedy	immunity	safety	😊
25	celebrate	wonderful	win	nice	ease	beautiful

Australia is the country that shows the most spikes on this word, surpassing all other countries in June 2020, but also showing many other peaks due to different events. For example, during September 2020, several anti-lockdown protests were organized in this country, as they were during July through November 2021. India, again, is the country that deviates the most from the rest, with a rather flat line except for two obvious spikes during December 2020 and December 2021. However,

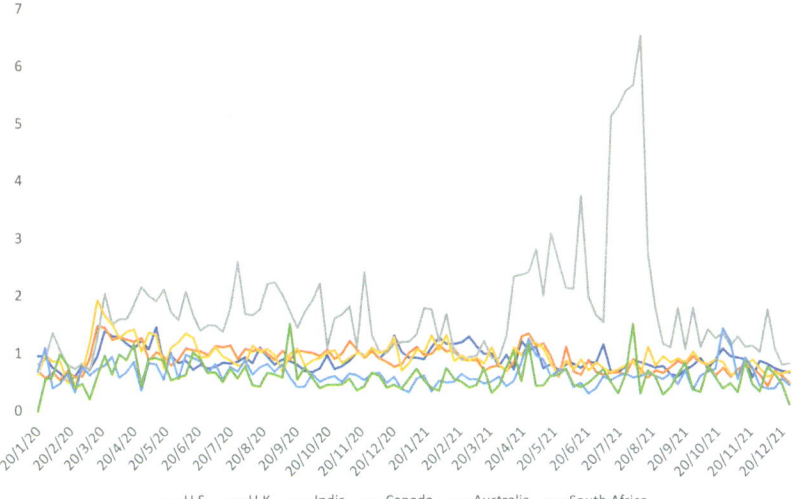

Fig. 6.5 Sentiment over time—'help'

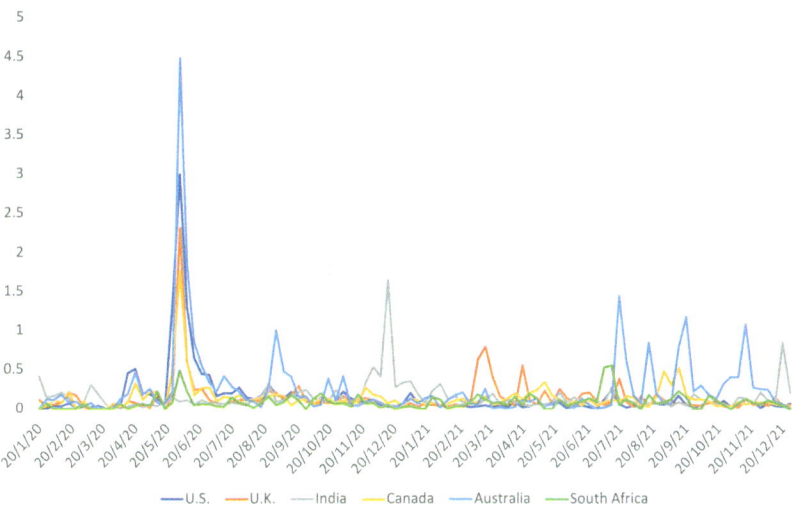

Fig. 6.6 Sentiment over time—'protest'

these demonstrations were most probably related to the farmers' protest as a reaction to the laws passed by the Indian government in September 2020.

6.3 The Role of Emojis in the Expression of Sentiment

There is little doubt that emojis contribute importantly to the emotional content of social media messages. They rank high in our lists of negative (Table 6.5) and positive (Table 6.6) terms of every country, and they are present in a large number of the examples provided in this chapter, which demonstrates the significant role they play. Emojis facilitate communication of subtle emotional cues by condensing ideas and emotions into a single icon or pictograph (Bai et al. 2019) and have a ubiquitous presence in social media all around the world (Ljubešić and Fišer 2016).

Emojis, like their less sophisticated text-based counterparts, emoticons, are said to fill the role of human facial expressions and gestures, absent in text-based communication, which is demonstrated by the fact that emojis that display facial expressions have been shown to elicit a similar neural time-course as actual human faces, although with lower attentional orientation response (Gantiva et al. 2020). In fact, research has shown how reaction times is slower when humans are confronted with messages where the text and the accompanying emoticon or emoji expresses conflictive valences, and the overall messages also tend to be interpreted as negative more often (Aldunate et al. 2018).

From a cultural perspective, however, the use of emojis is not homogeneous across nations and languages. Kejriwal et al. (2021), in a large-scale study that included 30 countries and as many languages on tens of millions of tweets, concluded that emoji usage is not only strongly dependent on cultural and geographical variables, but its diversity is also much more constrained in some languages and countries than others.

These conclusions are unquestionably supported by the data in this study. From a purely quantitative perspective, we can see in Table 6.5 that four negative emojis are included in the top 25 negative items for South Africa, whereas only one is present in the rest of the countries, which suggests that South African Twitter users tend to use a higher proportion of emojis in their tweets. However, an actual count of emojis in each of the corpora is necessary to confirm this hypothesis. The script used to achieve this task counts emojis using the *emoji* Python library to detect emojis and produces frequency counts per 1,000 words to account for the differences in corpus size across countries.

Figure 6.7 shows a visualization of the results, which clearly show that the use of emojis is much more frequent in the South African subcorpus, where 35.84 are found per 1,000 words, versus 18.33 on average (including South Africa; 14.83 excluding it).

This huge difference is also apparent when we attempt to plot the presence of specific emojis over time to make comparisons across countries. Figure 6.8 visualizes the relative frequency of the *loudly crying* emoji (😭), which can be used to unequivocally measure the level of sadness, unlike others whose interpretation may be more ambiguous, and their interpretation is more dependent on cultural factors (Godard and Holtzman 2022). The overall frequency of this emoji in the South African corpus is so much higher than in the rest of subcorpora that it dwarfs all other timelines.

Specifically, the frequency of the *loudly crying* emoji in the South African subcorpus was 12.28 times greater than the average of other countries. Comparative analysis revealed that the United States had the nearest frequency to South Africa, albeit still 5.80 times lower. The most substantial discrepancy was observed in the Indian subcorpus, where the emoji's frequency was a striking 19.25 times less than that of South Africa.

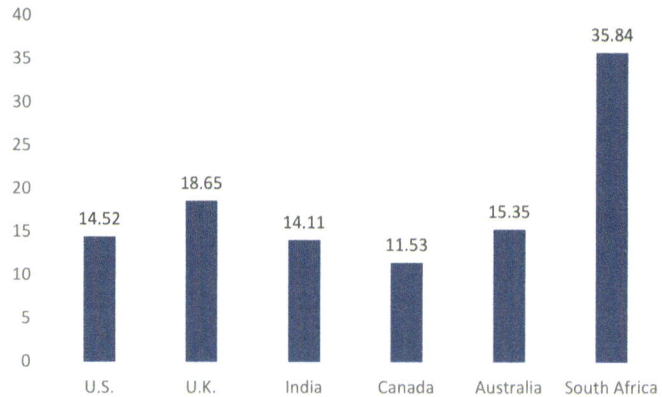

Fig. 6.7 Frequency of emojis (per 1,000 words) across countries

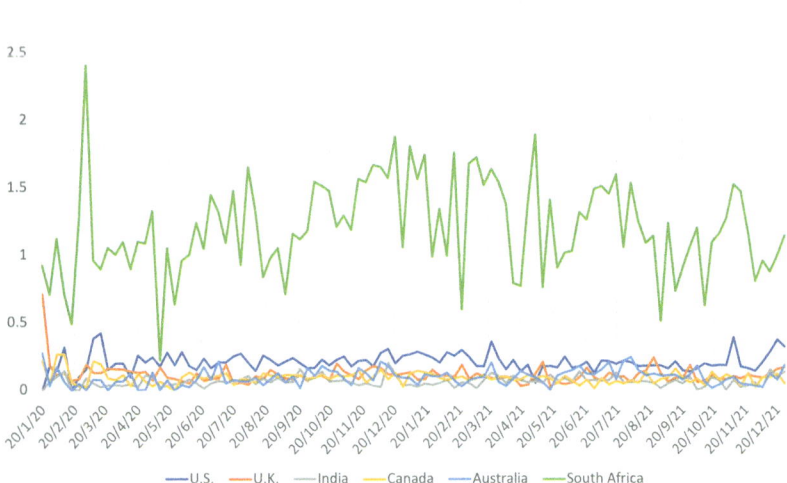

Fig. 6.8 Sentiment over time—'😭' (*loudly crying emoji*)

In order to offer a more complete overview of the use of emojis, Table 6.7 shows ranked lists of emojis, including their frequency (per 1,000 words) in each of the subcorpora.

The data in this table show some interesting differences among countries. For example, the *virus* emoji (🦠) is present in all of the subcorpora except, precisely, in South Africa; in fact, it ranks very low in the South African list of emojis (58th position). The same is true of the *syringe* emoji (💉), which ranks in 48th position. To easily check all differences in emoji use across countries, Table 6.8 summarizes them.

We can now see clearly that South Africa (8 differences with rest) and India (5 differences) are the two countries that deviate the most from the rest. Thus, the United States (3 differences), the United Kingdom (2 differences) and Canada (0 differences) share the most emojis with the rest, especially among themselves. Conversely, India and South Africa are the two countries that show most differences with the rest, and also among themselves.

The order in which the emojis rank in each country is also very telling. For example, the *praying hands* emoji is present in all lists, but it ranks at the very top in the case of India, a more spiritual country than the

Table 6.7 Top 25 emojis per country ranked by frequency (per 1,000 words)

	U.S.A.	U.K.	India	Canada	Australia	S. Africa
1	😂—0.606	😂—0.723	🙏—1.799	♥—0.346	😂—0.469	😂—1.923
2	😊—0.425	👍—0.478	♥—0.349	😊—0.309	😊—0.406	😭—1.777
3	🙏—0.362	♥—0.441	😂—0.290	😂—0.306	♥—0.335	😘—1.278
4	♥—0.321	🙏—0.399	👍—0.263	🙏—0.283	😉—0.317	🙏—0.923
5	😍—0.318	😍—0.389	😊—0.240	👌—0.263	🙏—0.291	♥—0.737
6	😁—0.293	😘—0.379	👌—0.217	😁—0.233	😁—0.284	♥—0.670
7	😘—0.269	👎—0.369	↓—0.170	👷—0.215	👌—0.275	😉—0.567
8	👷—0.253	😒—0.354	👏—0.157	😉—0.206	👍—0.272	👷—0.419
9	🙂—0.231	👷—0.321	😊—0.156	🙂—0.202	👏—0.260	😁—0.404
10	😉—0.216	🙂—0.306	😉—0.141	👍—0.167	😘—0.252	😜—0.392
11	👌—0.169	😁—0.285	😘—0.127	😘—0.160	👷—0.250	🔥—0.389
12	😢—0.124	😊—0.248	😭—0.110	👏—0.158	🙂—0.246	😩—0.389
13	👏—0.121	😊—0.195	🌷—0.104	💅—0.154	🙂—0.189	🙂—0.339
14	💅—0.118	😡—0.193	👉—0.098	💅—0.154	😡—0.179	😇—0.334
15	😜—0.115	💙—0.166	😍—0.090	😭—0.134	😭—0.162	😊—0.311
16	👍—0.114	😭—0.165	😁—0.089	😡—0.094	💍—0.160	😉—0.272
17	💍—0.109	🙏—0.156	💍—0.085	↓—0.092	😬—0.147	👇—0.271
18	😆—0.109	😊—0.137	🙂—0.083	😊—0.089	💅—0.136	💀—0.269
19	🙂—0.105	💅—0.134	💅—0.079	😊—0.088	😊—0.122	😊—0.262
20	🙏—0.094	😉—0.129	😡—0.073	🙏—0.085	😉—0.114	😘—0.258
21	😢—0.092	💍—0.129	😉—0.072	😩—0.077	🙏—0.114	🙏—0.231
22	👀—0.091	😠—0.128	😢—0.072	😟—0.076	👆—0.100	👎—0.204
23	🔥—0.090	😁—0.127	👆—0.070	😊—0.072	😊—0.096	😊—0.179
24	👑—0.089	💪—0.123	🙏—0.068	😊—0.066	😎—0.092	👀—0.175
25	‼—0.089	👆—0.123	🔥—0.068	♥—0.063	👆—0.089	💧—0.172

Table 6.8 Idiosyncratic uses of emojis by country

Country	Present but absent in rest	Absent but present in rest
U.S	😊 💋 ‼	
U.K.	💙 🧢	
India	💡 🧹 🥀 ❣	🧿
Canada Australia	😀	
South Africa	🎃 ☺ 🎮 💧	💅 ⚪ 🖊 🗡

rest. Again, we find evidence that social media language, both in terms of linguistic and paralinguistics elements, is a good reflection of the cultural, economic, and social differences that exist between societies when it comes to expressing their emotions in written text.

REFERENCES

Aldunate, Nerea, Mario Villena-González, Felipe Rojas-Thomas, Vladimir López, and Conrado A. Bosman. 2018. Mood Detection in Ambiguous Messages: The Interaction Between Text and Emoticons. *Frontiers in Psychology* 9.

Baccianella, Stefano, Andrea Esuli, and Fabrizio Sebastiani. 2010. SentiWordNet 3.0: An Enhanced Lexical Resource for Sentiment Analysis and Opinion Mining. In *Proceedings of the International Conference on Language Resources and Evaluation*, 2200–2204. Valletta, Malta.

Bai, Qiyu, Qi Dan, Zhe Mu, and Maokun Yang. 2019. A Systematic Review of Emoji: Current Research and Future Perspectives. *Frontiers in Psychology* 10: 2221. https://doi.org/10.3389/fpsyg.2019.02221.

Arrieta, Barredo, Natalia Díaz-Rodríguez. Alejandro, Javier Del Ser, Adrien Bennetot, Siham Tabik, Alberto Barbado, Salvador Garcia, et al. 2020. Explainable Artificial Intelligence (XAI): Concepts, Taxonomies, Opportunities and Challenges Toward Responsible AI. *Information Fusion* 58: 82–115. https://doi.org/10.1016/j.inffus.2019.12.012.

Brown, Tom, Benjamin Mann, Nick Ryder, Melanie Subbiah, Jared D Kaplan, Prafulla Dhariwal, Arvind Neelakantan, et al. 2020. Language Models Are Few-Shot Learners. In *Advances in Neural Information Processing Systems*, ed.

H. Larochelle, M. Ranzato, R. Hadsell, M. F. Balcan, and H. Lin, 33:1877–1901. Curran Associates, Inc.

Camacho-Collados, Jose, Kiamehr Rezaee, Talayeh Riahi, Asahi Ushio, Daniel Loureiro, Dimosthenis Antypas, Joanne Boisson, Luis Espinosa Anke, Fangyu Liu, and Eugenio Martínez Cámara. 2022. TweetNLP: Cutting-Edge Natural Language Processing for Social Media. In *Proceedings of the 2022 Conference on Empirical Methods in Natural Language Processing: System Demonstrations*, 38–49. Abu Dhabi, UAE: Association for Computational Linguistics.

Cambria, Erik, Soujanya Poria, Alexander Gelbukh, and Mike Thelwall. 2017. Sentiment Analysis Is a Big Suitcase. *IEEE Intelligent Systems*. IEEE.

Cambria, Erik, Yang Li, Frank Z. Xing, Soujanya Poria, and Kenneth Kwok. 2020. SenticNet 6: Ensemble Application of Symbolic and Subsymbolic AI for Sentiment Analysis. In *Proceedings of the 29th ACM International Conference on Information & Knowledge Management*, 105–114. CIKM '20. New York, NY, USA: Association for Computing Machinery. https://doi.org/10.1145/3340531.3412003.

Carretero, Marta, and Maite Taboada. 2014. Graduation within the scope of Attitude in English and Spanish Consumer Reviews of Books and Movies. In *Evaluation in Context*, 221–240. John Benjamins.

Devlin, Jacob, Ming-Wei Chang, Kenton Lee, and Kristina Toutanova. 2019. BERT: Pre-training of Deep Bidirectional Transformers for Language Understanding. In *Proceedings of the 2019 Conference of the North American Chapter of the Association for Computational Linguistics: Human Language Technologies, Volume 1 (Long and Short Papers)*, 4171–4186. Minneapolis, Minnesota: Association for Computational Linguistics. https://doi.org/10.18653/v1/N19-1423.

Godard, Rebecca, and Susan Holtzman. 2022. The Multidimensional Lexicon of Emojis: A New Tool to Assess the Emotional Content of Emojis. *Frontiers in Psychology* 13: 921388. https://doi.org/10.3389/fpsyg.2022.921388.

Gantiva, Carlos, Miguel Sotaquirá, Andrés Araujo, and Paula Cuervo. 2020. Cortical Processing of Human and Emoji Faces: An ERP Analysis. *Behaviour & Information Technology* 39: 935–943. United Kingdom: Taylor & Francis. https://doi.org/10.1080/0144929X.2019.1632933.

Grosan, Crina, and Ajith Abraham. 2011. *Intelligent Systems*. Intelligent Systems Reference Library. Berlin, Heidelberg: Springer Berlin Heidelberg. https://doi.org/10.1007/978-3-642-21004-4.

Hu, Minqing, and Bing Liu. 2004. Mining and Summarizing Customer Reviews. In *Proceedings of the Tenth ACM SIGKDD International Conference on Knowledge Discovery and Data Mining*, 168–177. Seattle, WA, USA: ACM. https://doi.org/10.1145/1014052.1014073.

Hutto, C., and E. Gilbert. 2014. VADER: A Parsimonious Rule-Based Model for Sentiment Analysis of Social Media Text. In *Proceedings of the International AAAI Conference on Web and Social Media*, 216–225.

Kennedy, Alistair, and Diana Inkpen. 2006. Sentiment Classification of Movie Reviews Using Contextual Valence Shifters. *Computational Intelligence* 22: 110–125. https://doi.org/10.1111/j.1467-8640.2006.00277.x.

Kejriwal, Mayank, Qile Wang, Hongyu Li, and Lu Wang. 2021. An Empirical Study of Emoji Usage on Twitter in Linguistic and National Contexts. *Online Social Networks and Media* 24: 100149. https://doi.org/10.1016/j.osnem.2021.100149.

Liu, Bing. 2012. Sentiment Analysis and Opinion Mining. *Synthesis Lectures on Human Language Technologies* 5: 1–167. Morgan & Claypool Publishers.

Liu, Yinhan, Myle Ott, Naman Goyal, Jingfei Du, Mandar Joshi, Danqi Chen, Omer Levy, Mike Lewis, Luke Zettlemoyer, and Veselin Stoyanov. 2019. RoBERTa: A Robustly Optimized BERT Pretraining Approach. arXiv. https://doi.org/10.48550/arXiv.1907.11692.

Ljubešić, Nikola, and Darja Fišer. 2016. A Global Analysis of Emoji Usage. In *Proceedings of the 10th Web as Corpus Workshop*, 82–89. Berlin: Association for Computational Linguistics. https://doi.org/10.18653/v1/W16-2610.

Medhat, Walaa, Ahmed Hassan, and Hoda Korashy. 2014. Sentiment Analysis Algorithms and Applications: A Survey. *Ain Shams Engineering Journal* 5: 1093–1113. Elsevier.

Mohammad, Saif M., and Peter D. Turney. 2010. Emotions evoked by Common Words and Phrases: Using Mechanical Turk to Create an Emotion Lexicon. In *Proceedings of the NAACL HLT 2010 Workshop on Computational Approaches to Analysis and Generation of Emotion in Text*, 26–34. Association for Computational Linguistics.

Moreno-Ortiz, Antonio. 2017. Lingmotif: Sentiment Analysis for the Digital Humanities. In *Proceedings of the 15th Conference of the European Chapter of the Association for Computational Linguistics*, 73–76. Valencia, Spain: Association for Computational Linguistics.

Moreno-Ortiz, Antonio. 2023. Lingmotif (version 2.0). Málaga. Spain: Universidad de Málaga.

Moreno-Ortiz, Antonio, and Chantal Pérez-Hernández. 2018. Lingmotif-lex: A Wide-Coverage, State-of-the-art Lexicon for Sentiment Analysis. In *Proceedings of the Eleventh International Conference on Language Resources and Evaluation (LREC 2018)*, 2653–2659. Miyazaki, Japan: European Language Resources Association (ELRA).

Moreno-Ortiz, Antonio, Chantal Pérez-Hernández, and Rodrigo Hidalgo-García. 2011. Domain-Neutral, Linguistically-Motivated Sentiment Analysis:

A Performance Evaluation. In *Actas del 3° Congreso Internacional de Lingüística de Corpus. Tecnologías de la Información y las Comunicaciones: Presente y Futuro en el Análisis de Corpus*, 847–856.

Pang, Bo, and Lillian Lee. 2008. Opinion Mining and Sentiment Analysis. In *Foundations and Trends in Information Retrieval* 2: 1–135. Now Publishers Inc.

Polanyi, Livia, and Annie Zaenen. 2006. Contextual Valence Shifters. In *Computing Attitude and Affect in Text: Theory and Applications*, 1–10. Dordrecht, The Netherlands: Springer. https://doi.org/10.1177/095792 65221076612.

Soo-Guan Khoo, Christopher, Armineh Nourbakhsh, and Jin-Cheon Na. 2012. Sentiment Analysis of Online News Text: A Case Study of Appraisal Theory. *Online Information Review* 36: 858–878. Emerald Group Publishing Limited. https://doi.org/10.1108/14684521211287936.

Stone, Philip J, and Earl B Hunt. 1963. A Computer Approach to Content Analysis: Studies Using the General Inquirer System. In *Proceedings of the May 21–23, 1963, Spring Joint Computer Conference*, 241–256. ACM.

Taboada, Maite, Julian Brooks, Milan Tofiloski, Kimberly Voll, and Manfred Stede. 2011. Lexicon-Based Methods for Sentiment Analysis. *Computational Linguistics* 37: 267–307.

Vaswani, Ashish, Noam Shazeer, Niki Parmar, Jakob Uszkoreit, Llion Jones, Aidan N. Gomez, Łukasz Kaiser, and Illia Polosukhin. 2017. Attention Is All You Need. In *Proceedings of the 31st International Conference on Neural Information Processing Systems*, 6000–6010. NIPS'17. Long Beach, California, USA: Curran Associates Inc.

Wang, Hao, Dogan Can, Abe Kazemzadeh, François Bar, and Shrikanth Narayanan. 2012. A System for Real-time Twitter Sentiment Analysis of 2012 U.S. Presidential Election Cycle. In *Proceedings of the ACL 2012 System Demonstrations*, 115–120. Jeju Island, Korea: Association for Computational Linguistics.

Wilson, Theresa, Janyce Wiebe, and Paul Hoffmann. 2005. Recognizing Contextual Polarity in Phrase-level Sentiment Analysis. In *Proceedings of the Conference on Human Language Technology and Empirical Methods in Natural Language Processing*, 347–354. HLT '05. Stroudsburg, PA, USA: Association for Computational Linguistics. https://doi.org/10.3115/1220575.122 0619.

Wolf, Thomas, Lysandre Debut, Victor Sanh, Julien Chaumond, Clement Delangue, Anthony Moi, Pierric Cistac, et al. 2020. Transformers: State-of-the-Art Natural Language Processing. In *Proceedings of the 2020 Conference on Empirical Methods in Natural Language Processing: System Demonstrations*, 38–45. Online: Association for Computational Linguistics.

Zhang, Lei, Shuai Wang, and Bing Liu. 2018. Deep Learning for Sentiment Analysis: A Survey. *Wires Data Mining and Knowledge Discovery* 8: e1253. https://doi.org/10.1002/widm.1253.

Open Access This chapter is licensed under the terms of the Creative Commons Attribution 4.0 International License (http://creativecommons.org/licenses/by/4.0/), which permits use, sharing, adaptation, distribution and reproduction in any medium or format, as long as you give appropriate credit to the original author(s) and the source, provide a link to the Creative Commons license and indicate if changes were made.

The images or other third party material in this chapter are included in the chapter's Creative Commons license, unless indicated otherwise in a credit line to the material. If material is not included in the chapter's Creative Commons license and your intended use is not permitted by statutory regulation or exceeds the permitted use, you will need to obtain permission directly from the copyright holder.

CHAPTER 7

Hashtags

Abstract The presence of certain textual elements specific to social media is ubiquitous and has transcended social media. Hashtags and emojis are now present in a number of discourse types and are even used in spoken language. While emojis carry out the function of expressing sentiment or emotions, as we saw in the previous chapter, hashtags attempt to condense a complex idea into a textual sequence of varying length with the aim of sharing and quickly disseminating it. This chapter contains a description of the most relevant hashtags used in the CCTC, focusing on the differences found among several countries, which reveal significant differences between them.

Keywords Hashtag analysis · Social issues · Internet memes · COVID-19 hashtags · Political polarization

According to Zappavigna (2011, 789), hashtags function as linguistic markers enacting the following social relation "search for me and affiliate with my value!" This is certainly the original function of hashtags, but their prevalence in social media is such that this original function has now been extended to fulfil more complex roles in the communication of the speakers' message itself, not just on Twitter/X or other social media platforms, but in offline written contexts and even face-to-face communication (Scott 2018).

Thus, hashtags have progressively become units of meaning that permit great creativity, as they function similarly to memes. From this perspective, hashtags successfully encapsulate an idea, socio-political view or vindication, which is then ready for fast and far-reaching dissemination on the Internet and beyond. This is exactly what internet memes pursue, as defined by Dawkins (1976), i.e. "a unit of cultural transmission".

Hashtags are commonly used in sociological studies to track online perception of current affairs, as their frequency and context can be used as a proxy to measure the stance that users have towards certain political or social events or ideologies. For example, Anderson (2016) tracked the use of the hashtags #BlackLivesMatter, #AllLivesMatters, and #BlueLivesMatters. The first one, which predated the Black Lives Matters organization, was used approximately 12 million times from July 2013 until March 2016, where the vast majority of the tweets were in solidarity with the movement, with only a small proportion (11%) used to criticise it. However, after the shootings of police officers in Dallas and Baton Rouge in July 2016, the three hashtags displayed increased frequency, accompanied by a change of tone changed around the #BlackLivesMatter hashtag, as well as a dramatic rise in the share of tweets criticising the Black Lives Matter movement.

A piece of research that shows how hashtags have transcended the social networking realm is the article by Dobrin (2020), who uses qualitative content analysis through the lens of cultural studies on a corpus of 200 articles where the hashtag #MeToo was included. The hashtag itself is found to be "a cultural object that perpetuates the movement's political agenda in the public sphere and bridges personal and collective experiences under the #MeToo myth" (p. 1). Obviously, the astounding success of the #MeToo hashtag on society has crossed borders and languages, and has made an exceptionally strong impact on general media and, ultimately, on society.

Research on the use of hashtags during the COVID-19 pandemic is also abundant, most of the the studies combine topic modelling and hashtag analysis, although some focus specifically on the latter, such as Cruickshank and Carley (2020)

7.1 Hashtags in the CCTC

The brief study that follows, which employs the same corpus as the preceding chapter, aims to provide a general overview of the most popular hashtags used during the pandemic in the top six countries by volume, highlighting their similarities and differences and how they reflect the societies that generated them. Hashtags are very easy to extract from text, as it only involves a simple regular expression, such as '#\w+'. The script I use extracts hashtags from each country subcorpus and generates counts and relative frequencies per 1,000 words, aggregated by week, so that the frequency of individual tags can be compared across countries and tracked over time. Table 7.1 shows the top 50 hashtags of each of the six countries in the corpus for the whole period.[1]

This table includes most of the hashtags common to all countries, which, if we account for variations of the same word (i.e. #COVID-19, #Covid_19, #Covid, etc.), is fairly limited: #COVID-19, #Coronavirus, #WearAMask, #vaccine, #lockdown, #StayHome, and #staysafe. In addition, a few others were present in all lists except #COVIDIOTS, only missing in India, where it ranks 80th, and South Africa, where it ranks very low (in 425th position), and #pandemic, only missing in South Africa, where it ranks 55th. Therefore, the most frequent type of hashtags across all countries were those of an exhortative nature, encouraging others to follow safety precautions.

The #COVIDIOTS hashtag goes a step beyond and aims to punish those that do not abide by these recommendations or laws, as examples (59) to (61) show.

59. If you think that please stop shopping in stores, just order things online. #COVIDIOTS Everything went down hill when Cats came out.
60. CDC: 38% of the attendees at an Arkansas church over a week contracted coronavirus #COVIDIOT #TrumpVirus #COVIDIOTS.
61. Let's hold back on what we WANT until a #COVID19Vaccine is available/working. #COVIDIOTS Great news for our community.

---

[1] The full list is included in the book's repository at https://osf.io/h5q4j/.

Table 7.1 Top 50 hashtags by country

U.S.A	U.K.	India	Canada	Australia	South Africa
#COVID19	#COVID19	#COVID19	#COVID19	#COVID19	#COVID19
#coronavirus	#lockdown	#coronavirus	#cdnpoli	#auspol	#lockdown
#COVID	#coronavirus	#COVID	#onpoli	#lockdown	#Covid19
#WearAMask	#COVID	#lockdown	#covid19	#COVID19Vic	#coronavirus
#covid19	#covid	#IndiaFightsCorona	#COVID	#coronavirus	#SouthAfrica
#pandemic	#covid19	#Covid19	#coronavirus	#covid19	#WearAMask
#covid	#Covid19	#India	#Covid19	#COVID	#covid19
#Covid19	#Covid19UK	#COVID19India	#pandemic	#COVID19Aus	#COVID
#Covid	#Covid	#Corona	#Canada	#COVID19nsw	#Covid19SA
#Coronavirus	#NHS	#Covid	#bcpoli	#covid	#StaySafe
#GetVaccinated	#WearAMask	#covid19	#covid	#Australia	#LockdownSA
#SocialDistancing	#SocialDistancing	#covid	#WearAMask	#Melbourne	#FamilyMeeting
#wearamask	#Covid_19	#Covid_19	#StayHome	#Covid19	#StayHome
#socialdistancing	#Lockdown	#StayHome	#Ontario	#springst	#cyrilramaphosa
#vaccine	#pandemic	#StaySafe	#ableg	#melbournelockdown	#Torment_Planet_Has_Neared
#Covid_19	#StaySafe	#pandemic	#lockdown	#melbourne	#Lockdown
#StayHome	#StayHome	#UnitingPeopleWithThePossibilities	#COVID19Ontario	#nswpol	#Covid_19
#MaskUp	#vaccine	#Sipgrab	#COVID19AB	#covidnsw	#StayAtHome
#CovidVaccine	#staysafe	#stayhome	#abpoli	#CovidVic	#CoronaVirusSA
#Trump	#Coronavirus	#Covid19IndiaHelp	#Toronto	#Covid	#Covid
#QuarantineLife	#London	#corona	#GetVaccinated	#Sydney	#FlattenTheCurve
#stayhome	#stayhome	#Nifty	#Covid	#WearAMask	#stayhome
#TrumpVirus	#Brexit	#staysafe	#vaccine	#stayhome	#covid
#quarantinelife	#mentalhealth	#india	#SocialDistancing	#Covid_19	#DJSBU
#COVIDIOTS	#COVIDIOTS	#Unite2FightCorona	#toronto	#pandemic	#ANC

7 HASHTAGS 173

U.S.A	U.K.	India	Canada	Australia	South Africa
#Florida	#socialdistancing	#Mumbai	#stayhome	#StayHome	#VoetsekANC
#lockdown	#coronavirusuk	#StayHomeStaySafe	#Covid_19	#Coronavirus	#staysafe
#vaccinated	#Torment_Planet_Has_Neared	#SocialDistancing	#socialdistancing	#China	#Sect. 59Investigation
#WearADamnMask	#london	#Delhi	#yyc	#NSW	#capetown
#staysafe	#StayAtHome	#WearAMask	#COVIDIOTS	#Victoria	#RacismMustFall
#Pandemic	#BorisJohnson	#vaccine	#canada	#IStandWithDan	#CoronaVirus
#BidenHarris2020	#CovidVaccine	#COVIDSecondWave	#yeg	#vaccine	#RacialProfiling
#GetVaccinatedNow	#Lockdown2	#COVID_19	#skpoli	#australia	#vaccines
#StayAtHome	#UK	#Maharashtra	#India	#SydneyLockdown	#southafrica
#COVID_19	#nhs	#CovidIndia	#StaySafe	#Lockdown	#level5
#covid_19	#Omicron	#Coronavirus	#NEWS	#covid19vic	#COVID19SA
#COVIDIOT	#COVID_19	#Omicron	#onted	#staysafe	#vaccine
#DeltaVariant	#covid_19	#Lockdown	#staysafe	#sydney	#sabcnews
#quarantine	#vaccination	#China	#Alberta	#GetVaccinated	#Covid19InSA
#MAGA	#uk	#CoronavirusIndia	#CovidVaccine	#COVIDIOTS	#Coronavirus
#BLM	#stayathome	#vaccination	#VoteFordOut2022	#covid_19	#COVID19SouthAfrica
#mask	#Scotland	#CovidVaccine	#Health	#qanda	#testkits
#BlackLivesMatter	#StayHomeSaveLives	#Odisha	#wearamask	#Torment_Planet_Has_Neared	#ItCanBe
#CDC	#art	#TamilNadu	#COVID19ON	#AusPol	#GautengCOVID19
#CoronaVirus	#lockdown2021	#covid_19	#Elxn44	#insiders	#covid19SA
#Texas	#ExcludedUK	#CoronavirusPandemic	#Omicron	#ScottyFromMarketing	#4IR
#SoundHound	#wellbeing	#COVIDEmergency	#Ottawa	#DeltaVariant	#LockdownHouseParty
#VaccinesWork	#community	#Telangana	#Vancouver	#Omicron	#SocialDistancing

(continued)

Table 7.1 (continued)

U.S.A	U.K.	India	Canada	Australia	South Africa
#Omicron	#lockdownuk	#UttarPradesh	#ldnont	#WHO	#Ramaphosa
#USA	#SuicideAwareness	#ChineseVirus	#Coronavirus	#coronavirusaustralia	#level3

All other hashtags are specific to each country. Table 7.2 lists them after removing those that simply refer to the country itself (e.g. #southafrica, #UK, #COVID19Aus).

Country-specific tags do provide a good picture of the particular social and political contexts. Some are irrelevant news aggregators, as in the case of Canada and Australia (e.g. #cdnpli, #bcpoli, #AusPol, #nswpol), but in general the differences are useful to study the idiosyncrasies of different countries and societies. In the United States and South Africa lists there is a significant presence of politics-related words. Both share racism-related tags: #BlackLivesMatter and #BLM in the former, #RacismMustFall, and #RacialProfiling in the latter. They also share elections-related tags (#BidenHarris2020, #VoetsekANC), as both countries had general elections during the period or recently before it (2020 in the United States, 2019 in South Africa).

The high position of the #BlackLivesMatter and #BLM tags during the two years covered by the corpus was no doubt due to the public outrage and subsequent protests caused by the death of George Floyd on June 6, 2020, which is clearly reflected in Fig. 7.1.

The political polarization of the United States is reflected more directly by the high-ranking #TrumpVirus and #MAGA tags, but also by the fact that there are several in reference to the use of facemasks (#MaskUp, #WearADamnMask), and vaccines (#GetVaccinated, #GetVaccinatedNow, #VaccinesWork), two aspects of the pandemic that became increasingly politicised. The fact that the only two geographical locations mentioned in the set of hashtags are Florida and Texas is also telling of the politicisation of the pandemic, as the Republican majority of these two States led to more permissive policies concerning stay-at-home orders and mask mandates. Similarly, although not present in the top 50 list, there is a plethora of tags that criticize the management of the pandemic by Trump's Administration: #TrumpLiesAmericansDie (position 95), #TrumpIsANationalDisgrace (110), #GOPBetrayedAmerica (121), #TrumpKnew (144), #TraitorTrump (196), #GOPDeathCult (213), #TrumpIsALaughingStock (214), #TrumpFailedAmerica (234), etc.

Other countries also display some politics-related tags: #Brexit in the United Kingdom, #VoteFordOut2022 in Canada, and #IStandWithDan in Australia. The Australian tag was deliberately created and made viral to support the Victorian State Government's handling of the pandemic, in reference to its Premier, Daniel Andrews, during the second wave in the

Table 7.2 Country-specific hashtags

U.S.A	U.K.	India	Canada	Australia	South Africa
#MaskUp	#NHS	#IndiaFightsCorona	#cdnpoli	#auspol	#FamilyMeeting
#Trump	#London	#Corona	#onpoli	#Melbourne	#cyrilramaphosa
#QuarantineLife	#Brexit	#UnitingPeopleWithThePossibilities		#springst	#FlattenTheCurve
#TrumpVirus	#mentalhealth	#Sirgrab	#bcpoli	#melbournelockdown	#DJSBU
#quarantinelife	#london	#Covid19IndiaHelp	#Ontario	#melbourne	#ANC
#Florida	#BorisJohnson	#corona	#ableg	#nswpol	#VoetsekANC
#vaccinated	#Lockdown2	#Nifty	#abpoli	#covidnsw	#Sect. 59Investigation
#WearADamnMask	#nhs	#india	#Toronto	#CovidVic	#capetown
#Pandemic	#stayathome	#Unite2FightCorona	#toronto	#Sydney	#RacismMustFall
#BidenHarris2020	#Scotland	#Mumbai	#yyc	#NSW	#RacialProfiling
#GetVaccinatedNow	#StayHomeSaveLives	#StayHomeStaySafe	#yeg	#Victoria	#level5
#COVIDIOT	#art	#Delhi	#skpoli	#IStandWithDan	#sabcnews
#quarantine	#lockdown2021	#COVIDSecondWave	#NEWS	#australia	#testkits
#MAGA	#ExcludedUK	#Maharashtra	#onted	#SydneyLockdown	#ItCanBe
#BLM	#wellbeing	#Odisha	#Alberta	#covid19vic	#GautengCOVID19
#mask	#community	#TamilNadu	#VoteFordOut2022	#sydney	#4IR
#BlackLivesMatter	#lockdownuk	#CoronavirusPandemic	#Health	#qanda	#LockdownHouseParty
#CDC	#SuicideAwareness	#COVIDEmergency	#COVID19ON	#AusPol	#Ramaphosa
#Texas	#CovidUK	#Telangana	#Elxn44	#insiders	#level3
#SoundHound		#UttarPradesh	#Ottawa	#ScottyFromMarketing	#ANCMustFall
#VaccinesWork		#ChineseVirus	#Vancouver	#WHO	

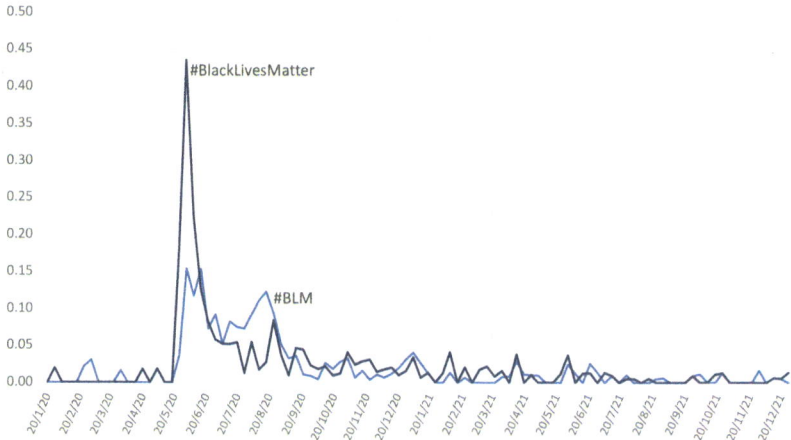

Fig. 7.1 Frequency of #BlackLivesMatter and #BLM (per 1,000 words)

second half of 2020. This hashtag was in opposition to the condemning #DictatorDan, which is in position 121 in terms of frequency in the CCTC.

Graham et al. (2021) conducted a comprehensive, mixed-methods study of this phenomenon, which showed how a small number of hyper-partisan pro- and anti-government campaigners were able to create ad hoc communities on Twitter that generated a considerable amount of political mobilisation. Their Twitter dataset contained data from March to September 2020 (nearly 400,000 tweets). Their quantitative data closely match ours for that period: a few weeks after #DictatorDan first appeared, #IStandWithDan quickly overwhelmed it, and then both tags fought for dominance over time, with a clear prevalence of the latter. Figure 7.2 plots the relative frequency of these two hashtags over the two years that our data cover.

It is surprising how this polarization was maintained long after the phenomenon started: although it subsided briefly at the end of 2020, it gathered considerable momentum at several points during 2021, which only goes to show how difficult it is to put out the flames of polarization once they have been ignited. It is also a good example of how social networks are used by political campaigners to gain support and votes, at the expense of social confrontation.

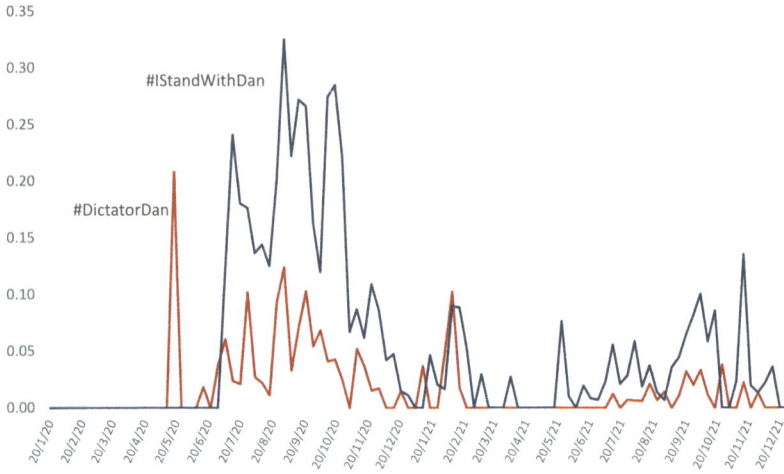

Fig. 7.2 Frequency of #DictatorDan vs. #IStandWithDan (per 1,000 words)

The mental health topic is only present in U.K.'s hashtags (#mentalhealth, #SuicideAwareness), although it is present in all countries with different relevance (as measured by their frequency): #mentalhealth is in 54th position in Canada, 69th in Australia, and 106th in the U.S. Again, we find significant differences between this group of countries, on the one hand, and South Africa and India, on the other; in the former, it is in position 220 and 438 in India. Figure 7.3 shows a visualization of these data based on relative frequency of the hashtag #mentalhealth in these countries.

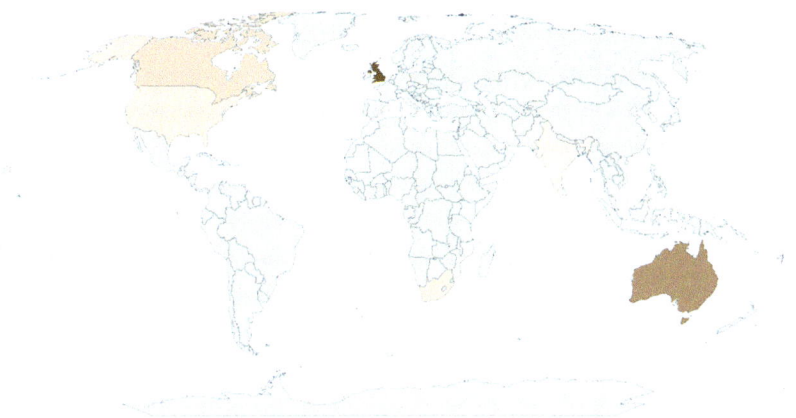

Fig. 7.3 Heatmap of #mentalhealth by country

References

Anderson, Monica. 2016. Social Media Conversations About Race. *Pew Research Center: Internet, Science & Tech.*

Cruickshank, Iain J., and Kathleen M. Carley. 2020. Characterizing Communities of Hashtag Usage on Twitter During the 2020 COVID-19 Pandemic by Multi-view Clustering. *Applied Network Science* 5: 66. https://doi.org/10.1007/s41109-020-00317-8.

Dawkins, Richard. 1976. *The Selfish Gene*. New York: Oxford University Press.

Dobrin, Diana. 2020. The Hashtag in Digital Activism: A Cultural Revolution. *Journal of Cultural Analysis and Social Change* 5: 1–03 Lectito Journals. https://doi.org/10.20897/jcasc/8298.

Graham, Timothy, Axel Bruns, Daniel Angus, Edward Hurcombe, and Sam Hames. 2021. #IStandWithDan versus #DictatorDan: The Polarised Dynamics of Twitter Discussions about Victoria's COVID-19 Restrictions. *Media International Australia* 179: 127–148. https://doi.org/10.1177/1329878X20981780.

Scott, Kate. 2018. "Hashtags Work Everywhere": The Pragmatic Functions of Spoken Hashtags. *Discourse, Context & Media* 22: 57–64. Discourse of Social Tagging. https://doi.org/10.1016/j.dcm.2017.07.002.

Zappavigna, Michele. 2011. Ambient Affiliation: A Linguistic Perspective on Twitter. *New Media & Society* 13: 788–806. Sage Publications. https://doi.org/10.1177/1461444810385097.

Open Access This chapter is licensed under the terms of the Creative Commons Attribution 4.0 International License (http://creativecommons.org/licenses/by/4.0/), which permits use, sharing, adaptation, distribution and reproduction in any medium or format, as long as you give appropriate credit to the original author(s) and the source, provide a link to the Creative Commons license and indicate if changes were made.

The images or other third party material in this chapter are included in the chapter's Creative Commons license, unless indicated otherwise in a credit line to the material. If material is not included in the chapter's Creative Commons license and your intended use is not permitted by statutory regulation or exceeds the permitted use, you will need to obtain permission directly from the copyright holder.

CHAPTER 8

Lessons Learned and Key Takeaways

Abstract This short chapter discusses the most relevant concluding remarks and observations from the research put forward in the previous chapters, including those regarding sampling techniques, analysis methods of keywords, topics, sentiment, and hashtags. Given the large amount of information that this chapter summarizes, readers are asked to refer to the individual chapters that discuss each of these topics in depth.

Keywords Social networks · Twitter · Data sampling · Keyword extraction · Topic modelling · Sentiment analysis · Hashtags

This book set out to pursue two objectives, one of a methodological nature (to describe available methods for extracting information from large social media corpora), and the other content-related: to distil specific information concerning the perceptions, attitudes, and concerns of English speakers around the world concerning the COVID-19 pandemic as expressed on social networks.

In each of the preceding chapters, I have presented and discussed a number of outstanding computational methods for extracting the concepts, ideas, topics, and opinions of Twitter users from large social media corpora. In the remainder of this section, I provide a summary of the most important conclusions mentioned in earlier chapters.

The first key takeaway, amply discussed in Chapter 3, is that large social media corpora are, not shockingly, too large to process in whole, and sampling strategies are necessary. However, using samples should not be considered a poor substitute for processing the whole corpus, as in most cases adequate sampling should produce very similar results, while optimizing time and resources. This is especially true in the case of social media corpora on a single major topic, as is the case here.

As for keyword extraction, it is quite apparent that different methods offer advantages and disadvantages, and many factors need to be considered when selecting one. Arguably, the most important criterion is the quality of results, which, as we have seen, is not easy to assess, and inherently conveys subjectivity: when offered to competing lists of keywords that are meant to summarize the themes and topics that a text contains, all we can do is "guess" what the actual topics are, and then assess the accuracy of the keyword lists against our mental image of those topics.

There are some more formal criteria that we can apply. For example, repetition in the form of synonyms or morphological variations is an undesirable feature, as is the inclusion of arbitrary n-grams instead of syntactically and semantically meaningful groupings for multi-word keywords.

Of all the keyword extraction methods surveyed, the best results for social media corpora—in terms of quality—are offered by the traditional Corpus Linguistics method, based on the use of a reference corpus, and graph-based approaches, which seem to complement each other. Unsupervised methods may be adequate in other scenarios, such as extracting keywords from single documents, which is in fact the type of application that they were created for. Finally, novel unsupervised methods based on large language models are promising, but at least in the case of the implementation that we have tested (KeyBERT), they still need considerable improvement and refinement to be successfully applied to large social media corpora.

Using basic set theory methods to compare sets of keywords can provide a clarifying image of the similarities and differences between them, and are therefore useful to evaluate extraction methods. This system also allows for the automatic generation of tables and graphs (Venn-type diagrams) that facilitate understanding and sharing results.

The potential of LLMs is much higher for topic extraction, as they can successfully fill a part of the process that has traditionally been left to the end user: labelling the extracted topics. Using the word embeddings contained in LLMs to extract topics also offers superior performance compared to "traditional" topic modelling algorithms (LDA and NMF). Together, these two features result in high-quality topic lists that accurately extract the essential themes contained in a large corpus. Furthermore, software libraries such as BERTopic make it extremely easy to use these advanced features, as they provide an abstraction layer over the complex lower-level processes (tokenization, embeddings creation, dimensionality reduction, clustering, etc.). If we bear in mind that the availability of LLMs is very recent, and that, with all certainty, more powerful, sophisticated models will become available in the future, it seems that this method of topic modelling will soon become the logical choice for most researchers. The one drawback they present is that using them requires specific hardware capable of parallel processing (GPUs or TPUs), which may not be available to some researchers, although cloud-based alternatives are available.

In terms of applicability and overall usefulness, topic modelling is probably a more versatile and powerful tool than keyword extraction, since it regards a topic as a set of related keywords, which are clustered using various techniques (co-occurrence in the case of traditional topic modelling, semantic similarity in the case of embeddings-based tools). Thus, an advanced topic modelling tool, such as BERTopic, coupled with LLM-based topic labelling, is capable of automatically distilling the relevant themes of a corpus, rank them by relevance, and list the keywords associated with each topic. This is not to say that keyword extraction tools are not useful, as they focus on the actual words, and score them individually, regardless of the topic they refer to, which is extremely valuable for terminology extraction and other linguistic applications. Extracting keywords is also computationally less demanding, and there are several user-friendly tools available, whereas topic modelling tools, especially advanced ones, require considerable computational resources and technical knowhow. Therefore, these techniques are complementary rather than antagonistic, and the choice between them may ultimately depend on the research objectives and the available resources.

The lists of topics extracted from the different subcorpora of the geotagged portion of the CCTC suggest that, while a core set of topics (prevention, testing, treatments, vaccination, safe practices, social impact, etc.) is present in all societies, there are significant differences between them that reflect and reveal their respective cultures.

Sentiment analysis is indispensable for analysing social media corpora, as well as any other emotionally charged text. While keywords and topics provide information as to what is being discussed, sentiment analysis tells us about the emotional perspectives and opinions on those topics, which is essential for understanding the speakers' feelings and attitudes, a crucial aspect of social communication in general, and computer-mediated communication in particular. Without some type of sentiment analysis, this key communicative dimension would remain concealed beneath the surface of individual words and topics.

The two types of approaches used in this field, machine learning and lexicon-based methods, produce valuable results and perfectly complement one another to facilitate quantitative and qualitative research by extracting insights from large amounts of texts. Although lexicon-based tools can classify documents with acceptable accuracy, machine learning classifiers, specifically neural networks based on transformers currently offer the state of the art and are particularly well suited to analyse Twitter/X data, as specific models exist that have been trained on vast amounts of tweets and offer excellent performance.

Comparing sentiment classification across countries yields unexpected results, as poorer economies that were hit harder by the pandemic tend to show higher sentiment scores, suggesting that those societies, being accustomed to harsher conditions and standards of living may be better equipped to deal with a sudden deterioration in living conditions.

On the other hand, lexicon-based tools excel at extracting the specific linguistic expressions that determine the semantic orientation of texts, which is critical to understand people's motivations and the nature of that sentiment. The negative words used to describe the pandemic's effects also indicate significant differences between nations, revealing the precise causes of human suffering, poverty being more prominent in less developed countries. There are also differences in the use of profanity and taboo words, with such countries using these terms significantly less frequently than more developed nations.

Emojis have become an essential tool for expressing emotions and attitudes in social media text, and as such they deserve special consideration. They often serve to make the intended sentiment explicit and provide a proper interpretation of the text.

Significant differences were also found in the use of emojis between different countries. South African social media users employ this expressive resource much more frequently than users in other countries, and the particular emojis also vary from the rest. India also displayed some important differences, for example, it was found to be the country where the "praying hands" emoji was used most frequently, indicating a more spiritual personality of the population.

Finally, hashtags can reveal important insights and are easy to identify and account for. For example, the frequency of racism-related hashtags clearly correlates with real-world events, as is the case with the killing of George Floyd by the police in the United States. It can also be used to track the development of political campaigns, as other authors have shown in previous research. Furthermore, the simple statistical study based on the frequency of use described in the previous chapter provides further evidence that some issues are more pressing than others in different cultures and economies. For example, hashtags related to mental health problems were considerably less frequent in less developed countries, which is probably an indication that the phrase and well-known meme "first world problems" does have a justification.

Ultimately, the experiments and studies conducted in this book have generated vast quantities of data, of which only a small subset have been fully described in some depth.[1] Readers are encouraged to take advantage of all the datasets generated, as they are sure to find additional insights than those explicitly discussed in the text.

---

[1] Moreno-Ortiz, A. (2024). LSMC Datasets. https://doi.org/10.17605/OSF.IO/H5Q4J.

Open Access This chapter is licensed under the terms of the Creative Commons Attribution 4.0 International License (http://creativecommons.org/licenses/by/4.0/), which permits use, sharing, adaptation, distribution and reproduction in any medium or format, as long as you give appropriate credit to the original author(s) and the source, provide a link to the Creative Commons license and indicate if changes were made.

The images or other third party material in this chapter are included in the chapter's Creative Commons license, unless indicated otherwise in a credit line to the material. If material is not included in the chapter's Creative Commons license and your intended use is not permitted by statutory regulation or exceeds the permitted use, you will need to obtain permission directly from the copyright holder.

Index

A
aboutness, 60, 62, 64, 70, 79, 86, 87
affective computing, 141
aggregated, 38, 39, 47, 76, 77, 84, 85, 104, 148, 152, 171
annotation, 8
Application Programming Interface (API), 6, 21, 24, 27, 33, 34, 37, 60, 119
appraisal, 12
Australia, 13, 48, 51, 96, 97, 147, 148, 150, 151, 155, 158, 164, 172–176, 178
Ayurvedic, 122, 129

B
Bapu, 113, 114, 121, 129
BERT, 26, 116, 117, 143
BERTopic, 105, 106, 116–120, 128, 130, 131, 133, 183
#BlackLivesMatter, 170, 173, 175–177
booster, 94, 95
Brexit, 121, 124, 129, 135, 136
#Brexit, 172, 175, 176

C
Canada, 48, 51, 147, 148, 150, 151, 155, 156, 158, 162, 164, 172–176, 178
Center for Disease Control (CDC), 112, 113, 122, 129, 171, 173, 176
Chen's Coronavirus Twitter Corpus (CCTC), 24, 26, 27, 37, 38, 40, 47, 51, 67, 84, 96, 105, 146, 147, 171, 177, 183
China, 4, 51, 78, 81, 89, 91, 93, 112, 122, 129, 148, 156
Chinese, 34, 78, 89, 91, 128, 129, 174, 176
classification, 8, 10, 20, 65, 142–144, 146–148
classifier, 10, 35, 74, 142, 146, 148, 152, 184
clustering, 104, 117, 118, 183
cluster sampling, 43, 44
coherence, 10, 104, 110
computational linguistics, 145
concordance, 61, 69, 70, 72, 90
concordancer, 61

concordancing, 7, 11, 22
Convolutional Neural Networks (CNN), 8, 13, 142, 156
co-occurrence, 77, 83, 107, 110, 115, 183
corona, 24, 78, 81, 82, 89, 91, 93, 96, 112, 114
coronavirus, 3, 4, 13, 21, 24, 60, 78, 79, 81, 82, 87, 91, 93, 95, 96, 112, 113, 122
Coronavirus Corpus, 12, 22
corpora, 11, 12, 21–23, 32, 33, 35, 37, 39, 41, 47, 60, 63, 64, 66, 67, 69, 72, 75, 79, 80, 132, 143, 146, 160
corpus, 1–3, 7–14, 19–27, 31, 32, 35–42, 44–47, 49–53, 60–73, 75–77, 79, 81, 82, 84–87, 89, 90, 97, 103–108, 110, 116–118, 132, 133, 136, 146, 147, 155, 157, 161, 170, 171, 175, 182, 183
cosine similarity, 96, 115
country-specific, 129, 175, 176
#COVIDIOTS, 171–173
COVID-19, 2–13, 20, 21, 23–27, 35, 47, 60, 75, 79, 108, 118, 121–127, 130, 133, 135, 136, 151, 152, 170, 171, 181
COVID-19 Open Research Dataset (CORD-19), 12, 19
covid shot, 95, 96
covid test, 79, 80, 82, 93, 95, 112, 113
CSV, 23, 36, 40, 68, 85, 86, 109, 116
c-TF-IDF, 133

D
data sampling, 41, 42
Delhi, 113, 124, 127, 130, 173, 176

Delta, 94, 95, 125, 126, 148, 151, 173
derogatory, 123, 126, 128
deterministic, 143–145
#DictatorDan, 177, 178
distant reading, 7, 10
dynamic topic modelling, 53, 105, 132, 133, 136

E
education, 8, 9, 11, 65, 128
embeddings, 26, 50, 84, 95, 96, 105, 115–118, 131, 136, 183
EmbedRank, 95
emergency, 81, 126, 153, 173, 176
emoji, 46, 89, 92, 157, 160–164, 184, 185
emoticons, 8, 160
emotion detection, 34, 142
explainability, 146

F
face masks/facemask, 5, 91, 93, 95, 109, 133, 175
fake, 4, 25, 122
filtering, 74, 108
focus corpus, 3, 63, 64, 66–69, 72, 73, 81, 92, 99

G
genres, 13, 32
geotagged, 3, 8, 23, 27, 41, 47–52, 77, 96, 105, 147, 183
GPT, 128, 143

H
hashtag, 32, 34, 36, 97, 98, 108, 169–172, 175–178, 185
help, 80, 109, 112, 113, 155–159

herd immunity, 93
HTML, 23, 87, 109, 131, 133
HuggingFace, 118, 146, 147
human-in-the-loop, 107

I
Ighalo, 78, 81
immunity, 94, 95, 157, 158
India, 10, 48, 49, 51, 53–55, 92, 96, 105, 106, 113, 114, 118, 119, 121–127, 129, 130, 134, 135, 147–158, 162, 164, 171–174, 176, 178, 185
infection, 91, 93, 95, 113, 125, 148, 153, 156
#IStandWithDan, 173, 175–178

J
jab, 82, 95, 96, 104, 113
jee, 92
JSON, 20, 36, 37, 40, 49, 52
JSONL, 46, 52, 77

K
Kea, 74
KeyBERT, 95–97, 119, 182
keyness, 62–64, 67–71, 95
keyphrase, 85, 96, 98, 104
keyword analysis, 10, 66, 67, 71
keyword extraction, 3, 6, 7, 14, 41, 46, 61, 64–69, 71–80, 83–87, 89, 91, 95, 96, 98, 119, 136, 182, 183
keyword list, 64, 66, 72, 76, 104, 182
keyword(s), 3, 6–8, 10, 13, 14, 21, 24, 27, 35, 41, 46, 59–98, 103, 104, 107, 109, 111, 113, 114, 117, 119, 120, 136, 182–184
keyword set, 67, 68, 81, 86, 87, 90
KP-Miner, 76

L
language model, 20, 26, 96, 105, 128, 143, 146, 147, 182
large language models (LLMs, 9, 95, 105, 119, 128, 136, 182, 183
Latent Dirichlet Allocation (LDA), 9, 10, 25, 105–110, 112–114, 117–119, 183
Latent Semantic Analysis, 105, 106
lemmatization, 10, 69, 87, 91, 108
lexicon-based, 142–146, 153, 184
Lingmotif, 2, 144, 146, 147, 157
Llama 2, 119–121, 128, 129
lockdown, 4, 8, 27, 35, 60, 76, 79, 80, 82, 98, 113, 114, 121, 123–125, 129, 131, 133, 148, 153–158, 171–173
London, 113, 172, 173, 176
long covid, 80, 82, 95, 113

M
machine learning (ML), 8, 20, 21, 73, 74, 142, 143, 145, 184
#MAGA, 173, 175, 176
masks, 121, 126, 127, 130
meme, 121, 170, 185
mental health, 25, 93, 95, 178, 185
#mentalhealth, 172, 176, 178, 179
metadata, 22, 23, 31, 32, 52, 53, 73, 74, 85
misinformation, 4, 5, 25, 35, 95, 128
Modi, Narendra, 113, 114, 122, 126, 130
MPQA, 144
multiphase sampling, 43, 44
multistage sampling, 43, 44
multi-word, 68, 71, 72, 75, 76, 81, 82, 84–89, 91–93, 95, 97, 182
mutual information, 110

N

Named entity recognition, 20, 84, 117
natural language processing (NLP), 7, 20, 21, 34, 73, 74, 76, 83, 84, 105, 115–118, 141–143, 145, 146
neet, 92
NFL, 121
n-gram, 21, 63, 68–72, 75, 77, 96–98, 114, 182
NHS, 122, 123, 129, 172, 173, 176
Non-negative Matrix Factorization (NMF), 105–109, 112–114, 117–119, 183
nursing homes, 93, 124, 129

O

Opinion Lexicon, 144
opinion mining, 141
outbreak, 5, 8, 13, 78, 79, 81, 89, 91, 93, 112, 121, 123–125, 129, 156

P

pandemic, 2–8, 11–13, 22, 25–27, 35, 48, 49, 75, 79–82, 89, 92–95, 97, 109, 112–114, 120–125, 129, 131, 133, 135, 148, 151–153, 155–157, 170–172, 175, 181, 184
passport, 82, 95, 104, 113, 123
PCR, 80, 82
Plotly, 110, 130, 133
pointers, 60–62, 103
political polarization, 4, 125, 175
predictive model, 74, 142
pre-processing, 10, 21, 24, 38, 76, 107–109, 118
pretrained, 20
pretraining, 146

probabilistic, 105, 107, 108, 143, 146
probability sampling, 42, 43
production rules, 142, 143
prompt, 119, 120
proportional-to-size sampling, 43–45
protest, 4, 123–125, 129, 130, 156–159, 175
PyLDAvis, 110
PyTextRank, 84, 85
Python, 21, 24, 37, 38, 84, 116, 160

Q

quarantine, 27, 81, 91, 109, 112, 153, 154, 156, 173, 176

R

Rapid Automatic Keyword Extraction (RAKE), 76–80, 99
Recurrent Neural Networks (RNN), 142
reference corpus, 11, 61–69, 71–73, 75, 81, 82, 85, 89, 92, 98, 182
reference-corpus method, 64, 66, 67, 71–73, 75, 80, 82, 84, 92, 98
relative frequency, 64, 68, 70, 71, 75, 161, 177, 178
repository, 2, 24, 41, 45, 50, 78, 81, 83, 85, 87, 97, 105, 110, 131, 147, 171
retweet, 21, 26, 32, 37, 38, 40, 41, 44, 45, 82
reviews, 2, 6, 82, 142
RoBERTa, 10, 26, 146

S

sampling, 41–44, 182
sampling methods, 41, 42, 46
sarcasm, 34, 35, 144, 152
score, 9, 10, 24, 62, 64, 68–71, 74–77, 81, 83–86, 97, 110, 142, 143, 147, 149, 154, 183, 184

semantic orientation, 142, 144, 146, 184
Sentence Transformers (S-BERT), 26, 117, 118
sentiment, 3, 6–10, 25, 34, 35, 41, 117, 141–149, 151–154, 157, 184
sentiment analysis, 3, 6–10, 25, 34, 41, 117, 141–146, 153, 184
sentiment classification, 10, 117, 143, 146, 148, 151, 152, 184
sentiment lexicon, 8, 142, 143
sentiment over time, 9, 10, 159, 162
SentiWordNet, 8, 144
shortage, 123, 124, 153
simple maths, 68
simple random sampling, 43
Sketch Engine, 2, 37, 53, 63, 68, 69, 80, 81, 84–95
SO-CAL, 144
social distancing, 4, 79, 80, 82, 93, 95, 112–114, 122, 123, 125
social media, 1, 3, 5–7, 9, 11, 20, 25, 27, 41, 62, 73, 89, 91, 93, 105, 107, 120, 142, 144, 160, 164, 169, 181, 182, 184
social media corpora, 1, 3, 41, 62, 73, 105, 181, 182, 184
social networking sites, 6, 32
social networks, 2–6, 35, 83, 177, 181
South Africa, 48, 51, 147, 150, 151, 155, 156, 160–162, 164, 171–176, 178
SpaCy, 84, 85, 108
stop-word, 10, 84, 107, 108
stratified sampling, 43
subcorpora, 13, 42, 52, 53, 65, 66, 69, 105, 118–121, 147, 157, 161, 162, 183

subcorpus, 42, 54, 55, 77, 85, 96, 106, 111, 118–120, 128, 133, 147, 155, 161, 171
subjective, 42, 64, 86, 87, 107, 141
#SuicideAwareness, 174, 176, 178
supervised, 73, 74
Support Vector Machines (SVM), 142, 145

T
term specificity, 75
TextRank, 77, 83, 84, 86, 87, 89, 91–95
text summarization, 83
TF-IDF, 74–80, 83
tokenization, 108, 118, 183
top2vec, 10, 105, 116
TopEx, 105, 116
topic, 2, 3, 6–10, 14, 25, 34, 35, 41, 50, 53, 60, 69, 73, 97, 104–107, 109–111, 114–116, 118–120, 128, 130–136, 154, 157, 170, 178, 182, 183
topic labelling, 183
topic modelling, 3, 6–10, 25, 41, 50, 73, 104, 105, 107, 111, 114–116, 132, 133, 136, 170, 183
topics over time, 10, 131–134, 154
transformers, 117, 119, 143, 145, 146, 184
trends, 4, 5, 7, 8, 10, 25, 54, 55, 124
Trump, Donald, 89, 91–93, 112, 113, 121–123, 129, 148, 155, 172, 175, 176
#TrumpVirus, 171, 172, 175, 176
TweetNLP, 146
Twitter, 1, 3, 5–9, 20, 21, 23, 24, 26, 27, 31–37, 41, 47, 60, 76, 77, 85, 89, 92, 134, 135, 146, 152, 155, 160, 169, 177, 181, 184

Twitter/X, 1, 5–7, 23, 25, 32, 33, 37, 169, 184

U
United Kingdom (U.K.), 11, 48, 49, 51, 77, 105, 106, 118, 119, 121, 129, 130, 133, 147, 150, 155, 156, 158, 162, 164, 172–176, 178
United States (U.S.), 5, 11, 26, 48, 49, 88, 89, 105, 110, 112, 118, 121–127, 129, 130, 134, 147, 148, 150, 155, 161, 162, 175, 178, 185
unsupervised, 73, 74, 77–81, 83, 99, 146, 182
URL, 22, 23, 107, 108
U.S.A., 48, 51, 119, 147, 151, 156, 158, 172–174

V
vaccines, 9, 10, 79, 95, 104, 128, 133, 134, 154, 173, 175

#VaccinesWork, 173, 175, 176
VADER, 8, 144
vax, 82
Venn diagram, 67, 86–89, 92
virus, 3, 5, 40, 41, 78, 79, 81, 91, 93, 96, 97, 112, 114, 128, 129, 133, 148, 152, 153, 155, 156, 162
visualization, 14, 109–111, 116, 130, 134, 148, 161, 178

W
#WearADamnMask, 173, 175, 176
word2vec, 115
word clusters, 7
word embeddings, 26, 84, 95, 96, 105, 115–117, 183

X
XML, 31, 36, 37, 52, 53, 77, 85

Y
Yake, 76–80, 83

Springer Nature

GPSR Compliance

The European Union's (EU) General Product Safety Regulation (GPSR) is a set of rules that requires consumer products to be safe and our obligations to ensure this.

If you have any concerns about our products, you can contact us on ProductSafety@springernature.com

In case Publisher is established outside the EU, the EU authorized representative is:

Springer Nature Customer Service Center GmbH
Europaplatz 3
69115 Heidelberg, Germany

The manufacturer's authorised representative in the EU is Springer Nature Customer Service Centre GmbH, Europaplatz 3, 69115 Heidelberg, Germany. If you have any concerns regarding our products, please contact ProductSafety@springernature.com

Printed and bound by CPI Group (UK) Ltd, Croydon, CR0 4YY
23/03/2026
02076401-0002